ISBN 978-1-331-14029-0
PIBN 10149616

1 MONTH OF
FREE
READING

at
www.ForgottenBooks.com

By purchasing this book you are eligible for one month membership to ForgottenBooks.com, giving you unlimited access to our entire collection of over 700,000 titles via our web site and mobile apps.

To claim your free month visit:

HISTORY

OF

THE SIEGE OF DELHI

BY

AN OFFICER WHO SERVED THERE.

William

WITH A SKETCH OF THE
LEADING EVENTS IN THE PUNJAUB CONNECTED WITH
THE GREAT REBELLION OF 1857.

EDINBURGH:
ADAM AND CHARLES BLACK.
1861.

PRINTED BY R. AND R. CLARK, EDINBURGH.

PREFACE.

No apology is needed for giving an account of the Siege of Delhi, a military achievement which must always be read with pleasure by all who love the glory of their country.

The narrative of the Rev. Mr. Rotton, though containing many valuable details, does not attempt to leave the stand-point he occupied as chaplain of the force. This excellent man had his mind too much imbued with the solemnity of his office, to be able to note all the military details. Some have found fault with his book as a history; but he never professes it to be one. It is a personal narrative of what came under his eye, or what he heard from trustworthy sources.

A pamphlet has been published by Colonel Norman, late Adjutant-general of the Indian army. It contains a complete account of the military operations and is ably and elegantly written ; but it is much to short and too full of technical details for popula reading. I am indebted to this distinguished office for the returns of killed and wounded, the strength of our force at different periods, and other details, with which, as deputy Adjutant-general, he was wel acquainted. Any other information derived through him will be acknowledged in its place. I have gaine a few facts from the published letters of Mr. Greathe and Major Hodson, which are always cited when the come. These books give much information, but, neve having been designed by either of their lamented authors for publication, are full of uncorrected mistakes The reader, who would trust to them for an account of the siege, would be apt to acquire a very imperfect idea of the operations, and give an undue share of credit to the friends of those gentlemen.

All information from other sources is acknow-ledged in the notes. I have occasionally corrected the mistakes of printed authorities, for in writing his-tory it is as necessary to pull up the weeds as to sow the good seed. Very little stress indeed has been laid on newspaper accounts, which throughout the siege were most meagre and untrustworthy.

The great bulk of the volume is written out of the manuscript notes of the author, who had the honour of being present during the whole of the siege operations.   He was an eyewitness of almost every battle described; went over the ground ; into the batteries ; talked with the soldiers, European and native ;   sifted accounts on the spot; and spent all his spare time in realising and recording the great events he witnessed. Those in the Punjaub and at Meerut are described from private sources, as letters and oral information ; when from printed books the reference is given.

The author hopes the public will support him in one innovation.   Our countrymen in India have used all their influence, direct and indirect, to be represented at home as perfectly faultless.   They must be painted without shade.   This perhaps has to a less extent prevailed in portraits of the scenes of the great rebellion, but the old style of art is too common. Englishmen in it are always drawn in chalk, if personal friends of the author, with a halo round their heads ; Hindostanis in charcoal.   It would be of no use for me to add another to the gallery.   The author has determined to try to paint people in their natural hues, Europeans an ordinary flesh-tint, Hindustanis

a copper colour. Some individuals will certainly b
disgusted. They would spoil the whole picture t
get themselves transfigured. The only thing they ca
do is to become as great and spotless as they wish t
be represented, which they will agree with me i
nothing very difficult, and then they will figur
accordingly in future history.

To the public I can say, with a good conscience
that I have always endeavoured to tell the truth an
conceal nothing; that I have no ill feeling agains
any human being that ever served at the siege; an
am not aware of the desire of adding to or detractin
from the exploits of any one. I hope that those, wit
whom I have had the honour to serve, will, allowin
for difference in matters of opinion, give their testi
mony to the general accuracy of this sketch of thei
exploits. Any corrections I may be favoured wit
I shall do my best to publish.

CONTENTS.

―――

CHAPTER I.

CHAPTER II.

CHAPTER III.

CHAPTER XII.

CHAPTER XIII.

APPENDIX.

SIEGE OF DELHI. ✳

CHAPTER I.

WITH Mahmud of Ghazni, A. D. 1001, and in the 391st year of the Hegira, the Mussulmans first entered India. His twelve expeditions were made rather for the acquisition of plunder than for the possession of the country, or the propagation of his faith; but after the followers of the Prophet had found their way into that beautiful land, they never again forgot it. A number of Mahomedan dynasties succeeded one another in Delhi. It was taken, and the inhabitants massacred by Timour Khan, in the year 1398, but soon passed to another family of kings, known in history as the House of Lodi. It was again conquered (1526) by Sultan Baber, the sixth in descent from Timour, at the head of an army drawn from his kingdom of Cabul. This was the first stable dynasty founded by the Mahomedans in India; and the student of Oriental history will always turn with pleasure to its

annals. The difficulties and dangers struggled wi
and overcome by its first princes, give to these pa
sages in the insipid chronicles of the East, the colou
ing of life and the charm of sympathy. A gre
historian of the West has remarked, that most king
if left alone, would sink to the level of the lowe
wretches on the earth. But this cannot be said
the first emperors of the race of Baber; the life
that prince, given in his memoirs, his never-endii
wars and misfortunes, his romantic adventures, h
generosity and devotion to his country, children, ar
friends, entitle him to an admiration, which me
elevation of rank can never obtain. The greatne
of Akber the royal philosopher, superintending tran
lations from the Sanscrit, disputing with moulvi
and missionaries on religion, holding the balance eve
between Hindoo and Mahomedan, and trying to cu:
the superstitions of each; the heroic prince slayii
Jei Mal with his own hand in the trenches, the ab
leader, the tamer of horses, yet a lover of peace ar
the fine arts, "affable and majestic, merciful ar
severe," has not yet been sufficiently recognised t
the learned men of Europe. Yet how much is l
superior to their Charlemagne, St. Louis, Otho, i
even to their Frederic the Great, or Charles V. ! Aftu
him we remark the magnificent Jehan, who built th

modern city of Delhi; and the able and politic Alamgir. The last-named emperor, generally called Aurangzib by Europeans, died in the fiftieth year of his reign, and the eighty-ninth of his life. He was one of the most skilful generals and able monarchs that ever lived in the East, but his religious zeal and exclusiveness disgusted the Hindoos, and his selfishness and suspicious temper estranged the Mahomedans. All his genius and incessant activity were insufficient to arrest the decline of the ruling race. All conquering tribes, existing as such, decay in India. Coming flushed with vigour from the cooler breezes of a less relaxing climate, they lose the desire as well as the necessity for exertion, amid the riches and luxuries which they have easily gained in one or two battles. The conquering Afghan built shady palaces, and planted gardens refreshed with fountains, and wore rich garments glittering with jewels; but his sword and spear became rusty, and he forgot the warlike exercises in which he took delight when a poor soldier in Cabul. His wife, who had gone to market in her bhoorkha, or cut grass for his horses in the clefts of the rocks, was now shut up in the rich zenana, which she rarely quitted. Hence half the race degenerated at once; and their children became feeble, relaxed, and indolent. Their rule only lasted

till some other tribe in its turn descended from tl
northern mountains, or till the children of the s(
shook off their degenerate oppressors.

And so Delhi was conquered, in the year 1739, l
the king of Persia, Nadir Shah ; and on an attempt
revolt, a terrible massacre of the inhabitants took plac
But this seizure was only for a time; Nadir Shah wei
away, never again to see India.   The two powe
which should destroy the Mogul emplre had con
into being during the life of Aurangzib.   It is not
our purpose to tell how the Mahrattas were raised l
the genius of Sivagi and his successors, from a bar
of robbers into a great power, which, but for tl
succour of the Persians under Ahmed Shah, 176
would have driven the Mahomedans out of India.

Nothing, however, could check the decline of tl
Mogul empire.   It sunk into a state of hopeless mil
rule and anarchy ; and Delhi was again seized by tl
Mahrattas, under Scindia, from whom it was wreste
by Lord Lake in the year 1803.

The blind old Emperor of Delhi, Shah Alun
whom he found in the palace, greeted the Britis
general as a deliverer, and seems to have expected t
be restored to a part of the inheritance of his famil;
He was left to reside in the palace ; allowed to kee
a guard of honour, and hold jurisdiction on thos

living within its walls, with a pension of twelve lacs of rupees a year. The whole of the Doab was joined to the British possessions, under whom it enjoyed a peace and tranquillity long unknown. The Mussulmans, however, still cherished the memory of their former empire. The kings of Delhi seem never to have abandoned their pretensions, and indeed, occasionally asserted them, though in an artful and cautious manner.

The history of the Sikhs is intimately connected with our story. They constitute a religious brotherhood, which was founded by Nanuk, a devotee and philosopher, who wandered through the world in search of the true religion, and returned to the Punjaub, his native country, about the end of the fifteenth century, to preach the result. He taught that forms of religion were not essential; that it was a good intention which was particularly pleasing to the Deity. His ideas of God and His worship were in the main good and pure, but mixed with Hindoo superstitions. His gospel was very successful. It had its apostles, saints, and martyrs. Thousands of Hindoos had been converted by the sword to Mahomedanism, and still hankered after the customs and superstitions of their fathers. But the Brahminical form of religion allows no return to those who

have abandoned its observances. The creed of Nanu
opened a door to the relapsing Mussulman, while
gratified the outraged self-respect of the lower caste
of Hindoos. " You make Mahomedans out of Hir
doos," said a Goroo, one of the successors of Nanul
to the badsha of Delhi : " I shall make Hindoos ou
of Mahomedans." Hence they were persecuted wit'
great cruelty by the Mahomedans. Tegh Bahadu
one of their Goroos, ninth in descent from Nanul
was dragged into the presence of the bigoted Aurang
zib. Though not regarded as an apostle, he was, a
the story goes, believed to be a mighty magician, an
was asked to give some display of his power. H
wrote a few words on a piece of paper, and stretchin
out his neck told the executioner to strike off hi
head. The credulous court was astonished to see i
fall on the ground. On the paper was found writtei
" He has given his head but not his secret," a pla
upon the words untranslatable into English. Hi
death made a deep impression on his followers, an
led his son and successor, Goroo Govind, to give
new form to their religion. The Sikhs were to follov
the profession of arms, always carry steel upo:
their persons, and never shave any hair. He mad
all the castes eat out of one dish. Henceforth the
formed one brotherhood. To the mild toleration c

Nanuk was added a political rancour to the Mussulman. A prophecy was cherished, that God was to grant them revenge for the death of their martyred Goroo ; and that the time would come, when they would storm and sack Delhi. They took up arms again and again to free themselves from the yoke of the Mahomedans ; they were beaten, chased into the hills, and almost extirpated. They rose, however, as the house of Timour Khan sank, and founded, a hundred miles from Delhi, the kingdoms of Patiala, Nabbha, and Jheend, but never gained many proselytes south of the Sutlej. In the country of the five rivers they became very numerous, and, under Runjit Singh, founded a large and powerful monarchy. That prudent ruler always avoided a collision with the English, but after his death his turbulent soldiery attacked the British power. Betrayed by their leaders, they still proved terrible enemies, but were conquered about 1847, and the whole Punjaub brought under British rule.

This immense accession of territory did not satisfy the Governor-General, Lord Dalhousie. A policy came into fashion, the programme of which was to seize all the independent states of India. A few common-places upon the predominance of the Anglo-Saxon race were thought sufficient to justify the

iniquity of the scheme. Lord Dalhousie followed i
up. He assembled an army, and, without any pro
vious declaration of war, or cause of hostility, an
contrary to the express promises of his own Govern
ment, stripped the King of Oude of all his posses
sions. The alleged cause was that the country wa
ill governed. The "atrocious Macchiavellism,"* tha
one power has a right to invade and seize upon th
dominions of another, because it believes it can gover
them better, might soothe the feeble disapproval which
the measure met with from some at home, but nobody
in the East believed we had such philanthropic motives
for the action. It was not forgotten how, a few years
before, we had sold the beautiful valley of Cashmere
for a sum of money, to Golab Singh, one of the most
odious tyrants that ever desolated Central Asia, and
had lent our troops to force the people to submit to
his hated sway. The Mahomedans have a close
sympathy with one another; to degrade a prince of
their religion is to put out one of the lights of
Islam. The King of Oude had long been our friend-
liest and truest ally. The country might be ill
governed; most eastern countries are so; but one
thing is clear, they preferred the rule of their native
princes to ours. Moreover, the great part of the

* Mill.

sepoys in our service came from Oude, where they retired after having gained their pension. Under the native rule they enjoyed privileges, such as exemption from some taxes, which were lost to them under that of the British. Hence even the Hindoo soldiers were very much disgusted with the seizure of Oude. They expressed their indignation in the most open manner, and told the King that, if he had resisted, they would have thrown down their arms and fought for him.*

To meet these immense additions to our territory there was no increase of the European troops in India. Some of them, indeed, had been sent away to the Russian war, and others to the recently conquered province of Pegu. The King of Oude's army amounted to nearly sixty thousand men, and large bodies were in the pay of the nobility. There were said to be two hundred and forty-six forts in the country, none of which were dismantled. We took into our service

* Major Bird, agent of the King of Oude, gave this last statement at a meeting in Manchester, 1st May 1857. (See *Lahore Chronicle*, July 15, 1857). As for the discontent of the sepoys, it was notorious, and remarked by every one who had an opportunity of noting it, and capacity for doing so. Lord Dalhousie had been warned beforehand by Colonel Sleeman, the Resident at Lucknow, that a mutiny of the native army would be the probable result of an annexation of Oude.

about one-fifth of the regular army, and disbanded th
rest, and, to keep all down, placed one regiment o
British soldiers in the city of Lucknow. Lord Da
housie, it is true, applied for more troops. The Go
vernment, however, seems to have thought, that, sinc
he could quietly seize upon a large kingdom withou
reckoning on any reinforcement, none was needed t
retain possession of it. Lord Dalhousie was a ma
of great administrative ability and energy, but every
thing he did seems to have drifted the native arm
to mutiny, a danger of which he certainly was no
sufficiently prescient.

Sir Charles Napier saw this tendency, and woul
have checked it [*] if he had remained Commander-in
Chief. A dangerous discontent appeared amongs
the sepoys in 1849, to dispel which, he thought i
necessary to keep out of operation a pay regulatio
of the Governor-General, who was at that time absen
on a sea voyage. The rising mutiny was quashed

---

[*] How like a prophecy are his words :—" Men from a
parts of Asia meet in Delhi, and some day or other muc
mischief will be hatched within those city walls, and n
European troops at hand. We shall see. I have no conf
dence in the allegiance of your high caste mercenaries."—
Letter to an artillery officer, published in *Bombay Telegrap
and Courier*, Sept. 30, 1857. He expresses the same view
in his published works.

and a regiment disbanded ; but the men had the satisfaction of seeing the great general rebuked by Lord Dalhousie, resign his command, and leave **India.**

On another occasion a native regiment resisted an order to go to Burmah, and Lord Dalhousie yielded. They were beginning to know their power.

The demeanour of the Governor-General was at the same time very displeasing to the native princes. One thing struck them in a tender part. Many of them had placed money in our funds, and Lord Dalhousie, without any warning, turned their five into a four per cent loan, a measure which, as might be expected, seriously damaged our credit in the money market. There is little doubt a series of intrigues was commenced against our power at this time by some of the leading men of Oude, with a view to compel us to abandon the country, as had happened in Cabul. The King of Delhi, Mohammed Bahadur Shah, who had long been discontented with the English, and had, nearly two years before, sent an envoy to the Shah of Persia to ask assistance against them, joined in the plot. The princes of his house, who knew that the British Government would not continue the title of King of Delhi to the heir-apparent, nor allow him to reside in the palace, were all eager

for rebellion. Efforts were made to corrupt the nativ
army. Pensions were paid to some of the nativ
officers ;* but little could be effected by bribery, an
their intrigues would perhaps have borne no fruit ha
it not been for a mistake of our own, which gave thei
the opportunity to gain over the Hindoos, by far th
preponderating element in our sepoy ranks, standin
in relation to the Mahomedans as five to one.

It is as difficult to make those in Europe undei
stand the importance of caste to a native, as t
make him perceive that it is unimportant with othe
people. Custom, public opinion, morality, and re
ligion, are the most powerful influences which act oi
human destiny. With the Hindoo all these ar
united into one, under the name of caste. A mai
who loses his caste loses his own self-respect ; h
feels as if he had committed a great crime. Every on
shuns him. A starving brother would not eat i
morsel of bread from his hand. His family, wh
suffer with him, deplore the shame and misery he ha

---

* One of the principal agitators in Oude, who also sen
agents to seduce the troops in our cantonments, is said t
have been a man called Mohsum-ood-dowlah.—See an articl
in *Friend of India*, March 10, 1859. The statements in it
though curious, are *valde probanda*, and after much flourishin,
lead at last to the cartridge question as the true cause of th
mutiny.

brought upon them. No one will give a daughter to him for a wife; he is cut off from all religious rites; if he dies, no one will come to his funeral; and he is taught to fear dreadful punishment in the next world. For time and for eternity he is a ruined man. The evils connected with this are excessive, yet the whole fabric of Hindoo morality (to whose precepts its votaries certainly give a more faithful obedience than Mahomedans or Christians in India do to those of their several creeds) rests upon this institution. A man is liable to the loss of caste by the commission of any flagrant immorality, by partaking of food that has been touched by men of lower caste, and especially by any use of the flesh of the cow, to kill which is considered an awful crime, requiring years of merciless penance. No Hindoo will even wash his hands with soap, as he suspects it to be made from the fat of that animal. If taken away for a venial offence, caste can be regained only by a ruinous fine, exacted in the shape of a feast to his brethren. A man of high caste, such as a Brahmin or Rajput, is thought entitled to great deference. It was principally from these two classes that our Bengal sepoys were recruited, simply because they contain the finest men, and make the bravest and most honourable soldiers. In stature and endurance

they surpassed any troops in the world. As men
high avoid the contact of men of low caste, the latt
were naturally excluded from the ranks. It wa
curious to see how the European officers becam
tinged with the prejudices of their sepoys, and value
natives by an imaginary scale, in which they kne
themselves to be at the bottom. For a Brahmi
sepoy to be deprived of his caste, was to him as cru
a calamity as for a peer of England to be lowered
the condition of a ticket-of-leave man.

It became necessary to use greased cartridges fo
the new rifle, which was to be supplied to the Beng
army. They were prepared near Calcutta by men o
the lowest caste, with the fat of the cow or pig, an
served to the sepoys at Barrackpore. They had t
bite the cartridges before loading. This was enoug
to destroy their caste. It is said that the first new
of their defilement was broken to them by one of th
Lascars, who had mixed the lard. He ostentatiousl
went up to a Brahmin soldier, and asked leave t
drink out of his lotah. The Brahmin, surprised
asked him how he could imagine he would defile hi
vessel by allowing him to touch it. The man retorted
that the sepoy's caste was gone, since they every da
put the fat of cows within their lips. The Hindo
struck with confusion, told the story to his comrade

Its truth was found to be undeniable. The men became enraged and suspicious. A report was spread that Lord Canning (who had succeeded Lord Dalhousie), had promised to convert all the sepoys to Christianity, which they believed could be accomplished by getting them to do something incompatible with their own religion, and making them perform some external rites. They had lost faith in our honour, and suspicion soon found ground to rest upon. They picked out, or imagined they picked out, little pieces of bone in their flour, which they supposed the merchants had been bribed to introduce, in order to carry out the same end.

The mere fear of being excommunicated by their brethren forced them to do something. They proclaimed their discontent to every one; incendiarism became common; and they held nightly meetings within their lines. All this was notorious in Calcutta towards the end of January 1857. The men believed themselves injured, and they had, so far at least, been injured by Government, though unintentionally; yet nothing was done to disabuse them of their suspicions, which were instantly caught up and skilfully worked upon, by letters and messengers to every regiment in the Bengal Presidency. Every native seemed to understand

the crisis, every European to mistake it; no expla
nation came from Government that their fears fo
their caste, which were built on a foundation o
fact, were idle, till these fables had become roote
beliefs in their minds. With a blindness commo
among men in authority, they imagined at head
quarters that they could suppress discontent by refu
ing to listen to it. The commander-in-chief, Genera
Anson, was fond of taking a little extra authority
such as giving General Orders regulating the civ
customs of the army; and he had caused man
Mahomedans to leave it, by an order for them t
shave their beards. Discontent of this kind woul
excite all his antipathies. One officer who made
report about it, was reproved for so doing. In th
meantime the story was spreading to every statio
in the Presidency, gained credence everywhere, an
is believed in India to this very day.

On the 24th February, a guard of the 34th Nativ
Infantry arrived at Berampore, about one hundre
miles to the north of Barrackpore. They told th
whole story of the greased cartridges, and of the plo
to ruin their caste; and the news had such an effec
on the regiment at the station, the 19th Nativ
Infantry, that next morning at parade the me
refused, and were only prevailed on by threats, t

take the cartridges, although there was nothing new about them.

That night they seized their arms, and assembled in open mutiny. A battery of native artillery, and a regiment of sowars were called out; but these being of little use against infantry, and themselves not to be trusted, the commanding officer was glad to order them away, on the assurance that the men would go quietly to their lines.

So helpless was the Government at Calcutta, that they were obliged to withdraw the only European regiment from Burmah to do something in Bengal. The 19th was ordered to Barrackpore to be disbanded; but ere it arrived, the first blood had been shed at that station. A sepoy of the 34th, called Mungul Pandy, openly trying to raise the men in mutiny, attacked and wounded the adjutant, Lieutenant Baugh, in presence of a guard of the regiment, who not only gave their officer no assistance while he was struggling for his life with the fanatic, but were upon the point of joining against him. The man was seized and hanged; and the jemadar of the guard, after an official delay of nearly a month (in order to make out his papers), met the same punishment. It was intended to disband the 34th regiment at once; but this was put off till the men were scarcely in time to

join the revolt up country. The 19th was disbande
on the last day of March, and the sepoys returned
their homes, spreading sedition in every station on tl
way. In the meantime the plot was ripening
over India. Almost every regiment was pledged
stand by the rest in defeuce of their caste.* T

* Our view is, that the mutiny was caused by a coml
nation amongst the sepoys to defend themselves from t
threatened deprivation of caste, taking afterwards a wider ai
We believe that the causes of no great historical moveme
whatever were more clearly proved ; but this very clearne
has made some people, who wished to shew superior peneti
tion, seek influences more obscure. Others have tried to dr:
attention to abuses in the army, by advertising them as caus
of the mutiny. The withdrawal of so many European offic
from their regiments, and the centralisation of power at hea
quarters, and consequent diminution of the authority of t
officers of corps have been assigned. But the mutiny oug]
under this view, to have begun with a relaxation of dis
pline in individual regiments, which most assuredly was r
the case.

Some time in February of 1857, a curious occurrence to
place. It began on the confines of Oude. A chokidar ran
to another village with two chapatties. He ordered his fello
official there to make ten more and give two to each of t
five nearest village chokidars, with the same instructions.
a few hours the whole country was in a stir, from chokid:
flying about with these cakes. The signal spread in
directions with wonderful celerity. The magistrates tried
stop it ; but, in spite of all they could do, it passed along
the borders of the Punjaub. There is reason to believe tl
this was originated by some intriguers of the old court

sepoys felt their power. From Calcutta to Meerut, about nine hundred miles, there was not a European regiment, save a weak one at Agra, and a few companies at Cawnpore. The quota of European troops in India was four thousand men lower than usual.

Lucknow. Its import has not been satisfactorily explained, and was probably not understood by many who helped it along. But the same thing occurred in 1860 in Behar, and about Jhansi, in connection with the discontent caused by the new income tax. It has been stated by a native authority, published by Mr. Russell of the Times (see *Friend of India*, 10th March 1859), that the first circulation of the chapatties was made at the suggestion of a learned and holy pundit, who told Rajah Madhoo Singh, that the people would rise in rebellion if it were done, and that the person in whose name the cakes were sent, would rule all India. This, however, is very doubtful. Almost all writers allow a considerable importance to the cartridge grievance, but no two agree as to the relative weight of any other cause. Colonel Bourchier (see " Eight Months' Campaign against the Bengal Sepoys") rejects them all in the words of General Nicholson, " neither greased cartridges, the annexation of Oude, nor the paucity of European officers were the causes. For years," he said, " I have watched the army, and felt sure, they only wanted their opportunity to try their strength with us." Very likely, if Nicholson had watched the army forty years sooner, he would have discovered the same tendency, as many great statesmen actually did. What would be said of a doctor giving evidence on the death of a man from loss of blood by a sword cut, who said it was not the wound that was the cause of death, for he had observed that the blood would leave the vessels whenever it had an opportunity ? There is not a particle of proof that any

The whole country was theirs whenever they cho:
to rise. The Punjaub might be expected to jo:
them with its warlike population. Their fellow-sepo:
who garrisoned its towns, greatly outnumbered tl
white regiments. They had conquered the country f:
the Company; why not take it for themselves? Amt
tious men there were in plenty to lead them—m:
who, in former days, would have entered into, a:
risen high in the service of the native princes; b:
to whose desire of power there was now no outl:
save by sweeping away the rule of the English, tl
most exclusive of castes. These men must have see
that it was impossible for the Government to car
out any scheme to ruin their ·caste. They n:
evidently entertained bolder ideas than that of su
cessful resistance. The horse that gets his own w:
never rests till he has thrown his rider. The mass
the sepoys, ignorant and passionate as children, w:
under the influence of such men, and driven rapid
on to rebellion. It was believed that we could reck:
on the assistance of the Mahomedan against t:

mutiny would have occurred in 1857 had it not been for t
greased cartridges. For a more copious account of the ori:
of the rebellion, see the "Red Pamphlet." Read also t
history of the mutiny at Vellore, caused by an attempt
interfere with the dress and religious customs of the Mad:
sepoys.

superstitions of the Hindoo. The Mahomedan had
no objection to the fat of the cow ; but the story went
that the cartridges were also greased with that of the
hog, to him an unclean animal. The Mussulmans of
India regard themselves as a caste, though they do
not hold to the idea, originally foreign to their creed,
with the tenacity of the Hindoos. And what a pro-
found ignorance of the followers of Islam, to imagine
they would stretch out a finger to save a threatened
Christian power !

Saving the instances given above, the outward
demeanour of the whole army remained as respectful
as usual. To their officers they vehemently denied
all intention of mutiny, though they confessed their
anxiety about their caste. Unfortunately their pro-
fessions were too much trusted. Old officers would
not believe that the men, along with whom they had
marched and fought for a generation, in whose chival-
rous honour their faith had never been shaken, and
whom they loved and were proud of, could prove
unfaithful to their salt. If they perceived any disaffection, it was in some other regiment than their
own. But a number of occurrences shewed the working of the poison. The newly-established rifle-depots
at Umballa and Sealkote called together a few men
from a great number of regiments only to concert

sedition. That a plot was formed at the first of thes
stations is certain. The soldiers there were very di
contented ; houses were set on fire almost every nig
by some unknown hand ; and one day, in a fit
excitement, they assembled on parade, broke into
bell of arms, and took their muskets.

It was only the energy and skill of Sir Hen
Lawrence that prevented an outbreak at Luckno
A mutinous regiment there had to be disarmed. Sti
it is wonderful how few Europeans appreciated th
greatness of the danger. None could deny that ther
was much excitement amongst the sepoys, fomente
by the native press, and worked upon by disaffecte
persons ; but further than this they could not se
The mind of the natives, however, was troubled ; the
either knew more or understood better than th
Europeans. They felt something dreadful was a
hand. Those who had money, hid it in the eartl
and fear was in the hearts of all ; the jackals wer
heard to howl more dismally at night ; the dogs t
weep round the villages ; and voices came from th
jungle crying, mar, mar (smite, smite).

CHAPTER II.

At Meerut it had been reported that the sepoys there had vowed not to touch any cartridges whatsoever. As this was the only cantonment in India where the European force was stronger than the native, no better opportunity could be found of shewing that we were determined to break such a dangerous combination. A parade of the 3d Native Cavalry was ordered. It was told them that they were expected to be a pattern to the other men; that they need not bite the cartridges, which were the same they had always used, but open them with the finger. They sent in a very respectful petition, stating that they did not wish to become the object of the scorn of their companions, and praying the parade to be deferred till the excitement was over. The parade took place, and the cartridges were offered to ninety carabiniers, a proportion of whom had been given by each troop; five men accepted them; eighty-five refused. They were instantly put under arrest, tried by court-martial, and condemned to hard labour for ten years. On the morning of the 9th May 1857,

a parade was held of all the force in Meerut. Tl
60th Rifles, the Carabiniers, Major Tombs' troop
Horse Artillery, and a field battery, were drawn v
against the native regiments, the 3d Light Cavalr
and the 11th and 20th Native Infantry, so that an
resistance on their part would be followed by instal
slaughter. The eighty-five high-caste troopers wei
brought on the ground, stripped of their uniform, an
the irons hammered on their limbs by the artillel
smiths. They were condemned to work on the road
for ten years. The only sign of emotion noticed wa
one deep sigh, which burst at once from all the blac
battalions. The condemned men were sent **away 1**
jail, and the parade dissolved. General Hewitt, i
command of the station, went away, to write **a con**
placent report of the affair to headquarters. Th
disposition of the sepoys, he remarked, was excellen
Private letters from officers of the 11th and 20tl
said this too. The native regiments returned to thei
huts ; nothing particular was noticed even by th
European sergeant-majors who live in the line
Next day was Sunday. It passed away drowsily
though uneasy rumours flitted up and down. Peopl
were preparing to go to the evening service, or t
take a ride at sunset.

At five o'clock a rocket is let off in the sepo

lines ; there is a tumultuous gathering ; they seize their arms and fire at their officers, four of whom drop. The 3d Light Cavalry mount their horses ; some officers ride in amongst them trying to pacify them, but none listen ; there is such a clamour that no word can be heard ; some are struck at and wounded. A part of them gallop away to the jail, whirling their sabres over their heads. One of their officers is carried along with them. There is only a native guard at the jail ; the doors are thrown open with shouts ; they set their imprisoned comrades free. A smith is at hand, who knocks off their chains. The officer, who was much beloved in his regiment, entreated the men not to accept their freedom in such a way, and said he would get their pardon if they stayed. They embraced him with tears, but said, after what had happened, they never could trust the Company any more. Fourteen hundred convicts are at the same time let loose, who rush eagerly away to reap the harvest of plunder and violence. A part of the sowars, with the 20th, went to the lines of the 11th to turn the tide of disaffection in its ranks, for it was not yet entirely gained over. Colonel Finnis was there endeavouring to address the men and keep them to their duty. They instantly fired at the un-fortunate gentleman, whose death decided the waver-

ing regiment. The sepoys of the 11th now join
with the rest, but protected the officers and ladie
It was the plan of the mutineers to set upon ai
massacre the Europeans assembled in church. Fort
nately the signal was given too early. The sepo
fall upon and kill everybody they meet ; joined wit
the rabble of the bazaars, they run to plunder tl
long lines of beautiful cottages in which the Eur
pean families resided. They push their muskets in
the thatch and fire ; in a few minutes they are all
a blaze. They break in at the glass doors, plund
and destroy everything, and search everywhere wit
bloodthirsty eagerness for the " Feringhee suars
Ladies and children are seized with exultation, an
tormented to death. The Europeans who get clea
fly away to the English barracks. Some hide a
night in the gardens and compounds, hoping evei
moment to hear the voices of their countrymen 1
their rescue. All the bungalows in the native line
. are burned and sacked. For two hours the work (
hell goes on,—tumult, murder, pillage, conflagration
they fight for the spoil and kill one another. An
what are our soldiers doing ? They are all armed an
ready, panting with fury, eager to rescue their dyin
countrywomen, eager for blood and vengeance,—th
noble soldiers of our race, able to slaughter twent

times their number of sepoys. General Hewitt's order comes ;—what is it? "Defend your lines!" The general is explaining to his staff (most of whom acquiesce) the proper course to pursue :* The sepoys are scattered over a wide space ; the armed budmashes of the Sudder are with them, plundering, killing, and burning. We cannot save houses fired almost simultaneously. After all, the mischief is probably over. Look, there is the last of the bungalows on fire! How can we get at them? Lead out some troops to one point, they will go to another. Chase them out of the sepoy cantonment, they will unquestionably run to destroy our own. I object to leave a guard ;—to divide our force is to destroy the whole. Before he could be prevailed on to make a cautious movement against the rebels, they had completed the destruction of all the houses south of the nullah, and had taken the road to Delhi. We came up with a large body of them, who fled into a tope. We fired grape into it ; but they probably suffered no loss in the darkness. They were not followed far. The station was now clear of them, and General Hewitt's duty was done. An old sepoy officer, he

* The arguments used by himself and his "Friend" in the "Lahore Chronicle," July 22, 1857, are here given in a condensed form.

exaggerated the prowess of the natives, and could n
think himself strong enough to march a detachme
on Delhi. He sent messengers to Brigadier Grav
who commanded there, to warn him what he mig
expect ; and marched back his men, " to strength
the barracks, and take precautions against attacl
The bazaar people and Goojur villagers continu
plundering the lines all night. Some time after l
took sick leave to the hills, and finally left for Europ
protesting on the way, that if he had had to mana
the thing over again, he could not have done
otherwise.

As the morning broke on the smoking rui
and trampled gardens, those who had been hiding
night ventured out, and the Europeans came an
brought away their dead. Many of them were
mutilated that their features could not be recognise
Thirty-one bodies of Europeans were buried. T
British in India live in cottages, generally surround
by a large compound and garden ; and this, though
then rendered them less capable of mutual defen
gave them a greater chance of escaping by flight.
was no doubt to this circumstance, and to their bei
well mounted, that many Europeans owed their liv
during the murderous times of the mutiny. Scen
of horrid cruelty had been acted, which were exa

gerated tenfold by popular report. The Oriental, who had played the hypocrite so long, now appeared in all the lurid cruelty of his character. The rage and fury of the Europeans were indescribable, especially as it was known that some of the worst outrages had been done by the people of the Sudder bazaar. Thirteen artillerymen rushed through it, killing all who came in their way.

Meanwhile the mutineers were speeding the live-long night to Delhi, where they arrived early the next morning, 11th May 1857. The cavalry, who had got a-head of them, secured the bridge of boats over the Jumna. The situation of Brigadier Graves at Delhi was as bad as could be. By a stipulation with the King, no European troops could be placed there; the Government, however, had judged it a convenient place for the greatest magazine in India. The city was inhabited by a large Mahomedan population, who clustered round the king, and clung to the traditions of their former greatness. The princes and courtiers passed their lives in luxury and debauchery of every kind. The wickedness of Delhi was a proverb all over India. The Mahomedans seem to have had some idea of the coming revolt. A placard in Persian was posted up on the walls of the Jumna Musjid (or great mosque of Delhi), in the beginning of April, announ-

cing that the king of Persia was coming to drive t
infidels out of India.

It may be well to premise, that the palace wa
look over the causeway which leads from the bridg
and, a little farther on, along the river face, stood t
magazine, the Delhi College, the houses of the ci
employés, and the warehouses of the European me
chants, which were all within the walls. The Cas
mere gate led out to the native cantonment, which l
on the farther slope of a ridge of hill about two mil
off. The commissioner, Mr. Simon Fraser, was arous
by the report that some sowars had entered t
city very early in the morning, announcing that th
had killed many Europeans in Meerut, and that a
the regiments were behind, intending to do the sar
at Delhi. He endeavoured to make such arrang
ments as would prevent the rabble of the city fro
rising. Sir T. Metcalfe, who was with him, went
the magazine to get a couple of guns to guard t
bridge. It was too late. Some of the sowars rode i
to the commissioner, who had been joined by Capta
Douglas of the palace guards, and Mr. Hutchinso
The last gentleman was wounded, but the commi
sioner shot a sowar with his own hand. His cha
rassies deserting him, he went into the palace
ask aid from the king, which was promised. In tl

meantime, all the mutinous regiments had arrived;—
about half-past seven A.M. they were seen crossing the
bridge in open column, headed by the cavalry, and
were at once admitted at the palace gates, which they
entered cheering. The commissioner, after being cut
down by a lapidary, who resided within the palace
walls, was despatched by several of the king's servants, who then ran up stairs to the apartments of
Captain Douglas, living also, with Mr. Jennings
the chaplain, within the walls. The door of the
room where these unfortunate gentlemen, with some
friends and two ladies,* were assembled, was beaten
open, and they were all murdered. The mutineers
caused a servant to point out the body of Captain
Douglas, to ensure he had not escaped.

Joined by the palace guards, they then rushed to

---

* Miss Jennings, the daughter of the chaplain, was murdered at once by the side of her father. I am particular about
the fate of this unfortunate young lady, because false accounts
of it were spread abroad, which have even got into printed
books. (See Red Pamphlet). The interests of truth compel
me to spoil the effect of the very graphic passage in the same
work, where the author describes Brigadier Graves leading the
54th "out of the Cashmere gate" against the rebels, "advancing from the Hindun." The Hindun was ten miles off, and
the 54th were led *into* the Cashmere gate, not out of it.
Everything in his description is turned outside-in as it
goes on.

the civil lines. In a few minutes the beautiful qu:
ter was grim with uproar and murder, fire and p
lage. Few who lived within the city walls were al
to escape. Whole families were butchered. You:
girls, who had that morning gently awoke in th(
peaceful homes, were dragged over the threshc
across the dead bodies of their parents by hideo
miscreants. Modesty and decency were outraged
the open streets. One lady, in defence of her chil
shot two of the wretches with her husband's pisto.
when a sepoy ran his bayonet through her back. Tl
sowars distinguished themselves by their blood-thirs:
ness. The populace were abreast of the sepoys. Tl
houses were gutted. Every thing was broken, sca
tered about, or snatched away. They kept prowlii
into every corner, till the burning roofs drove the:
out. The treasury and the Delhi bank were brok(
open, and rupees by bundles carried off.

On the first news of the approach of the insu
gents, Brigadier Graves had sent a circular to tl
European residents, bidding them repair to the Fl:
Staff tower beside the cantonment. It overlookt
both the sepoy lines and the city ; and, being on tl
road to Umballa, was in every way favourable as
place of refuge ; but, unfortunately, to many tl
order came too late. At the same time two guns an

the 54th Native Infantry were ordered to proceed to
the city. The regiment seemed willing and loyal,
marched away quietly, passed through the Cashmere
gate, and came in sight of the tumult a little farther
on. The sowars instantly rode up to them with the
greatest confidence, and singled out their European
officers, whom the men suffered to be shot and cut
down without any apparent concern. Many of the
54th now joined the mutineers, and ran to take a
share in the plunder. There was a guard of fifty
men of the 38th at the Cashmere gate. The officer
in command seeing all this, ordered it to be closed,
lest the mutiny should spread back to the cantonments. At the same time the guard would do
nothing against the mutineers, and refused any assistance to the colonel of the 54th, who was cut down
by some sowars almost at their feet. At this moment
the two guns which had come on behind, escorted by
the grenadier companies of the 54th, under Major
Paterson,* entered the gate, and his men remaining
for the time obedient, the tumult flowed back towards
the city. Major Paterson was told that the rest of
the regiment had run away to the Subzi Mundi, and
some of them actually returned by his orders to the

* The evidence of Major Paterson was given at the trial
of the King of Delhi.—Blue book, p. 95.

Cashmere gate, followed by the sowars inciting th
to mutiny.   The news of the disaffection of the 5
soon reached cantonments, and produced great
citement among the sepoys who still remained
their lines. Some left to join the rest in the c
The brigadier sent two more guns and some co
panies of the 74th to the Cashmere gate. Tl
reached it about this time, but the officers w
unable to do anything with their men, beyond send
in the bodies of the murdered officers of the 54
They were brought up in a bullock cart to the fl
staff. The sepoys pointed to them and cried to
crowd of Europeans there—"The Company wis
to take away our caste, on this account have
killed them." They became every moment m
excited and threatening in their demeanour.

A party of the 38th, who had mutinied on t
ridge near their lines, met two guns of the batte
which were returning to cantonment agreeably
orders. They fired at Captain de Teissier, who l
ridden up to bring the artillery to the flag-staff. :
escaped with difficulty, but the guns were turr
back with the 38th mutineers, to join the rest in t
city. Reaching the Cashmere gate just as Ma
Abbot, commanding the detachment of the 74th, v
leaving it, he asked them why they had return

The gunners looked sulky, and gave evasive replies, upon which he ordered his own men, who were already falling off and joining the mutineers, quickly away to cantonments, and told the gunners to follow. All his officers had not passed the gate when the deserters from the 38th came up, seized, and shut it, and then commenced firing at the officers and some ladies from the Residency, who had, so far at least, managed to escape. Anxiety to share in the plunder lured the wretches away ; and some of the officers and ladies succeeded in dropping down the wall from the bastions, and scrambling, stunned and bruised, out of the ditch. A party of them escaped on foot, through incredible dangers and hardships, to Meerut. Major Abbot wished to bring back his men to their rescue ; but the sepoys made it clear that if they turned, it would be to join, not to prevent the mas⁻ sacre. The sole part our officers were suffered to play in this cruel tragedy was that of victims or spectators.

The magazine, which was within the city walls, not far from the palace, was, of course, in danger from the very beginning. The officers in charge had seen the mutineers crossing the bridge in the morn⁻ ing, and Lieutenant Willoughby had gone with Sir T. Metcalfe to endeavour to get the gates closed. On his return he found eight of the officers attached to

the establishment, Lieutenants Forrest and Rayn
Conductors Buckley, Shaw, and Scully, Sub-conduc
Crowe, and Sergeants Edward and Stewart, with
native lascars and servants. Preparations w
instantly begun for the defence of the magazine*
the arrival of relief from Meerut, which none doubt
was at hand. It consisted of a number of buildir
enclosed by a high wall. The gates were closed a
barricaded. Inside the gate leading to the park w
placed two six-pounders, doubly charged with gra
The two sergeants stood by with lighted match
ready, if that gate should be attacked, to fire **both**
once, and fall back upon the body of the magazir
At the principal gate two guns were put in positic
with a chevaux-de-frise on the inside ; **and a litt**
behind, but bearing upon the same point, were tv
others. Farther in were placed four more **piec**
commanding two cross passages. **A train was la**
to the powder magazine, **ready** to be fired on a giv
signal. Arms were put in the hands of the nati
establishment, which they took sulkily. **They we**
getting insolent and disobedient, the Mussulma

---

* This account is condensed from the official report
Lieutenant Forrest. See *Times*, 17th September 1857. Al
a short narrative by him in the *Lahore Chronicle*, July 15t
of the same year.

particularly so. Scarcely had these arrangements been made when the palace guards appeared, and demanded the magazine in the name of the Badsha of Delhi. No answer was given.

The king, they heard soon after, had sent word, that ladders would be immediately brought from the palace to scale the walls. The natives in the magazine scarcely concealed their hostility. One man was seen to be communicating with the mutineers outside, through the gate, and ordered to be shot if he was observed doing so again. The enemy, who had thus learnt what was ready for them, did not attempt to force the gates ; but in a short while the scaling ladders arrived. On their being placed against the walls, the whole of the lascars deserted, climbing over the sloped sheds on the inside and down the ladders. It was found they had hid the priming pouches. The enemy now appeared in hundreds on the walls. The guns were immediately pointed at them, and worked as quickly as was possible, considering the fewness of the party. Nine Britons alone in that great Mahomedan city, betrayed and given up even by their own countrymen, they thought of nothing but holding their post to the death. The enemy kept firing down upon them. In a few minutes several of the little band were wounded ; it was clear that in a

few more they would be all shot. Willoughby tl
gave the signal for firing the powder store. Scul
who had distinguished himself even here by his d
perate coolness, in the most careful and methodi
manner lighted the trains. The explosion took pl
almost immediately. The wall adjoining was thro
upon the ground; numbers of the enemy were bur
among the ruins; and thousands of bullets from t
cartridges in store were hurled far off, striking do
people in the streets. What is astonishing, half t
defenders of the magazine crept out alive, ha
stunned, blackened, scorched, and bruised, but al
to make their way through the sally port by the riv
for the Cashmere gate. Lieutenants Forrest and Ra
nor, and Conductor Buckley succeeded in escaping
Meerut. Willoughby was seen at the Cashmere ga
and set out for Meerut with three more, who were
murdered in a village on the road. Scully, who w
much hurt, was killed, when trying to escape, by
sowar. The explosion of the magazine was of cour
seen from the flag-staff tower; and was heard eve
at Meerut.

On the return of Major Abbot's party, it becar
clear that there was no hope of the sepoys, who we
still in the lines, remaining in their duty; inde
there was danger every minute of their setting up

the Europeans assembled round the flag-staff, whose lives were really in their power. Several parties of fugitives had already left for Umballa or Meerut. That morning the men did not appear ripe for revolt; but they were gradually infected by bad example. Sepoys from the mutinied regiments appeared in their lines, and urged them to join. About sunset those men of the 38th who had not deserted, and had remained quiet, few of them having been in the city, told their colonel and adjutant to go away, for they would serve the Company no longer. A general flight had already taken place; the brigadier was one of the last to leave.

Thus was Delhi lost; though one thing is beyond doubt, that had even a few squadrons of the carabiniers dashed into the city an hour or two after the mutineers from Meerut, or had four hundred of the Rifles filed over the bridge about noon, myriads of graves might have now been empty. Even the King of Delhi could not believe that there was no pursuit. He sent out a man on a sowaree camel along the Meerut road, who returned with the report that there were no European troops within twenty miles.*

---

* This fact was given to Mr. Rotton by the deputy-collector of Delhi. The reverend gentleman evidently believes that the mutiny of all the sepoys in the lines was caused by the report of the messenger.

The cantonment was soon pillaged and burn
The savage villagers from the neighbourhood, cal
Goojurs, had been hovering round it from the mo
ing, anxious to snatch some of the beautiful thi
they had often admired, as they looked through
screens at the doors, when bringing their produce
their heads to sell.   They now appeared with swo
and cudgels, squabbling with the sepoys for a share
the plunder.

Many of the Europeans trying to escape were
upon by the villagers on the road, stripped of th
clothes, and insulted.   As they were seen toil
along half-naked in the hot sun, the people wo
cry out, where were their servants, punkahs, and i
water?   Many were killed.   The Mahomedan
lagers distinguished themselves by their crue.
The greater part, however, got at last to Umballa
Meerut.   Some were protected and kindly treated
weeks in Hindoo villages, till the advance of our ar
enabled them to get off with safety.

The first news of all these doings was borne al
the telegraph from Delhi.   The signaller sent w
that the sepoys from Meerut were burning the hous
and he must now try to escape; but the poor n
perished before the message left the office in Umba
It was passed along to Lahore.   We had thus

first move all over the Punjaub. It was said that the leaders of the revolt had arranged, that a simultaneous outbreak should take place in every station in the Bengal Presidency; and writers on the mutiny are eloquent on the terrible danger which we escaped by the premature rising at Meerut. History, however, shews that such secrets, necessarily confided to so many, are always betrayed; while common sense and a knowledge of the native character lead to the conclusion that such would have also been the case in the present instance. The powers of deception of the Hindustani are wonderful; but among a number of them there are always some traitors. After all, the mutineers had no reason to complain of ill luck in the beginning of the rebellion.

CHAPTER III.

THE effect produced by the news of these massac
was such as no one who saw it will ever forget, nor 1
one who did not, will ever realise. The idea that
natives would dare to rebel was sufficient to sti1
fury the mind of the Anglo-Indian, like all conqu
ing races, imperious and passionate. But on its be
known that not only was such the case, but that
rebels were our own sepoys—of all classes in In
the most honoured, petted, and trusted—the ven
of ingratitude maddened the sores of pride ; and w1
it was added that they had poured out and defi
our kindly English blood, no words can express
burning desire of vengeance that followed.

European families in India are generally rela
to one another. In almost every station some vic
had kindred, always many friends. Public hat
and private wrong went together, while indignat
and thirst for vengeance kept fear and alarm at a (
tance, if these could ever have entered the minds (
race of soldiers. The English, generally so cold {
stiff, were roused as children of one mighty mot1

The energy that now appeared, struck the natives with astonishment. For years they had never seen their conquerors venture out in the sun, scarcely crossing the court-yard without an umbrella; now they rode all day in the hot wind, changing their luxurious messes for a morsel of unleavened bread and a drink of muddy water. They now saw everything and did everything for themselves. The European soldier mounted guard, and did sentry duty for the first time in India. A single glance shewed all, that it was only by doing and daring, as had never been done and dared before, that we could gain vengeance or save ourselves. There was every ground to believe that the Doab and all its garrisons were gone.

The horizon in the Punjaub seemed to forebode inevitable storm. That country was full of a robust and manly population, totally dissimilar to us in religion, language, manners, and tone of thought. Most to be feared were the Sikhs, trained to war from their infancy, and despising everything else; among whom were scattered the old soldiers of Rungit Singh, still chafing at their discomfiture in the battles of the Sutlej, and eager to resume the profession of arms. Many large towns were left under the charge of two or three European Magis-

trates and the native police. The army we l
there had never been thought too large to garris
it; and now all the native portion must be coun
against us. Could we hold the Punjaub with ι
rest, or dare to detach a single man to avenge ι
massacres of Delhi? We had but eleven regime
of infantry, as many troops and batteries of artille
and one cavalry regiment, to hold all the Punja
from Kurnaul to Peshawur, about fourteen milli(
of souls. There were twenty-nine native regime
of Poorbeah infantry, with four of Sikhs, and ten
cavalry, four being Punjaubee, eleven troops and b
teries of artillery, in all about thirty thousand men
be watched and kept down. To those who read arij
the lessons given at Meerut and Delhi, not one
these regiments was to be trusted ; and all, save (
or two, and the Sikhs and Ghoorkas, sided against
in the end. There was, besides, a long frontier to
guarded where all wished us ill. No one would hι
been astonished at Golab Singh doing any thing b,
or treacherous. He might even have used his naι
deeply tarnished as it was, to raise the old Sikh w
cry down the five rivers. Our whole Peshawur fr
tier was hemmed in by those untameable hill-tril
with whom we were almost constantly at war.
the north-west was Cabul, with our old enemy D

Mohammed ruling over it still; behind him Persia and Russia. To the west was the state of Bawulpore, the rajah of which, though a prince of our own raising, began instantly to intrigue, till reminded by the chief commissioner that those who made could yet unmake. To the south was our recent conquest of Scinde, full of fierce Beloochies, and fraught with the deepest Mahomedan fanaticism. The Hindoo tribes that lived amongst the Himalayan range on the northeast, might not be very formidable, from their want of union, ·but could do us much mischief by plundering our hill-stations, which to them seemed so many rich palaces.

It was at first hoped that the mutiny would not spread; but this chimera every post went to destroy. There was nothing for it, but to meet the dangers as they came. Moreover, some advantages appeared in our position, on which at the outset we had not calculated. The Sikhs, who before us ruled the Punjaub, had little reason to feel confidence in their old leaders, many of whom too were dead, others in exile. The Mahomedans, who remembered how their mosques had been turned into stables, and the tombs of their saints into pigstyes, under the rule of the Sikhs, were not anxious to have such lords again. The Sikhs on their side hesitated to promote

a revolt, which might place the King of De
again over the Punjaub, and they were unwill
to aid the revengeful Mussulman, in carrying aw
the silver gates, and polluting the holy tank of
Goroo-ka-Durbar of Umritsur.

The money-making Hindoos had not forgot
the rapacious soldiery of Shere Singh, and the for
contributions which the former rajahs in Lahore l
wrung out of their hoards. They could make m
money, and keep it all, under the sway of the wh
people, and this was enough for them. Besides, 1
whole Punjaub proper, save the trans-Indus stai
had been disarmed; and although men might l
wise, and talk of whole parks of artillery hidden
the sand, and though no doubt individuals could
their hands on concealed arms, there can be no qu
tion that, in the event of a rising, they would ha
been very much at a loss for weapons, especially fi
arms.

Another impulse, the most powerful of all, so
shewed itself. An old grudge existed between
Poorbeahs and Punjaubees, which had, since the Si
wars, grown into ferocious hatred. After the batt
on the Sutlej, the Poorbeah sepoys had swagge
through every village in the Punjaub, and boasted
every bazaar, that they had conquered the country, a

that one Poorbeah could fight ten Punjaubees. Poorbeah soldiers garrisoned their cities, and Poorbeah employés stood between the European magistrate and the people, hoodwinking justice and fingering bribes. We soon perceived that the mutineers could gain no sympathy in the Punjaub, and that Sikh regiments were eager to fight them. Every deserter was brought in by the villagers. The great height and strange accent of the sepoys gave them no chance of escape. When it was known that an army would be marched to take Delhi, the old prophecy revived amongst the Sikhs. The time had come when they were to take revenge on the house of Timour Khan for the death of Tegh Bahadur.

In another chapter it will be related how these feelings were worked upon and taken advantage of by the ability of the Government. At present it is sufficient to remark, that no invasion came from without, that all the Punjaub across the Sutlej remained quiet, and that we had the assistance of the population in dealing with the evil-disposed sepoys in its cantonments. On the first telegram of the Delhi mutiny, Mr. Montgomery, the judicial commissioner, who was acting at Lahore for Sir John Lawrence, then absent at Bawul Pindi, determined, with the concurrence and approval of the commander, Brigadier Cor-

bett, to disarm the four native regiments at Lahc
They were ordered to parade on the morning of {
13th May, and three thousand five hundred m
piled arms before three hundred European infant
and a dozen horse artillery guns.

The wisdom of this procedure was much qu
tioned, and even Sir John Lawrence, on his retu
was dissatisfied with Mr. Montgomery ; but in a d
or two news came from Ferozepore, a station to t
north of Umballa, which vindicated the foresight
that gentleman.   On the first word of what had ha
pened at Delhi, Brigadier Innes ordered a parade
the troops there,—two native regiments, the 57th a
45th infantry, H. M.'s 61st, and a battery of artille
The sepoys had laid a plan of rising two days lat
The 57th were to have stormed the intrenched arsen
as a company of theirs was in charge ; the 45
cavalry to have cut off the officers, and then attack
the Europeans, who, they expected, would be tryi
to retake the arsenal.   A detachment of Europe
troops was sent to guard this important magazu
The native regiments were marched out of canto
ments by different roads ;—no attempt was made
disarm them.   The 45th passed the arsenal on t
way, and seeing all their hopes of success vanishi
suddenly, they attempted to break in at the gates ;.

only one company of Europeans had arrived, who,
however, drove them back. The insurgents then procured scaling-ladders, placed them against the walls,
and actually succeeded in getting into the intrench-
ments, where they were again met by the same Europeans, just as the company of the 57th, still on duty
there, were loading their muskets to join them. Two
more European companies now came up, and the
natives were beaten back, and many of them killed.

The whole affair was out of concert ;—the 57th did
not join in it, and the 10th cavalry made a show of
taking our side. If they had done so seriously, they
might have cut off all the mutineers, who were driven,
with numbers sadly diminished, out of the station.
The 57th were disarmed and the regiment disbanded ;
but there were not more than a dozen sepoys to hear
the sentence ; the rest of them had deserted to
Delhi.

On the 16th, Sir John Lawrence telegraphed to
Jullundur to secure the fort of Phillour. Two
marches to the south, and commanding the bridge
over the Sutlej, it contained the only magazine that
could now furnish us with a siege train. It was held
by the 3d Native Infantry, who, it was said, had made
up their minds to seize it on the very day on the
morning of which a company of Europeans and two

D

horse artillery guns from Jullundur quietly p:
through the gates. The native guard there star
them as if they had been spectres; and had not
sence of mind left even to give a military s:
From what evils did not the message of the unf
nate signaller at Delhi save us! Without that
gram we had been lost!

Where, in the meantime, was the commande
chief? He was out of the reach of the electric
deep amongst the hills. About forty miles from
balla rises, abrupt from the plain in awful precip
the mountain ridge of Kussowlie. On the top o
wild pine-clad hill, six thousand feet high, in the
climate in which Europeans delight, are barracks
houses, with the station church. Here was the '
Foot. In the second range, about ten miles off, st
the bare and bleak mountain, on the summit of w
is the station of Dugshai, then sheltering the 1st I
liers. Still deeper in, but much lower, in a
tropical climate, are the barracks and white bunga
of Sabbathoo, where were the 2d Fusiliers. A'
thirty miles farther on, far out of the sight of I
surrounded by awful ghauts and precipices, there
mighty hill eight thousand feet high. On its to
a somewhat larger space of level ground than is (
mouly seen among these mountains, ever so won

fully steep. A wandering Englishman had once come to this desert, where the most far-fetched fancy of a native could never have dreamt of building anything but the low stone hut for the poor mountaineer, who would turn the nearest waterfall to irrigate each narrow shelf of soil, which his rude ploughshare scratched on the edge of the abyss. The stranger returned with a report that the climate was as cool as his own England, and soon the first cottage was built in Simla, —a marvel to the untaught hillmen in the stony ravines below. In a few years Simla was a city. A thousand houses and pleasant cottages, reached by stairs and narrow winding paths, nestled on every nook, amongst the Himalayan pines, yews, and rhododendrons, that shade the rocks from the ever powerful sun of India, but let through the breezes that cross from the crescent of eternal snow, whose spotless zigzag line refreshes the eye turned upon the northern range. Here the fainting invalid finds he can live again, as the cool air fills his chest. The breath of the grave does not mount so high. Here young officers come to spend their months of privileged leave ;—ladies come to escape the heat of the plains. Incessant toil has widened the ways round the hill, and the eye, unaccustomed to such giddy heights, is kept steady by the sight of stout wooden

palings, which run along their free sides. By tu:
the taxes for the village roads in India to an
work, a path has been cut, blasted, or built on st
along the most awful precipices and the hi;
mountains in our globe, hundreds of **miles away**
the far distant valleys of Bunawer, between the ;
of eternal snow, where those of our officers wh
more manly or less gay, may betake themselv
hunt the bear, or bag game strange to the Euro
sportsman. In the narrow and crowded baza
Simla can be seen all the races of the hills and p
of India ;—the shivering little Bengali, the
manly-looking Poorbeah, the Punjaubee, the c
merchant of Cashmere, and the Tartar **peasan**
Ladak, flying from the cruelty of Golab Singh,
come to labour for the lords of India.

In this pleasant retreat was General **Anson,**—
posed, like all commanders-in-chief, to be **listenii**
reports from every station in India, conveyed thr
the proper channels, and according to the regulat
His excellency was now and then madé a
uneasy at queer stories of threatened revolt am
the sepoys. He hoped, above all **things, that it w**
not break out till the hot season was past, and
rains dried up, when, like Noah's dove, he w
descend from his Ararat, bearing an olive branch,

restoring peace. Besides, there was no danger. Reports and enclosures from all parts of India had been arranged by skilful secretaries, working on the discoveries of successive governors-general, commanders-in-chief, and courts of directors, to converge from all parts of India, like rays of light through a series of lenses, to shed a focus of light on Headquarters. Its lustre shone yet undimmed. The dak runners were borne down under the weight of official documents in clumsy envelopes;—the resumé of which was, that the Bengal army was sound at heart. Yet there must have been for once some aberration—something must have gone wrong in the exquisite adjustment; for there was Captain Barnard, aid-de-camp, who had ridden express from Umballa with the telegram announcing the mutiny of six regiments. Moreover, on the 13th, came in a note from General Hewitt, that the native troops at Meerut had risen, and that the Europeans "were defending their barracks!"

General Anson never shewed the great qualities looked for in one intrusted with such a momentous charge as that of the army of India; but there is reason to believe him to have been a man of considerable ability. To say that he was now roused by the crisis is not much to his praise; but his future

arrangements seem to have been as good as th
cumstances allowed. The three regiments in the
were instantly ordered down to Umballa by f
marches.

It was an interesting subject of observation,
the European constitution would bear up agains
transition, within a few hours, from repose in a
perate, to exertion in a tropical climate. Here
were none of the gradual changes of temper
which prepare the constitution, even of the trav
by the swiftest steamer. In one march they we
the hot wind, the thermometer rising thirty deg
They stood the fatigue admirably, but on their ar
at Umballa cholera appeared to a most fatal ex
brought on, it was thought, by their drinking v
out of the stagnant pools on the road.

Here was gathered the small force which the
mander, a few days before, of the largest arm
Asia, could now call around him ;—two troop
Horse Artillery, the 9th Lancers, the three regin
from the hills, besides three more of native tr
whom it would be more correct to count agains
The Ghoorka regiment at Juttog, near Simla,
ordered to Phillour, to escort down a siege train
serious act of insubordination, however, was
mitted in this valuable regiment. One of its

panies rose, and, after having robbed the treasury of Kussowlie, set out for Simla, plundering the commander-in-chief's baggage, and threatening to murder some Europeans whom they met on the way. The regiment at Juttog was in a very excited state, and a general flight of the residents in Simla, which was full of families come up from the plains, took place. This affair caused much talk;—it appears that all the officers at that sanitarium had not shewn the chivalry one might have expected from gentlemen, to whom had fallen the defence of so many fair ladies. Fortunately the Ghoorkas were soothed down by a few concessions, necessary under the circumstances, and the prospect of going to fight the Poorbeahs, to whom they bore no good will, soon put them into proper humour. They delivered up the men who had plundered the treasury, and afterwards marched to Saharunpore, where they did good service. It is said that the chief cause of discontent in the regiment was, that no guard was to be left in their absence, to watch the conduct of their burly dames among the handsome hillmen of Sarmoor.

The siege train had to go down with a most untrustworthy escort of sepoys, but arrived in safety, —the bridge over the Sutlej being washed away a short while after it had crossed.

Every one saw the necessity of mar
quickly as possible upon Delhi ; but there
the means of at once getting ready so large ‹
men for a campaign in the hot season. Wag
camels had to be hired or seized for the bag
tents, spare ammunition to be provided, ai
bearers for the wounded to be collected.

Great anxiety was felt as to the behavio
Rajah of Patiala, the largest of the allied Sil
near Umballa. Treachery on his part mig
proved our destruction. It is true he was b
treaty to assist us, and we could have marc
force in a few hours on his capital, if he had
But every one knew that an Asiatic would n
hostility in this way. The danger was in his
against us while we were on the road to D
his falling upon Umballa, and inciting the
to sack the four Himalayan stations which wer
his own territory. Our communications v
Punjaub would then be stopped, the trunk ro
ning a considerable way through the Patiala
The smaller Sikh states, Nabbha and Jheen‹
have followed, and the chiefs deeper in t
would have rushed to share the spoils of Siml
Rajah of Patiala, besides, belonged to the olde
of name amongst the Sikhs, and his call mig

his brethren across the Sutlej against us. It is said
he took two days to deliberate whose side he would
adopt, after which we received the cheering assurance
of his assistance. He offered us troops, lent us money,
and sent his camels and elephants to help our commissariat.

After much ado, on the night of the 17th May
1857, two horse artillery guns, a squadron of the
Lancers, and four companies of the 1st Fusiliers, left
for Kurnanl, where they arrived on the forenoon of
the 19th, having made one of the marches in the sun.

The rest of the force followed as they could get
equipment,—the advanced detachment pushing on to
Paneeput, a large Mahomedan city, where the Rajah
of Jheend, with eight hundred men, was already in
the field. Four companies were left in Umballa, to
which some of the Patiala troops were added. An
intrenchment was thrown round the church as a place
of refuge. All the women, and those soldiers who
from sickness were unfit for duty, were sent up to the
hills.

On the 25th the Commander-in-chief reached
Kurnaul, but was next day seized with cholera, and
died on the 27th. He was succeeded, in command of
the field force, by Major-General Sir Henry Barnard.
As the hot season had now set in, the marches of the

main body were made by night. During the
men lay overpowered in their tents, sleeping
could, or wearying till the terrible heat wou
off. No one was to be seen out of doors. W
temperature rises a degree or two above blood
is to a European a daily illness, from which
recover every night, but which will wear hi1
by degrees, if he has not strength to rally. '
evening all again became life and bustle, and
a few hours after, the tents were struck, and th
arranged for the march—a great novelty to ε
campaigner. The nights were delicious, th
bright in the dark deep sky, the fire-flies flashi
bush to bush, and the air, which in Europ
have been called warm and close, was cool and
ing to the cheek that had felt the hot wind
the day. Along the road came the heavy rol
guns, mixed with the jingling of bits, and the
ing of the steel scabbards of the cavalry. The i
marched on behind with a dull deep tread
lines of baggage, camels, and bullock carts, v
innumerable sutlers and camp servants, toile
for miles in the rear, while the gigantic el
stalked over bush and stone by the side of tl
Yet our hearts were full of bitterness. Hov
had led, in the opposite direction, the very

with whom they were now going down to fight ;—
led them to dethrone Dost Mohammed,—to avenge
our countrymen lying bloody and cold in the Kyber
Pass, or to turn the doubtful tide of war against
the Sikhs! We felt as if our dearest friends had
betrayed us.

On the 3d of June, five villagers were seized, who
had grossly insulted two ladies escaping on foot from
Delhi. There was little doubt of their guilt, and
none of their condemnation, although some of the
witnesses had disappeared. They were all sentenced
to be hanged. They deserved their fate, yet a few
regretted the fierce desire for blood, which began to
manifest itself on every possible occasion.

Officers now went to courts-martial declaring they
would hang the prisoners, whether guilty or innocent,
and the provost-marshall had his cart waiting for them
at the tent door. Some brought the names of offending
villages, and applied to get them destroyed, and plundered on the strength of vague report. The fierceness
of the men increased every day, often venting itself
upon the camp servants, many of whom ran away.
These prisoners, during the few hours between their
trial and execution, were unceasingly tormented by the
soldiers. They pulled their hair, pricked them with
their bayonets, and forced them to eat cow's flesh,

while officers stood by approving. **The fury**
of the peasants, a tall powerful young Jat, bro
in boasting and curses as he was led to exe
The village was burnt and plundered; they
not even the house of the old zamindarin, w
in vain tried to save the ladies from insult. I
and humane men began to fear, that our ju
geance on Delhi would be stained with a
massacre of the inhabitants, and a course of j
slaughter, which would surpass the horrors
Reign of Terror. But the slightest whisper (
thing short of indiscriminate vengeance was in
silenced by twenty voices. How dangerous i
intrust to mankind the power of taking ev
justest retribution!

Our advanced body, which was sent on to
two marches from Delhi, could now gain a mo
tinct knowledge of the position of the mutineer
and of the state of the country.* The ki
hoisted the green flag, and proclaimed himself e
of India. He had held a durbar, where forty
and native chiefs had pugaries put on their he
his hand. He had taken the revolted regimer
his service, and promised them the same pa
gave. Eight of our treasuries had been plu

* The reports of spies are here given.

and secured on his account; but some of the richest had become the prey of the sepoys, who could scarcely walk under the weight of the rupees which they carried about them. Some of the luckiest had prudently departed for their homes. In the city they were very disorderly, and rifled the passers by at the bridge of boats. During the first two or three days, many shops of the native merchants had been plundered. The men gave up the habit of paying for anything, snatching from the bazaars whatever they wished. The merchants in revenge gave them false gold pieces for their bulky rupees. They however kept up their military discipline, and talked bravely.

Forty-nine Europeans, principally women and children, had been imprisoned within the palace walls, where they were treated with great cruelty, and where the sepoys are said to have amused themselves by presenting their loaded muskets, to the terror of their unhappy victims. The king, after having for a week enjoyed the novel spectacle of so many European suppliants, gave them up to the soldiers, who murdered them all at once "with sword and gun." Their bodies were piled in a rotting heap at the Cashmere gate.

A great part of the weapons in the arsenal had been carried off by private marauders, and the large gunpowder magazine outside the city had been half

emptied by the Goojurs. The rest was
within the walls, where quantities of gun ca
seized on, and sold by the khulashies ; musk
swords were going for a few annas. What re
of the stores was secured by order of the ki
the bastions were mounted with cannon.

The cavalry were anxious for an attacl
Meerut ; and the whole force had got as far o
way as the gates of the city, but were prever
disagreement from proceeding further.

The country around was in a state of a
Along the road the staging bungalows were b
and the telegraph wire broken and half carrie(
The fierce peasantry, known by the names of (
and Ranghurs, at once threw off our rule ; but s
with the intention of submitting to any other,
some of the leading men got commissions fr
king of Delhi, to hold the districts in his
Half a century of peace and order had nc
weakened their instincts.* They at once r
to the old freebooting state, in which they ha
in the times of the Mahratta forays. Any or
turing near their villages, whether servant

* See General Report on the Administration of
jaub Territories from 1856-7 1857-8 inclusive, etc.
1858, passim.

Company or the Badsha, was rifled with the utmost impartiality.   Goojur ho ya Oojur, you are either Goojur or Oojur, was their motto.   The larger villages plundered and oppressed the smaller ones.   Villagers turned out with matchlock, sword, and spear, and fought with one another about boundary questions, decided half a century ago.   Hundreds of heads of cattle changed hands.   Murders and robberies were committed unpunished in the open day.   A peaceable man could not go into the bazaar without the chance of being rifled or beaten, or finding his wife carried away on his return.   Some cities, as Umballa, Kurnaul, Lodiana, and Ferozepore, were kept under ; but in the open country this state of things existed from Delhi over the whole of the Cis-Sutlej states, which were inhabited by the same turbulent tribes.   The country around the most northern of these cities was almost as little under our power as that behind Delhi ; nor could our magistrates resume their functions till after the termination of the siege.

A body of the mutineers, with one of the princes of Delhi, had gone out on the 23d May to the contiguous districts, and raised the troops we had in Rohtuck, Hansi, and Hissar.   The treasuries were plundered, and some barbarous murders of the English residents took place.

We had very little intelligence about wl
going on below Delhi.   The telegraph wire, sti
down by Agra, was broken, after having cc
various embarrassing messages from the Gc
General, such as, "Make short work of Delhi
heard, with satisfaction, that he had taken m
to stop the China expedition ; and trusted
have troops sent from home overland to our i
was hoped in camp, however, that a blow st
Delhi might save the rest of the army froi
rebellion.   Indeed many could scarcely belie
the sepoys there would not run away on our ap
or come out with clasped hands to solicit
But the rebellion spread ; all the troops in th
revolted ; at Rohilcund an old pensioner
government, Khan Bahadur, made himself
and a boy of the royal house of Oude was pli
the throne at Lucknow.   The contingents
placed to ensure the vassalage of the M
Rajahs, Scindia and Holkar, in Central Ind
also carried away.   Fortunately for us these
did not join the mutineers, but used their
endeavours to delay their march to Delhi ; a
they were unable to keep their own trooj
joining and sympathising with them.

The mutiny at Delhi may be taken as a sj

of what went on at all these places ; everywhere the same strange and trusting confidence of the officers ; the same protestations of fidelity of the sepoys ; then a sudden rising and plundering of the station. Sometimes a part of the officers managed to escape; at other places they were all massacred ; more rarely they were allowed by their men to leave unharmed. It is not our purpose to give the various dates of mutiny at the separate stations ; suffice it to say, that the King of Delhi had the prospect of getting a large army of our own raising and training to serve against us, and all the country garrisoned by the revolted troops. In addition, the villages round about Benares, Patna, Goruckpore, and Northern Behar, passed from our rule ; and a great part of the unfortunate European officers with their wives and children were cruelly put to death. The rest had to fly for their lives, with the loss of all their property. Our weak European detachments were beleaguered by terrible odds in Cawnpore and Lucknow ; in the Doab, Agra alone remained to us, like the last leaf on an autumnal tree. What was singular, the rebellion stopped at the frontier of the Bengal Presidency. It did not spread amongst the men of the Bombay or Madras Army, though the former contained a considerable proportion of Oude sepoys, who did not reach the

height necessary for admission into that o:
Much excitement and sedition appeared, '
were always quelled ere they could pass i:
rebellion. It would be difficult to define th
opinion amongst the peaceable populatior
Doab. From the immense variety of races a
in India, a general proposition about the wl
have little truth. The magistrates of course l
from their districts, where, in some cases, the
were taken by petty rajahs, nawabs, and oth
chiefs ; some acting against, some for us, the
number trying to keep on good terms w
parties. In many districts all authority wa:
off, save that of the village headmen. The
dans were generally hostile to us ; the Hind
less so. If the higher classes were more o:
than the lower, it was because they knew
resources better. Many ignorant people
that there were very few more British in
besides those who appeared in India. It wa
sally believed, that the rule of the Compan}
ever passed away, like that of the Moguls
rattas. Many regretted it. The general voice
that a better government they never had h
we had held the balance of justice even ;
been the friends of the poor man. There

doubt that, had we been driven away, future genera-
tions would have remembered us with affectionate
and mythical regret.

Our whole force having been gathered together,
now marched on Alipore, ten miles from Delhi, where
it waited for the Meerut Brigade and the siege train.
The troops at Meerut had been ordered to join us,
leaving a sufficient number with General Hewitt to
defend the station. Another mishap had taken place
there. On the 16th May, a corps of Sappers from
Roorkhee had mutinied, and shot their captain and a
native officer on the road. It was said that this was
the deed of two or three miscreants, and that the body
of the men were well disposed; but half of them
ran away through pure fright, and took the road to
Delhi. They passed in front of our field-battery
loaded with grape, telling the Artillery officer, that
they were going to punish a village where a havildar
of theirs had been murdered. Their manner was so
plausible that he not only allowed them to get clear
off, but stopped Lieutenant MacKenzie, who was
pursuing them with his score of faithful Sowars.
The Carabiniers, however, came soon after; but
the greater part of the Sappers got clear off. About
fifty of them were overtaken. These sought refuge
in a tope, where they fought to the last man. This

desertion at the commencement of a siege w
cularly annoying.

The Meerut troops, according to the order,
out and encamped on 30th May at Ghazeeo
gur, about ten miles from Delhi, on the ban]
Hindun, where their videttes reported that th
was at hand.　Their force had marched out,
intention of cutting off the brigade ere it cor
headquarters.　The result proved how de
General Hewitt had miscalculated the milit
racter of the sepoys.　Our troops immediatel:
the suspension bridge to meet them.　Th
advanced along the causeway beyond, availi:
selves of the cover of its walls as the enemy
while Major Tombs, by a skilful and rapid m
took them in flank with his horse artille
They almost immediately retreated, pursue
Carabiniers, and leaving five pieces of artille
hands, after having themselves fired some of t
munition waggons.　Our principal loss w
one of these exploding among the men.　Th
felt that this defeat was most disgraceful '
selves, and most detrimental to their cau:
Hindoo sepoys reproached the Mahome
deluding them, and expressed their doub'
whether the Company had really wished t

their caste.* The Goojurs in the neighbouring villages fell upon many of the fugitives, stripping them of all the plunder which they carried with them, and even of their arms and clothes. The King of Delhi loudly reproached them with their cowardice, and the loss of their guns. They returned next day, and fought much more stoutly, but were again beaten back. In these affairs we lost four officers, and fifty men. We had seven cases of sunstroke, two of them fatal. Everybody was well pleased that the Meerut force should have had a separate opportunity of proving their courage. On the 7th June they joined headquarters at Alipore; and the men were received with loud cheers, as they marched in with the captured guns.

As a counter-stroke to this success, a most disastrous affair took place on the night of the 7th June, at Jullundur,† which might be considered the gate of the Punjaub, across the Sutlej. Two regiments of infantry and one of light cavalry mutinied, killed

---

* Trial of the King of Delhi, p. 93.

† For a very detailed account of this affair see Mr. Cooper's " Crisis in the Punjaub." I suppress the materials I have collected for want of space. In the " Crisis " is a letter from Brigadier Johnstone, defending himself from two several accusations, which, he says, were made against him, namely, of over haste, and also of over slackness in the pursuit. His reply completely clears him of the first charge. He asks, " Is it possible for Europeans to have accomplished

and wounded several of their officers, and c
burning and plundering the station for man
unmolested by the European regiment and
troops of horse artillery there. They were
to get away unharmed, taking of course t
to Delhi. The 3d Native Infantry joine
at Phillour. The deputy-commissioner at
Mr. Ricketts, had cut down the bridge over th
and had Brigadier Johnstone made a singl
march, they might have been all destroyed
were crossing the river, which they did in thr
boats, taking a long time, at a ferry that h
unfortunately forgotten and left unguarded
troops were led in pursuit of them ; but were
to march only ten miles the first day, and
or thirteen in the evening. The old gene
much exhausted, and did not bring in his
Lodiana, a distance of three ordinary marches,
night of the 9th June. The mutineers had
meantime entered the city, notwithstanding th
resistance of Mr. Ricketts, with some comp
Rothney's Sikhs, and two Nabbha guns.
Native Infantry guard in the Fort there
thirty miles in thirteen hours, having been under
whole of the previous night ?" The Duke of Welling
said, in India, once marched his men twenty-five miles,
forty-seven, after a rest of eight hours.

joined them, they were in possession of the largest powder magazine in the country. Some of the powder they wetted, took a supply for themselves, and **left the** rest. The lives of the residents were saved by the loyalty of the Sikhs, though some of their houses were plundered by the mutineers, aided by the Cashmeree population of that great cloth-manufacturing town. They then left. The pursuit was given up, after having been carried on for twenty **miles further.**

CHAPTER IV.

WHILE the army remained at Alipore, the
suffered more perhaps from impatience at th
than from the choking heat of their close an
encampment. The spirit of the men was rat
which animated their ancestors, the fierce and
thirsty worshippers of Odin, than that wh
British soldier breathes on European battle
The fury and horror with which the recita
massacres at Meerut and Delhi had been hea
stirred afresh by the news of the murders a
and Hissar, which some who had escaped had
into camp. Many an oath was sworn th
would grant no mercy to a black face. Th
matic nature of the British soldier disappear
the burning desire of havoc and revenge.
doubted of a complete and easy victory.
the men believed that one battle would de
fate of the mutinous regiments. They would
the morning ; they would drink their grog i
at night.

On its being known that a battle was to be fought on the morrow, the sick in the hospitals declared they would remain there no longer. Many hardly able to walk suffered on in silence, or lay in the corners of the tents imploring their comrades not to tell they were ill, in case they should be kept in hospital on the day of battle. Every man whose strength was not hopelessly gone was let out, and few returned for **days after.**

The same sentiments of animosity filled the breasts of the officers, and the same confidence of victory. Although it was known that the sepoys still kept up an appearance of discipline, and had fought with much spirit at the last affair at the Hindun, the European mind could not banish the idea, that they were going out to meet a disorderly horde of murderers and mutineers, who would fly, without any attempt at rallying, from the severe chastisement they must receive, if they attempted to meet a British army in **the field.**

They sternly calculated the chances of hunting down the fugitives, who might escape the conquering bayonets and swords of their men; lists of all the mutinous regiments existed; their names, families, and villages, could be ascertained; a price would be put on their heads, they would be hunted as the Thugs

E

had been hunted through British India, and
the native States. Their breasts would k
satisfaction if death had passed over one nam
rolls, till the last fugitive was dragged from h;
place and met his doom.

An equal assurance did not prevail in tl
camp. They had taken up a strong position
road a few miles from Delhi, and waited th
of their old conquerors and former masters, c
mind their own exploits and depreciating tho
white people, enumerating the occasions,
fancied, where the Feringhees had flincl
they conquered. Still the terror of the wl
which had ruled Hindostan for a hundred y
not to be dispelled in a day. They could n
the thoughts of their shameful discomfiture
Hindun out of their minds, facile as they w(
uneasy feeling that boasting was not victory
traction defeat; that it was one thing to massa
officers and their wives and children in
cantonment, and quite another to meet their
countrymen in open battle, gnawed at thei
hearts. Hindostan was theirs not yet. T
powerful motives for making a desperate r(
The religious fanaticism both of the Mahom(
the Hindoo had been deeply roused. The

hatred which a subdued race bears to its conquerors, the ferocious thirst of blood which the massacres had nourished but not satisfied, the consciousness that they had offended the British power beyond every chance of forgiveness, all determined them to offer the bravest resistance in their power. The one side resolved to fight desperately, the other to conquer pitilessly.

Two or three hours after sunset were occupied in a few quiet and well-understood preparations for the engagement of the morrow. The position of the enemy was chosen with that shrewd appreciation of the advantages of ground which the natives shewed throughout the war. A large serai stood on the right of the road ; a short way in front of it was a small mound on which they had made a sand-bag battery, mounting three heavy guns and a howitzer. To the right of the serai was a small village, whose mud walls, and enclosures, and gardens, offered a good cover for infantry. Their position was a strong one, and required to be approached with care and judgment. Their numbers were also considerable, consisting of seven entire regiments, and two detachments of infantry, and two regiments of cavalry. Their ranks were swelled by deserters and fugitives from Ferozepore, Meerut, and Umballa, by soldiers on furlough, by police, and chuprassies

of all kinds, as well as by volunteers from
and Goojur villages around. Their guns were
by the men of the 3d Company, 7th Native B
Artillery; by the gun lascars of the magaz
artillerymen of the Palace Guards, and m:
retired Golundazes living in the city.

At midnight Brigadier Grant set out w
horse artillery guns, and three squadrons of
Lancers, guided by Lieutenant Hodson, witl
Native Horse. They crossed the bridge, and
bullock track which led them, through the ⟨
country, again over the canal. They move
its banks in order to come upon the flank
enemy, while Sir Henry Barnard should m
attack with the main column in front. Th
however, were bad, and full of ruts and water
which so much hindered the progress of th
that the discharges of cannon, the regular f
musketry, and the flight of flocks of birds fi
left, told them the battle had commenced befo
arrival. At half-past four in the morning tl
body, which had set out at two o'clock, cam
the village of Badle-Serai. The sepoys imm
opened fire from the battery in front of th
Then were heard the deep shouts of the Eur
and the yells of the sepoys. With deadlier

two foes had never met. Our artillery advanced
hastily and fired ; the infantry deployed on each side
of the road. Their cannon told on our ranks ; one of
our waggons was blown up, and the bullock drivers of
our heavy guns ran away. Captain Money's troop of
horse artillery galloped up, unlimbered, and fired
with great judgment and precision ; but it was evident
that the enemy's guns in their strong and sheltered
position could not be silenced. Our men began to
fall quickly ; the musketry fire of the sepoys was
regular and well sustained ; the second brigade had
fallen behind, and was not yet in sight. One round
shot carried off the leg of Captain Money's trumpeter,
and mortally wounded Colonel Chester, the Adjutant-
General. Captain Russell, another of the staff, was
killed ; several horses fell ; Sir Henry Barnard said
he had never witnessed such a concentrated fire, even
before Sebastopol. The 75th, who had been lying
down in line, and the 1st Fusiliers, were ordered to
charge upon the heavy battery. An unfortunate
delay took place in making the regiment form square,
in order to meet the attack of some cavalry, which
turned out to be our own. The ground was broken,
and covered with water, from a great fall of rain a
few days before. The enemy's guns were pointed at
the advancing line, as it struggled through the mud.

Many a brave heart beat high as the hurl
iron swept past, giving fearful evidence of il
on the bodies and limbs of the heroic r
Seventy men were killed and wounded in
minutes. Captain Harrison was shot throt
head, and seven officers were wounded. Tl
neither flinched nor stayed, but rushed u]
guns, driving out the Golundazes and infan'
defended them, at the point of the bayonet.
Fusiliers carried an enclosure and some hou
ting them on fire ; supported by them the 7£
on the serai, break in the gates, and bayc
defenders. Some of the sepoys fought des]
some stood stupified and met their fate, others
clasped their hands, imploring the mercy wh'
themselves had never granted, and which the
they would not obtain. A Mussulman fans
taken in the serai, and hanged on the spot.

The 2d Brigade, under Brigadier Grav
appeared on the enemy's right. Brigadier H(
the lancers took them in rear on the left,
guns came up one by one, as they could ma
push through the water-courses which cross
way. The lancers fell upon their foe at oi
persed those opposed to them, and took two gui

his own hand. The enemy took to flight on all sides, some across the plain under the fire of our artillery, which, however, could do little execution among men dispersed here and there. A charge of the carabiniers might have cut down hundreds of them. The great part retreated to the right, their cavalry and guns along the road. The rest were soon beyond the reach of our infantry, among the broken ground, full of gardens, houses, and ruins, which extended towards the city. The artillery drove on as quickly as the infantry could follow, firing now and then on the flying enemy, killing a few men, and taking two guns. The Afghan chief, Lall Fishan Khan, who with some horsemen had followed our star from Meerut, was heard crying out, his stout old heart big with the enthusiasm of the moment, " Another such day and I shall be a Christian ;" and, sad to tell, an English deserter from Meerut had been struck down fighting in the sepoy ranks, and was recognised by his former comrades.*

A feeble attempt was made to rally when the fugitives had gained the ridge overlooking the city, which they had left with loud boastings. Our force then divided ; Sir Henry Barnard's column took its

* I was assured of the truth of this by several of the Rifles, to which corps he belonged.

way across the plain, where the last kin
house of Toghlak had contended for the 1
Delhi with the Tartar hordes of Timou
Crossing the half-ruined bridge over the c
force was fired down upon by some guns w
stopped beside the Flagstaff Tower, but tl
were ill directed, breaking down the tomb
the churchyard to the right. The parad
with the blackened shells of the officers' bi
now came into view. A little above were t
huts. A light was eagerly thrown upon t
and a column of smoke and flame told to
fied citizens the fate of the dwellings of the
Captain Money's troop then wheeled to the
the Flagstaff. The firing was admirable. Tl
fled after a few shots, leaving three guns
them, and disappeared down the covered ros
led to the city.

The other column under General Wilsc
through the suburbs of the Subzi-Mundi, wh
quite deserted, our soldiers breaking into th
and setting them on fire. They neared tl
gate of Delhi, and then turned to the left, a
ridge which looks down upon the city. The
the conquering squadron was seen they w
upon from the walls, the round shot almost

their white pugaries. They pushed hastily under shelter of the walls and gates of a large stone building called Hindoo Rao's House, where they met with the victorious column of Sir Henry Barnard, and the Ghoorkas, who had ascended the front of the hill. The enemy had taken the range of the house, and the justness of their aim was surprising. A gun limber was blown up, and the clothes of a young officer of artillery caught fire ; he was most cruelly burned.

The hill, which Hindoo Rao's house surmounts, commands a fine view of Delhi, the ill-fated city. Among the capitals of the earth, there was none more beautiful. The eye ran along the wide circuit of its ramparts, with their picturesque gates and bastions half hid among the trees, resting on the palace of the old Mogul conquerors with its green gardens and lofty red walls, along which to the eastern side of the city ran the waters of the Jumna, commanded by the old towers of Selim Ghar, and crossed by its bridge of boats. A thousand mosques and stately houses, and the long line of Chandney Choke, the principal bazaar of the city, with its rows of trees, broke the monotony of streets and lanes. It seemed half buried in green, every hovel having its little enclosure and garden. The giant domes and lofty

minarets of the Jumna Musjid towered abov
if reared by the hands of Titans.

Beyond were the endless ruins of old D
remains of a mighty race, whose strength a
had passed away, though its descendants w
there, to defile their fathers' graves by their
impure deeds. All looked quiet in the br
vertical sun; there was no sign of war s
occasional gun, its white smoke rising am
trees; but by the gates, and in the bazaars,
the steps of the great mosque, trembling crow
listening to the tidings of the victory of the Fer

It was now about noon; the sun was striki.
right upon our heads, and the hot wind bl
the blast of a furnace. Several of the men fe
from sunstroke; but the fatigues of the day w
nigh over, and the large trees at the foot of
' Rao's hill sheltered them from the direct ray
sun. The wounded were placed in the old
ment hospital, and cared for by the medical s

The native followers of the camp had
means shared the confidence of the British; a
had been hanged the day before, for having
some soldiers that they would be beaten
morrow. This, however, did not seem to conv
other natives of the superiority of our star.

The baggage had been left at Alipore under a guard, and was ordered forward after the battle. But a panic thrice arose on the road. The followers, servants, and camel-drivers, turned and fled, or hid themselves among the bushes and hollows by the sides of the road, causing the utmost confusion, and some damage to the effects and cattle. When they had finally arrived, the soldiers' tents were hastily erected on the parade ground, and the men got under cover. Some sepoys shewed themselves at the gates below Hindoo Rao's house, and a cannonade was opened from the walls on our picquets on the ridge. This movement, however, was a mere bravado. On some troops being marched towards the place, they retired into the city. Our loss in this battle was no greater than fifty-three men killed, and one hundred and thirty-two wounded. Among these, four officers had died, and thirteen were wounded. The steady dash of our troops in carrying the position, had prevented the affair being bloody. The loss of the enemy was certainly more than double, and thirteen guns were left in our hands, two of them twenty-four pounders. Of these, eight were taken at Badle-Serai, two on the road to Delhi, and three at the Flagstaff tower. Many of the sepoys never appeared again; the terror of some was so great, that they ran in at the gates on the one side of the city, and out through those on the other.

An attack upon Delhi that evening might have been successful. Many of the inhabitants, well disposed to us, afterwards said, that if we had broken into the town that night, only a very feeble resistance could have been offered. The battle had not lasted long; our men had made only one march. To say, that after a few hours rest they would not have been able for further fight, would be to underrate half the fatigues, which, after months of sickness and exhaustion, they endured. To blow open a gate was surely as easy that night as on the morning of the 14th September. Moreover, if they were wearied, so were their opponents. The troops might have been marched down near the walls, by roads almost covered from the enemy's artillery. The risk of failure appears slight, compared with the enormous advantages of our gaining the city and magazine, which would have paralyzed the insurrection, then spreading all over the country.

The battle of Badle-Serai was one of many engagements, fought with small numbers, yet of great mark in the world's history. The effect of the victory was not felt below Delhi, but acted most favourably in tranquilizing the Punjaub, where our defeat would have led to the destruction of all the Europeans in **the north-west.**

At this date our army sat down before Delhi, remaining in the position we had taken on the evening of the 8th June. Fortunately it was a strong one. The tents were pitched upon the parade ground of the mutinous regiments, about two miles from the city, separated by a long ridge of hill, that rose in broken ground on the banks of the Jumna to our left, and, smoothing down at the top, extended to our extreme right. It was crossed towards the left by the grand trunk road, marked here and there by the telegraph posts, from which still hung broken pieces of wire. A little further to the right, on the ridge of the hill, stood the tower called the Flagstaff;* and, still further along, an old mosque, both occupied by picquets of our men. To the extreme right was the hill on which were placed our heavy batteries. Its top was crowned by the building called Hindoo Rao's house, from an old Mahratta chieftain who had lived there. All these points were connected by a road which ran along the summit of the hill. Its sides are formed by out-

---

* It was about 150 feet high, with two terraces, and ascended by an inside winding stair. A cart load of dead bodies was found there; no doubt those of the murdered officers of the 54th Native Infantry.

cropping strata of sandstone and gneiss, w
tier above tier.

From every part of this hill a view of De
be obtained, as the ridge neared the town frc
right. The best view was at Hindoo Rao
only a mile from Delhi. Part of the slope
our camp was covered by the now ruined ht
mutinous regiments, and the burnt hot
trampled-down gardens of the unfortunate
Broken articles of furniture, fragments of
leaves of books, and pieces of music flying
the compounds, recalled the scenes of rap
had been enacted there. Behind the camp
canal, which separated it from the plain bey
covered the whole of our rear, though it cor
in somewhat narrow bounds. Its banks w
but it was crossed everywhere by bridges.*
into the river on the north side of Delhi.
flank was covered by the Jumna, which her
very wide bend, enclosing a large space, w
elephants, camels, and cattle, might feed i
On our right, below Hindoo Rao's hill, was
on which were placed three heavy guns. I

---

* Much of this is taken from a description of ot
written by the author from the camp, and which a
the *Times*.

a small elevation was occupied by a Mahomedan Cemetery; an ancient garden, surrounded by a lofty wall, ran abreast of it to the canal. Three quarters of a mile farther on to the right, began the beautiful suburb, called the Subzi-Mundi, full of country-houses, enclosures and gardens, in which a number of desperate fights afterwards took place between our men and the enemy.

Nearer the city, and lying between Hindoo Rao's hill and the one to the right called the Eedgah, were the suburbs of Kissengunge and Paharipore. The ground between the ridge and the city was much broken, full of houses, old mosques, tombs, and ruins of all sorts, with clumps of trees and gardens. The defences of Delhi had a circumference of seven miles. They consisted of a parapet wall, with bastions at considerable distances, mounting generally ten or twelve guns. The walls were covered for one-third of their height by a glacis, and had in front a ditch twenty-four feet deep.* The river completely covered one face of the city, and our attack was entirely confined to the north side, so that there never was any

* For a more detailed description of the fortifications, see chap. xii.

The population of Delhi was above 150,000, but it covered a great deal more ground than a European city containing the same number of inhabitants.

real investment. To all intents, Delhi, save on the north access, was as open as if we had been a hundred miles off. To the south were the wide and vast ruins of the ancient city. The opposite side of the river was in the hands of the enemy, who thus had free communication in all directions, and, as will be seen, could render ours very insecure. The key of our position was the Subzi-Mundi, whence they could turn our right and cut off our road to Umballa, upon which we rested.

CHAPTER V.

MAJOR GENERAL REID had arrived, after a fatiguing journey from Rawul Pindi, just before the battle of Badle-Serai. By virtue of seniority he had a right to the command of the force, which his delicate health prevented him from taking. Sir Henry Barnard remained at the head of affairs as formerly. The morning after the battle the Guides entered camp under the command of Captain Daly. They were already well known as one of the finest regiments in India. They were almost all of Afghan and Persian race, and consisted of three troops of cavalry, perhaps the best riders in our pay, and six companies or infantry armed with the rifle. They had marched in this the hottest time of the year from near Peshawur to Delhi, a distance of five hundred and eighty miles, in twenty-two days. Their stately height and military bearing made all who saw them feel proud to have such aid. They came in as firm and light as if they had marched only a mile.

The same morning a number of soldiers were

E 2

crowded together, taking a leisurely view of the
city from the mosque on the ridge, about a mile
off, when a shot was fired from the walls, which
killed one and mortally wounded four of them.
It soon became known to every body that the
enemy had some excellent marksmen at their guns,
and had the range of every place on the ridge well
ascertained. A paper in native characters, noting the
relative distances of the different points, was even
said to have been picked up at Hindoo Rao's house;
and the Meerut force, while encamped by the Hindun,
had heard their artillery practising. In the afternoon
an attack was made upon Hindoo Rao's hill by a
body of sepoys from Delhi. The Guides, who were
much concerned at the battle of the 8th having been
fought without them, were sent to support the picquet.
A deal of skirmishing and fighting took place amongst
the thickets and broken ground between the hill and
the city. The 3d Cavalry, the originators of the
mutiny, fought hand to hand with the Guides, but
not long. The enemy was beaten with considerable
loss and chased under the walls. Lieutenant Quentin
Battye, in command of the mounted division of the
Guides, fell mortally wounded by a bullet from the
ramparts. He was a young man of great promise, a
good swordsman, and an excellent rider; and his

impatience to have an occasion for distinguishing himself in the field, had been remarked at every station he passed on the march. He died in his first battle, murmuring with his failing voice the old Roman saying, that it is well and proper for a man to die for his country.

It seemed to be the intention of the general to make regular approaches ; batteries were piled on the front of Hindoo Rao's hill about fifteen hundred yards from the city. The two twenty-four pounders taken from the enemy were the heaviest pieces we had. We had no balls for them, but those fired at us by the enemy were picked up and returned. Most of the shots sent without effect at our batteries, fell among the trees at the foot of the farther side of the hill. It was a dangerous place to pass, and was called "The valley of the shadow of death." Here half-naked wretches were seen watching from some cover the balls as they fell. On finding one, they would bring it into the batteries, to claim the promised four annas. No doubt spies found their way under this pretext to inspect our works. People too would venture through a heavy fire to sell their fruit and milk to the artillerymen. Our officers, however, did not like to frighten them away by inquiries, as supplies were by no means steady, and there were too many natives in camp for us to hope that any secret could be long kept. Great efforts were made to silence the enemy's batteries, and shells were occasionally thrown into the town. The houses in the quarter most exposed to our range were abandoned; but it soon became clear that we had not superiority in our artillery-fire sufficient to extinguish theirs. Although we had the advantage of a higher position, the distance of our batteries was such as to expose us to the fire of all the bastions on one side of Delhi. We had not enough of sappers to make approaches, and too few soldiers to guard our parallels. The materiel of the enemy was much more abundant; ammunition and guns they drew from the great magazine in their hands, as they needed them. They had evidently plenty of trained artillerymen. Their gunners were often led to the batteries, and kept to their posts by parties of cavalry; they, however, did their work well. From an object of contempt, their skill became one of wonder and admiration, perhaps too great. Some artillery officers protested their practice was better than our own. Many believed that their fire was under the superintendence of Europeans.* Two

* The overrated influence given to the three European officers to account for the obstinacy of the Sikh war, and the story of Russians directing the Chinese at our repulse on the

men with solar helmets could be seen by the help of our best glasses in their batteries, but no one who knew how much of the work in India was really done by natives, wondered at the practical skill they now shewed.

The enemy did not appear to be discouraged by the repulses they had met with. According to our spies, their spirits were kept up by the prospect of large reinforcements from almost every station in Hindostan. They said our loss was as great at Badle-Serai as their own. The 60th Native Infantry marched in from Rohtuck to join them. This regiment had been sent to pacify the districts there. The commander, Colonel Seaton, had treated with contempt any surmise of their disloyalty, and many of the officers were out shooting when the men rose. They all escaped ; several sepoys assisted them on horseback, and came with them. This took place on the 10th June. The men must have got news of the battle of the 8th. It was one of the first proofs that such a partial success could not allay the revolt. Indeed, the fugitive officers would have been set upon by the villagers, had they not said that the men were marching quietly on behind them. Attacks were

Peiho, shew how ready Europeans are to attribute a strenuous resistance to the aid of men of their own race.

made almost daily upon some part of our position.
Our little force was kept in continual alarm. Knowing the effects of the sun on the European frame, the
enemy generally commenced these onsets during the
sultriest parts of the day. If even one picquet was
attacked, our whole force was turned out. The infantry stood in line before their tents, the cavalry sat
on horseback, and the artillery were at the guns. No
thermometrical statement can give any one, who has
never been in a tropical country, any idea of the
flashing, stupifying glare, and the agonizing heat of
an Indian sun. Indeed hundreds of Europeans in
India had never suffered its direct rays before. To
move about is exhaustion; to remain still, intolerable distress. The strength of the men bore up sur-
prisingly against everything; but they could not
conceal their impatience at being made the victims
of these ceaseless alarms; especially, as often happened, when they were merely sent into their tents
again, after two or three hours exposure to the sun.
It seemed as if the general was playing the enemy's
game. He was exposing them to a real danger to
avert an imaginary one. The responsibility of a
commander is very serious, and it would be rash to
blame him for his vigilance; but certainly the alarms
were often puerile. One night the whole camp was

roused and under arms. An elephant having thrown off its driver, who had gone to sleep on its back, ran away, and frightened a sentry. An aid-de-camp rode into camp at full gallop. Some sowars had been seen issuing from the Lahore gate; the whole force was paraded in the sun for several hours, and then ordered to return to their tents, save those who went to the hospital. One well-known officer felt so sure of discerning between a false alarm and a real one, that he often sent his men under cover, in anticipation of the order, which never failed to come an hour or two after. If there were many false alarms, neither were real ones few. Scarcely a day passed without an attack on Hindoo Rao's hill, or one or other of our picquets. Fresh mutinous regiments began to come in, and as they came, the constant message was "jao laro," "go and fight." Till they had met the white people, they got no pay, and were not allowed to enter within the walls. The enemy always avoided a pitched battle, and courted that system of desultory fighting, in which the strength of the native soldiers is best brought out. Among the broken and rocky ground, full of jungle and trees, and every level plot covered with gardens, groves, and ruins, separating the city from the ridge, and under shelter of their own artillery on the walls, with the city to afford them a refuge in case of defeat, they had the very arena which they would have chosen above all others. Naturally patient, artful, and stealthy, the Hindostani seemed more fitted for such warfare than the European, who, disdaining the advantages of cover, fluttered with fury and impatience, till, worn out and stupified by the heat, he was often shot down, as he pressed incautiously forward to close with his wily foe, who was loading and firing behind some bush or rock.

Our soldiers have been regarded as deficient in intelligence, because they appear to possess it in a less degree than troops whose officers pass their lives in exercising them, just as the British have been said not to be a military people, because their armies do not make the showy appearance of nations, who spend longer time on the parade ground, and yet shew no superiority on the field of battle. In this species of skirmishing, though the least of all fitted for their nature, they made a rapid and visible improvement, and were ably manœuvred by their officers. The sepoy forces were apparently well handled, their native officers shewing conspicuous courage. Their voices were often heard urging on the men, calling them pigs and camel drivers, and challenging the Feringhees to come nearer. One advantage they had was, that they could lead fresh men against us on every occasion, while, from the fewness of our numbers, we were compelled to bring the same troops into action sometimes twice or thrice a day. Though never defeated, and almost always driving the enemy before them, our men were hard pressed and overworked. The post of honour was Hindoo Rao's hill; and round it most of the affrays took place. It was held by Major Reid with the Sirmoor battalion, and two companies of Rifles. His losses were afterwards filled up by the infantry of the Guides. The Goorkhas were crowded into the large house from which the place took its name. Its walls were shattered with shells and round shot, which now and then struck through the chambers. Ten men were killed and wounded in the house by one shot, and seven by another the same day. Nobody there was secure of his life for an instant. Through the whole siege Major Reid kept to his post; "He never quitted the ridge save to attack the enemy below it, and never once visited the camp, until carried to it wounded on the day of the final assault."[*]

The Guides and Goorkhas were adepts in skirmishing; their being on our side was one of the hundred chances which saved us from utter destruction. Trained in danger from infancy, among the

[*] Norman.

F

robber tribes of his frontier, the Afghan soldier was
more than a match for the Poorbeah. He hated the
Hindoo for his idolatry, and his fellow Mahomedan
in the sepoy ranks, for his Hindoo prejudices and
exclusiveness. He despised them both as servile
races. The name of Patan or Conqueror, which is
given in India to the native of Cabool and his
descendants, was a proof of his superiority. The
European he regarded with manly admiration. Each
knew that the other could use his weapons well. His
aquiline nose, sloping forehead, sharply traced line of
eyebrow, and fair complexion, shewed he belonged to
a different race from the Hindustani. The Goorkhas,
though perhaps not so skilful, were equally brave and
faithful. Originally descended from the Hindoo
inhabitants of the plains, their ancestors had conquered
the wide mountainous district of Nepaul. Though
probably mixed with the vanquished Budhist race,
they still retained the Hindoo faith, but neglected
many of the arbitrary rules of caste. They eat flesh
and drink wine; hence all fellowship is avoided by
the people of Hindostan, to whom they bear a
rancorous hatred.* They are perhaps fonder than

* Sir C. Napier proposed to raise forty thousand of them,
to secure us against the preponderance of the Brahminical
element in the army. Perhaps so many could not be got.

A story which was much relished in the camp was told of

any other race in India of the company of Europeans. They are very short in stature, with deep chests and wide shoulders, flat-nosed, broad-faced, and singularly ugly, but exceedingly daring, active, and athletic. Pitiless and bloodthirsty when roused, they still preserve a high ideal of honour, such as has been so long borne by the tribes of Rajpootana. Great temptations and immense bribes were offered to seduce them from our service. Even during action, voices were heard urging them to change sides. The Rifles found frequent occasions of shewing the use they could make of their pieces; and had we been able to spare others to guard the batteries, they might have been most usefully employed in picking off the enemy's artillerymen.* Our other regiments were

a Ghoorka and a Rifleman, who had followed a Brahmin soldier in one of these skirmishes. The last took refuge in a house, and closed the door. The Rifleman tried to push it open, but the Ghoorka went to the window, and coiling his compact little person into its smallest compass, waited for his enemy. Soon the point of a musket, then a head and long neck appeared. The Ghoorka sprang up, and seizing him by the locks, which clustered out of the back of his pugarie, he cut off his head with his cookry, ere the Brahmin could invoke Mahadeo. The little man was brought along with his trophy by the Rifleman, to receive the applause of his comrades, who were in the mood to enjoy a joke of this kind.

* On one occasion, ten Riflemen at the Sammy-house made such execution amongst the gunners at the Moree bastion, that the battery was for a time abandoned.

not yet armed with the rifle. This was the last great contest fought with the old musket.[*]

During this never-ending fighting, our loss in killed and wounded was serious; that of the enemy undoubtedly very great. As they were almost continually beaten back, their wounded were killed by our men, and whenever we had a chance of closing with them, they met with a rough handling. As the sepoys generally carried all their newly acquired plunder and savings on their persons, often in the form of gold moyadors, valuable spoil was sometimes taken from the bodies of the slain. To narrate each daily encounter would be tiresome. It is enough to describe the most notable.

After unsuccessful attacks on the 10th and 11th June, on the morning of the 12th a number of their infantry collected in the gardens and covered ground near Sir T. Metcalfe's house. This was a short distance from the Flagstaff tower, where two light guns were placed under Lieutenant Bishop and a detachment of the 75th. The enemy stole along among the trees, and gathered about two hundred men in the racket-court close by the tower. They gained the

---

[*] Some of the regiments that arrived later were armed with the rifle. The enemy also had riflemen, whom they used as sharpshooters.

brow of the ridge to the left, to take the guns in
flank. These were hastily turned; but the enemy
advanced in skirmishing order with great quickness
and spirit. Captain Knox of the 75th was killed
with several men. The infantry sheltered themselves
behind the tower, and the sepoys came within
twenty yards of the guns. Four artillerymen were
shot down, and the guns would have been lost, had
not the 75th, recovering from their surprise, come
forward and driven them back. This was so near the
camp, that some of the bullets fell amongst the tents.
Aid was at hand, and the Pandies were pursued with
loss; fifty or sixty of them were said to have been
killed in the compound of Metcalfe's house, but no
more than seven or eight bodies were found round
the Flagstaff. They were all Hindoos.

A little after, an attack was made on the Hindoo
Rao picquet, and large bodies of the enemy passed
through the Subzi-Mundi into the gardens and
thickets, close up to the mound on the right flank
of our camp. Some guns were brought up to play
upon them, and they were driven out with great loss
by the 1st Fusiliers. Twenty of them were caught
in the corner of a compound, and killed by the
bayonet. Some more took refuge in a serai. It was
surrounded, the door broken open, and all killed;

seventy corpses were counted. The attack on Hindoo
Rao's was repulsed with effect by the Guides and
Rifles. Many of the men slain belonged to the 60th
Native Infantry, which had been sent to meet its
trial fight. These attacks were no doubt meant to be
simultaneous, but, owing to the bad arrangement or
insubordination in their ranks, took place at different
periods of the day. We thus gained an easy victory
with little loss. Great discouragement was felt in
the city. Our spies reported they had five hundred
missing. Perhaps this calculation was too high.

The difficulty of our position was not understood
in the stations in the Punjaub. All waited with
sleepless anxiety for the news of the fall of Delhi,
which most of them expected would come in a few
days. Officers, too, marching down to the camp,
expressed their fears, that the city would be taken
before they could possibly reach it. Some false
reports of its capture appeared in the Anglo-Indian
newspapers. Much impatience and irritation were
shewn at the delay. Voices were loud at every mess.
Most of the officers in camp said we ought to go in at
once. Among so many good officers, there were
plainly few generals. Sir Henry Barnard seemed at
last driven to do something. The whole camp was
roused at dead of night. Two infantry regiments

were moved off towards the city. Two gates were to be blown in to give an entrance to our infantry, of which not more than eighteen hundred could be brought up. Directions were sent to withdraw the picquets, which made up half our little force; but Brigadier Graves, who was in command of an important one, refused to do so, without a written order signed by the general and two witnesses.

Sir Henry Barnard was weighing the dangers of the undertaking; and the return of the aid-de-camp from his fruitless ride, inclined him to abandon the attempt. The assault would most probably have failed. The dawn was at hand; we could not hope to succeed with the enemy on the alert. It was best as it was. A party, who went down by the gates, said all was quiet; but there were some people lying outside them, who would most likely have started on our approach. Even had we got in, our force was too weak to have kept up a prolonged struggle in the streets, and to have held both our own camp and that part of the city which we might have gained against the enemy, who were receiving powerful reinforcements every day. Repulse would have been destruction.

To prevent an attack like that of the 12th upon the Flagstaff tower, a large picquet was placed near Metcalfe's house. They occupied a strong position

on a small rising ground surrounded by trees,
the stables, the walls of which were heighte
sandbags. The thickets round about were cut
as we could spare men to do it. Without forci
picquet, the enemy could not pass in any nun
our left, which was closed in by Metcalfe's
standing hard by on the now half dried cha
the Jumna. It was attacked on the 15th ii
force; some fighting took place between the
and the 75th. Four horse artillery guns were b
down, and the sepoys driven away after a
struggle. Two or three days after, the enemy
on a constant fire from all their heavy artillery.
was no doubt to prevent us noticing a battery,
they were constructing on the right of Hindo
hill to enfilade our whole position. Men wer
carrying baskets of earth, and some force was evi
collected across the road to our right. It was
sary to prevent this. About four hundred 1
the 1st Fusiliers and 60th Rifles, with Tombs
of horse artillery, thirty horsemen of the Guid
a few sappers and miners, were got ready. Th
mand was given to Major Tombs. Their desti
was kept secret. Orders were given and co
manded to confound the enemy's spies. Majo
descended from Hindoo Rao's with the rifle

Ghoorkas, while Tombs advanced towards the enemy's left, and our batteries poured their fire on the Lahore gate, whose guns might have reached our squadrons. At first their cavalry, seeing the fewness of our sowars, prepared to charge them, but recoiled at sight of our troops coming up behind. Their infantry, taken by surprise, fled without offering the least resistance, many leaving their arms and clothes behind them. Some threw themselves into a mosque. The walls of its courtyard were loopholed, and they began to fire at our men. Tombs had two horses killed under him. His bold bearing and loud voice made him the aim of the enemy. He ordered the riflemen to go up and fire into the loopholes till the doors could be forced. A train of gunpowder was got ready; a bag was attached to the gates; they were blown open, and thirty-nine sepoys were killed in the mosque. A nine pounder gun was taken. Major Reid on his side was also successful. He destroyed a battery and magazine, and set a village and serai on fire. Our whole loss was only three killed and fifteen wounded; Captain Brown of the Fusiliers, dangerously. A great peril averted by such small loss lightened the hearts of our men, and made them despise everything about the enemy, save their long shots.

Sir Henry Barnard shewed his admiration of the

gallantry and conduct of Tombs, in the most
siastic manner. During the interview it was
a bullet had cut his arm. The same evening
general appeared for a few minutes in the mess-
the Umballa artillery, and gave the highest an
heartfelt praise to the young officer. He had
seen greater coolness and courage, and a more
knowledge of his profession, than had been she
Major Tombs. This time the voice of the car
also that of headquarters. Considerable dissatis
existed on the publication of general orders p
officers who had not distinguished themselve
had no opportunities of so doing, and neglectin
who had borne the brunt of the fighting.]
such complaint could be made in this case.

Tombs was henceforth the hero of the forc
had reached the aim of a soldier's life. On 1
entry into the Company's army, he had serve
great distinction in the wars of the Punjaub, a
talents had been marked by the keen and wise
Sir Charles Napier. He had been made breve
when only a lieutenant of artillery. His galla
Ghazeeoodeenuggur had made him conspicuo
the beginning of the siege of Delhi. He had]
to this date five horses shot under him.
seemed to seek him out only to leave him unt

At this time he was in the flower of manhood ; above the middle height, broad shouldered, deep chested, and very handsomely made. He had coal-black hair, and beauty and strength seemed to struggle with one another in his countenance. Another name which began to vie with Harry Tombs was that of Hodson. They seemed to have little in common save distinguished soldiership. Hodson entered the Company's army as a cadet of infantry, rather older and better educated than cadets generally are. He gained great credit as a daring partisan officer in the wars of the Punjaub. After they were over, Sir Henry Lawrence had tried him in various tasks ; and by his countenance he rose to the command of the newly raised Guides. From this height he was pre-cipitated by an accusation of mismanagement in his regimental accounts. The opening of the mutiny found him doing duty with his original regiment, the 1st Fusiliers. But though the accusation, of which he was never found guilty, and which there is reason for believing was groundless,* still weighed him down, he was too well fitted for those dreadful times to keep

* All this was written before a perusal of the life of Hodson, published by his brother. It of course contains an elaborate and, as far as it goes, a successful defence of the hero. Nothing may be thought incredible of the Audit Office, which has ever shewed the most ostentatious suspicion of military

the level of a subaltern.　He was placed at the head
of the Intelligence department.　Wherever danger
was, there also was Hodson ; whenever the enemy
came out of the gates, Hodson was seen, with his
loose hanging rein, followed by a dozen of wild-look-
ing sowars, leaning easily on their carabines at full
gallop.　In a quarter of an hour he was back with
the news of their whereabouts.　He had also been
charged to raise a new native regiment of irregular
horse, an undertaking almost impossible in those
times of dissolution and desertion.　In figure he was
tall and spare.　His light reddish hair left the top of
his head uncovered.　He had a high forehead, aquiline nose, and haughty Roman features ; there was a
light in his eye which looked as if half kindled.　His
manners were distant and supercilious ; ordinarily he
spoke little and answered in few words.　His dress
was plain, but that of a man continually in the
saddle.　Tombs, on the contrary, understood the effect
of dress, was fond of speaking, especially on military
matters, and, though impatient of flattery, seemed to
care more about the good opinion of others.

officers, and is often allowed to treat them with great harshness ; but probably the haughtiness of Hodson's character
raised him many enemies, who formed a combination against
him.　We also see from his letters that he had plenty concealed vanity.

CHAPTER VI.

THE spies had brought us news that a large reinforcement had come to our enemies. It was the brigade from Nysseerabad ; two regiments of native infantry, and a company, and horse battery of artillery. It was not allowed to enter the city, but encamped beyond the Lahore gate. They were to fight us on the 19th. This reinforcement must have been pleasing to them. The irregular cavalry at Haupper had taken a courier, bearing an order to the Bareilly mutineers to send guns and men quickly, as most of the sappers in Delhi had been killed ; to eat their dinner in Rohilcund, and wash their hands in Delhi. Our glasses on the ridge were kept open all day to watch for the apprehended attack. The usual time went by,—our fears had half passed away with the fierceness of the noontide heat, when a powerful force was seen in motion. It was thought that the attack would fall on some one of our picquets, and they were reinforced. The enemy disappeared amongst the gardens to our right. The first news of their destination was brought

in by some flying sowars of the Rajah of Jheend. The
blow was to be struck on the rear. Half our camels
were out feeding on the plain ; and the terrified
camel-drivers fled into camp, bewailing the loss of
their property. The camp followers, many of whom
had built their huts beyond the canal, came after them,
spreading panic and confusion everywhere. The attack
must be met at once. Very few troops were in camp.
They were sent out as they could be got. The horse
artillery were first on the ground ; twelve guns of
three troops, the rest being at picquet ;—they fell
upon the enemy, who shewed a wide crescent-shaped
front. For a short time the artillery bore the whole
weight of their assailants. Without support, they kept
them back by the skill and rapidity of their movements, but they soon perceived they had met no every-
day enemy. The Nysseerabad brigade began that
evening to form a reputation which it held till the
end of the war. No corps of the rebel army kept up
its discipline and organization so steadily throughout. Their horse artillery bore on its guns the figure
of a mural crown, in commemoration of its illustrious
deeds in the famous defence of Jellalabad against the
Afghan. Their fire was steady and well-distributed,
and, being supported by infantry in covered ground,
it placed our guns in great danger Tombs, on the

right, found himself under a severe musketry fire from a number of men in a thicket near an old gate, against whom his artillery was useless. A portion of the Guide cavalry came up. " Daly, if you do not charge ;" said Tombs to their leader, " my guns are taken." Daly spurred into the bushes ;—scarcely a dozen of his men followed him. He returned with a bullet in his shoulder ; but the momentary diversion saved the guns. Captain Money's troop took ground on the left, towards the Subzi-Mundi ; and, though taken in flank and exposed to a heavy fire, gained ground upon the enemy, who brought their artillery against him. Captain Money had his horse killed under him, and one of his guns disabled. Another gun, belonging to the 3d troop, 3d Brigade, under Lieutenant Bishop, who was wounded, was also dismounted, and for the time abandoned.* The lancers

* This affair was fought almost entirely by the Artillery. Hodson writes (Letter, 20th June), " The enemy came down and attacked our rear, and a sharp conflict ensued between some two thousand sepoys with six guns, and three hundred Europeans with one gun." The reader may, by comparing this with the text, judge of the errors which creep into history Hodson's Letters are full of uncorrected mistakes. He, however, was ill about this time. In the same letter he says, p. 209, " The consequence is (of Becher and Daly's being wounded), that I have in effect to see to the whole work of the Quartermaster-General of the army, and, in addition, the

came up, charging the enemy, who took them in flank in a lane, and inflicted some loss. **Brigadier Hope Grant**, who held the command of the troops, had his horse killed under him, and was with difficulty rescued by some men of the lancers and his two native orderlies. The confusion was very great, and was increased by the dusk coming on. Our force was too small and too scattered to press back the enemy at all points,—ou one wing there was fighting more than a mile from the camp ; on the other they approached so near, that their grape shot fell on the banks of the canal. Our troops, hurrying up without any plan, were fighting, each body for itself. It was difficult to find where they were, or to distinguish them from the enemy. The lancers were fired upon by our own artillery, and Captain Money was twice asked to turn his guns on the carabiniers. One of Major Scott's waggons was blown up ;—every one thought it belonged to the enemy. Very few infantry could be spared from camp, and they did not come up till it was beginning to turn dark. With their aid we began to push the enemy back. For a while

General has begged me, as a personal favour, to take command of the Guides until Daly has recovered." It is scarcely necessary to notice the strange blunder of Mr. Rotton, that the Ochterloney gardens were the scene of the fight. It took place on the plain beyond.

the darkness was divided here and there by the flashes of the artillery. Gradually they ceased, and our men returned slowly to camp, bringing the wounded on the gun-waggons, but not with the joy of men coming safe out of deadly battle. Exaggerated accounts of our loss and confusion were spread amongst the men. Even in the mess-tents, where the truth was better known, the conversation was low and sad. It was the first time the enemy had met us on what could be called equal terms. Colonel Becher, Quartermaster-general, was wounded ; Colonel Yule's charger had come in riderless ; some of the infantry had been seen flinching ; Daly of the Guides was hit at last ; a great many officers and men were knocked over ; four guns were disabled ; and the Pandies had kindled their fires in our rear. What would be their boasting, as they cooked their meal, that we were surrounded by a chain of iron—and what joy in the city, that they had met the white people, and parted fairly ! Not to return flying through the gates was a triumph. Very large reinforcements were on the point of entering Delhi. What would happen if they could hold a position to our rear, or if such an action took place every time a new mutinous regiment came in ?—Should we be able to hold our position, or keep the road clear behind us ?—Well, we had done it as

yet, and might do so still. Let them boast to-night,
to-morrow would dawn upon another tale!

At the first breath of the morning our men rose
from their uneasy sleep, and a strong body went to
the rear to drive away the enemy. We came upon
a sight which convinced us that their loss could
not have been light. At one spot alone forty of
them were lying, their bodies torn by the ghastly
wounds of cannon-shot, the faces of some twisted
with agony, others sleeping quietly. There was a
havildar, with the mural crown on his hat and a
medal on his breast. Some were still alive; one man
stated that he had come along with the brigade from
Nysseerabad, a solitary deserter from the 1st Bombay
Light Cavalry. He was spared at the request of the
Rajah of Jheend. He said they were refused admit-
tance into Delhi, and ordered to go and fight, after
which they would get ten rupees a month, and two
hundred at once. Fifty-five horses were said to have
been counted lying on the ground where the Jellalabad battery had fought. The body of Colonel Yule
was found, rifled and mutilated. A village about a
mile farther on was occupied by the enemy. Probably a large number had gone to the city. At any
rate no attempt was made to cope with us; a few
shells drove them out. A gun, on which some wounded

men were strapped, was overtaken, and brought in. Our force had scarcely entered camp when some Pandies came back, and wheeled up a gun so near our tents, that the round-shot passed through the Head-quarter camp. Having executed this bravado, they again galloped off. The alarm of the camp-followers across the canal was renewed ; they rushed with one accord to the nearest bridge. Terrified men, unman-ageable camels, women unveiled, sedate-looking ele-phants, frightened horses, sulky oxen, and deserted children, were seen crushing over and against one another, across the narrow broken bridge, like a swollen lake disgorging itself by a small stream. Soldiers were mixed up with them, rushing to the front, knocking them about without any apology, and troopers trying, with much swearing, to push their frightened horses against the stream. Our forces had turned out upon the plain, and clouds of dust hindered us from seeing what was going on ; our artillery was blazing away at the imaginary enemy ; and a regiment of infantry was made to lie down by a wary old brigadier, to avoid vollies that never came.

It was found that our loss in this affair amounted to three officers and nineteen men killed, and seven officers and seventy men wounded, and sixty horses.

hors de combat. One of the officers killed, and four
of those wounded were attached to the 60th Rifles.
Most of the camels were found, and the abandoned
gun was brought back in a waggon by some men,
who volunteered to go out and seek for it that same
night. A picquet was established in the rear, to
guard against such attacks for the future, and two
heavy guns were mounted. Like the Metcalfe picquet, it would have been useful before the enemy had
taught us the weakness of the point; but our force
was so small and hard-worked, that it was a problem
to get reliefs, and, at the same time, leave a few men
in camp.

On the 21st one of the bridges across the canal
was blown up by us. It would have been as well if
this, too, had been done before the 19th. As a counter-
part, the bridge over the Jumna at Bagput had fallen
into the hands of the enemy. It had been left in the
charge of the magistrate, Mr. Campbell, with one
hundred and fifty sowars of Nabbha and Patiala.
They were attacked by a large insurgent force of
Goojurs, and retired over the bridge. The sowars lost
heart, and on the enemy crossing, refused to charge
them or fight any more. As they could not be
trusted, the magistrate, with two European officers
who were with him, galloped off with the news to

camp. Our communication with Meerut was thus cut off; and, though we did not care very much, so long as the road to Umballa was kept clear, it was determined to get the bridge repaired, and send out the whole of the Jheend force to guard it. Many of the boats were collected, and the bridge put together. In a few days it was again lost. On the news that the enemy were coming out from Delhi to attack them, the whole force ran away without seeing a hostile face, or getting proof that they were really coming. The bridge was left as it was; the officer with the force not even getting the boats pulled to our side of the river. The enemy found their way to it when they knew no one was there, burnt some of the boats, and plundered the place. The officer with the Jbeend force was much blamed, and was removed from his place. Hodson was sent to find out the real state of things; he succeeded in recovering most of the boats, and floating them down to camp, but saw nothing of the enemy.

The road to Umballa was guarded by troops of the Patiala Rajah, and remained pretty clear. If the enemy had made proper use of their numerous cavalry, we might have been put to very serious straits. All our news came this way; letters from Calcutta had to double the Point de Galle and come up the Indus.

The telegraph wire ran from Umballa up country,[*] though now and then broken. The stoppage of our communication with Calcutta was generally acknowledged to be an advantage. The Punjaub government could act for itself. Agra, the seat of the Lieutenant-Governor, stood insulated amidst the storm of rebellion that had submerged the Doab. Now and then a courier appeared in our camp, with a letter concealed about his person. We were ever dreaming of reinforcements from Cawnpore. Sometimes we heard they were half-way ; sometimes that they had reached Allygur ; and then no more of them.

The enemy in the meantime were making use of their new gunners. The practice against us at Hindoo Rao's was excellent. Not a foot of ground they could strike was left unswept by their fire. From the distance of their batteries the flash of the guns could be seen long before the shot reached us. Men were kept on the look out to warn our soldiers to keep behind the works when a shot was coming. Although we had given up hopes of making approaches, we still replied and sometimes tried to silence their batteries.

---

[*] Going *down* country is following the flow of the rivers Jumna and Ganges towards the sea ; going *up* country, the reverse, and, beyond them, towards the sources of the Indus in the Punjaub.

One of their best gunners was killed at this time. The enemy evidently liked firing, and often threw shells into our camp. Most of them fell short, or burst in the air; but now and then one alighted among the tents.

They still kept up the forms of military discipline. They posted sentries, and we could hear at night the fire of their patrols; but so many regiments had come flown with mutiny and plunder that it became difficult to manage them. It was said that the 60th Infantry, which deserted from Rhotuck, not getting a share of the plunder already divided, refused to fight any more, and had encamped three miles from the town; and that a body of men had made over the bridge to desert, pursued by a regiment of cavalry and some guns. They were seen crossing the bridge from our batteries, and the guns were heard firing.

About this time, the mutineers from Jullundur reached the city, three regiments of infantry, and the 6th Light Cavalry. Our men, however, had three days' cessation from fighting. Glad to get the heat of the day past, even under the shelter of a thin web of canvas, such as were not at picquet slept off the time in their crowded tents. Experience taught them to take repose while they could get it. The health of the men was as good as could have been looked for in cantonments.

Months before this a prophecy had been widely spread, that the rule of the Company would expire with the hundredth year. It had begun on the field of Plassey, consequently must end on the centenary of that battle. This was the 23d June; "Let the soldiers go and smite the Feringhees without fear." The astrologers had calculated it ; the holy Brahmins had read it ; the spirits of the conjurors and the dice of the soothsayers all told the same tale. It was written, that assuredly on this day the reign of the white people would be over. Fanaticism and super- stition flowed into the same stream. It was also the first day of the new moon, sacred with the Maho- medan, and the Jattra, the commencement of the night of the gods, a festival of the worshippers of Vishnu and Juggernaut. It was very well known in our camp, that on this day we should have a hard struggle for existence ; perhaps our weak force would be annihilated under the swarms of the enemy. The day before, every one thought anxiously of the morrow ; the most careless were sobered ; some thought wist- fully of their wives and children in the hills, some made their wills ; the more religious said their prayers.

The enemy did not keep us long waiting. About three o'clock in the morning a cannonade was opened from the walls, and their whole force came out, and occupied the Subzi-Mundi and Kissengunge. From these points they could enfilade both our camp and batteries. Our infantry was moved up against them, and a small body of cavalry and artillery was sent to the rear, to cover the entrance of Major Olpherts' reinforcement and baggage, into the camp. This was the pursuing force from Jullundur; and consisted of four guns of the 1st European troop, 1st Brigade Horse Artillery; part of a native troop, commanded by Captain Renny; a company of the 75th Foot, some men of the 2d Fusiliers, the 4th Sikh Infantry, and a wing of the 2d Punjaub Cavalry; the whole numbering no more than eight hundred and fifty men. He was not impeded on his way. Some horsemen appeared on the road, but a cannon-shot brought down four or five of them, and scared the rest away.

Our infantry in the meantime was struggling with the enemy for the Subzi-Mundi. The sepoys held the houses and serais, and from their flat roofs poured their fire upon our men. We cleared the streets several times, but whenever we tried to force the houses, the enemy swarmed back through every opening. The odds were too great; we were thrice within the place, and thrice out again. Sometimes the battle came so near, that the shouts of the men and the

words of command could be heard by our artillery at
the foot of the mound, waiting to cover the infantry
should they be driven in ; sometimes it seemed as if
our troops were driving them far before them. The
footsore infantry, who had marched twenty miles that
morning, had to be called out after an hour's rest.
The Sikhs did much havoc, falling upon the enemy,
who mistook them for one of their own regiments.
The command of the force engaged was held by
Brigadier Showers. Perhaps it would have been
better had everything been left to his well-known
gallantry and discretion. Sir Henry Barnard stood
upon the mound, saying, he could know the course of
a battle from the smoke. But the officers complained
that the order to retreat would come when they were
driving the enemy back, and the order to advance
when they had the worst of it. That whole hot
tropical day did they fight, till the men began to fall
down with heat and exhaustion. Towards evening
the enemy retired, evacuating the Subzi-Mundi,*
which, before sunset, was in our possession.

We had one officer, Lieutenant Jackson, 2d

---

* It is clear from this, that we were not worsted in this
engagement (although some people have said so). However,
it is incorrect to state, that this battle was a complete victory,
as some have done.

Fusiliers, and thirty-eight men killed; Colonel Welsh-man, 1st Fusiliers, dangerously, two other officers severely wounded, with one hundred and eighteen men. The enemy must have lost between three and five hundred men. The result of this affair freed our minds from a great load of anxiety. We knew it was a fearful danger tided over. The enemy would not make such an effort every day. Blows that strain the hand are not often struck. The spies reported that the enemy were very much depressed. Their prophets had deceived them; it was not our fate to be destroyed. Instead of the expected victory, they had returned, baffled and disgraced, with waggons full of dead and wounded. And what would it be if, after all, these white people conquered? Were there so many more men in Villait like those who fought them day after day? They played their game badly, but they still had many men on the board. They ought to have held and strengthened the Subzi-Mundi and Kissengunge, and, by shelling our camp, forced us to attack them at a disadvantage. Perhaps their upstart generals had not sufficient authority to hold them to the post. Our play was clear; we moved into the Subzi-Mundi, and placed a picquet there. Our men were lodged in a serai, and in some strong houses, and across the road, towards Hindoo Rao's house, in a temple called the Sammy house. Thcs were hastily fortified, and a breast-work afterwards run along the ridge to our main batteries. The enemy could not now come along the road to the rear, without being exposed to the fire of our men. The reinforcements we had got did not tend to raise our spirits They had expected to find us either in Delhi, or on the eve of capturing it; and were alarmed and shocked to perceive that we were the besieged, and not the besiegers, with strength hardly sufficient to keep off destruction from day to day. What was to be the end of all this? If the same men went out daily to fight, they must be all killed in the end, even if they were never defeated. The resources of the enemy were exhaustless; the whole of the Bengal army was against us. We knew nothing of what was going on in Calcutta, and cared nothing. There was no help there; even if it had been two days' march off, or if a railway had run from thence into our camp, there were no troops to send. The prevailing tone of conversation was most desponding; at messes the necessity of retreating to Umballa was openly discussed. To the more clear-sighted retreat implied the death of every European in the Northwest. A beaten army could never rule the Punjaub. To the more determined death seemed preferable.

Our eyes were turned to our own island, far away across the jungles, the mountains, and the sea ; and we knew that, even if we all perished, yet would our avengers one day stand upon our dust.

About this time Brigadier Chamberlain, who had been appointed Adjutant-General, arrived in camp. Much was expected of him. Everything will be right, they used to say, when Chamberlain comes! and all took courage when they saw his stern pale face. He had been known as a cavalry officer of desperate daring ; and had gained great praise for the determined manner in which he headed the moveable column through the Punjaub. Promotion in the Bengal army went by seniority, and was very slow. Military genius, even of the highest kind, was little marked, and could not raise a man. There was a shorter road, however ;—to risk life desperately on every possible occasion, to play ten to one with death, and nourish a reckless fatalism. In this way hundreds perished, but a few, covered with wounds and glory, succeeded in climbing to high command. Chamberlain, Nicholson, and Hodson, were men of this stamp, whose courage had been tried to the utmost, but who had scarcely yet proved their judgment and capacity to direct the motions of armies. Hence our generals were of two sorts, either daring, guerilla leaders,

prompt, skilful, and full of vigour, but generally rash
and lavish of blood; or worn out old men, who had
gained their rank by living long, unnerved by age
and the exhausting climate of India, perfectly inca-
pable of doing the rough work required of them,
but with rank and influence sufficient to obstruct
those who were able to do it. There were several old
officers like these in camp, whom everybody wished
away ; though some veterans still retained vigour and
energy enough to keep abreast of young men. Experience is very valuable in India, but only men of
ability will learn from it.

The enemy, though there were frequent alarms
and skirmishes, did not make any serious move for
some time. Everybody was disgusted at the waste
of men and ammunition that took place in these useless affairs. Instead of keeping behind our breastworks, our officers could never resist the temptation
of fighting the enemy on their own ground ; and
though a soldier would often go out and return with
his cartridge-box empty, without having seen the top
of an enemy's pugarie, still we were continually
losing men who might have been spared. On the
27th June, for example, an attack was made on the
Metcalfe and Subzi-Mundi picquets. The enemy
were repulsed with considerable loss. We had sixty-

two men hors de combat ; and on the 30th a skirmish took place near the Eedgah, when Lieutenant Yorke, 4th Sikhs, was mortally wounded, some said by one of his own men, and Lieutenant Blair of the 2d Fusiliers dangerously.

On the 27th the rains began, to every one an immense relief. We could now go out during the day without danger of sun stroke ; and although, when the sun broke out, the close damp heat was most distressing, it lasted only for a time, and the nights were always cooler.

On the 28th a European regiment reached camp, Her Majesty's 8th, numbering four hundred men, about the strength to which almost every regiment in camp was reduced. We had got the rest of the guns of Major Olpherts, and Captain Renny and some foot artillery from Lahore, with a body of newly raised Sikh artillery, old gunners, who talked in the batteries of what they had done against us at Feroshuher and Chillianwallah. Her Majesty's 61st regiment, 1st Punjaub Infantry (Rifles), and a squadron of the 5th Punjaub Cavalry, came a little while after. Our strength now amounted to six thousand six hundred men.

A company of the 3d Native Infantry, which had come down with a convoy from Phillour, before the

regiment mutinied, was disarmed, and the men ordered
to their homes for six months, to report themselves to
the nearest civilian, somewhere, doubtless, in lower
Bengal. They were known to be seditious, and we
were glad to get rid of them, even in this humorous
manner. What could we do with men good for
nothing but to corrupt the rest, and send news to the
enemy? The sepoys were sulky and insolent, holding up their red coats, and asking what return they
could have for spending their money upon what was
now quite useless, and never becoming. They collected their clothes and dishes and went away.

Our camp was beginning to extend itself by many
new accessions. Native merchants, too, began to
appear; and the price of provisions, which at first
was very high, fell, especially after the bridges over
the canal were destroyed. Our commissariat, under
the charge of Colonel Thomson, was perfect; no
convoy was ever surprised by the enemy, and the
soldier never wanted his grog a day.* The medical

---

* No merchant was allowed to sell any spirituous liquor
in camp; but an allowance of rum was given daily to the
Europeans, and also to the Ghoorkas and Sikhs. By the
Ghoorkas it was highly valued, although their pay in the hills
was too low to allow them to become habitual drinkers. The
Sikhs sold it, if they could, to Europeans. This was the
cause of many a case of drunkenness. The craving for drink

arrangements were as good as could be in the case. Two or three houses in the cantonment, that had escaped destruction, were used by some regiments as hospitals, but the sick, in general, were found to do better in tents. Though quinine was scarce we had always medicine, and a sufficient number of surgeons and apothecaries, and plenty of servants, even natives, to fan those who were very weak. The health of the men bore up well. The surgical operations were wonderfully successful. Cholera, dysentery, and fever were never absent, but not remarkably frequent. The wounded were despatched from time to time, in litters and covered waggons, to Umballa, where a great field hospital was established, under the care of Dr. Balfour, and the worst cases were sent from thence to the hills. The disposition of the men, both in camp and hospital, was stout and hearty, even gay ; or if sad, only for a moment. ·

Our camp began to have more the appearance of

with the latter was excessive. It was one of their keenest pangs on going into the hospital, that it was taken from them. On the walls of houses near their picquets demands for increased allowances were written in chalk. Some were very amusing—" We haven't half plenty of grog." " Gif us enoffe grog." " Plenty grog, plenty work." " Give us two totts and we'll go in," (i.e., to Delhi). " More grog." Then again, by a more sentimental hand—" You may talk of Salamanca, but future ages will talk of Delhi."

a town. The cantonment roads were very useful, and
the native merchants repaired and reoccupied the
shops of the old regimental bazaar. As the canal
was close behind, our space was rather confined.
Although · many of the native followers and cattle
were on the gardens and plains on the other side,
there were still too many crowded together beside the
troops ; and the little churchyard near was full of
dead.   It was difficult to keep in cleanness a place
covered by so many men and cattle. Outside the
camp it was worse ; a border of filth and rottenness,
heaped with dead camels and horses, repelled all who
ventured out to seek a little pure air. The favourite
ride was along the ridge, though sometimes a round
shot whizzed by.   The Quartermaster's department
was continually criticised ; they did all they could
however.

The scene was a very curious one.   It is thus
described in a letter, written at the time :*—What
a sight our camp would be, even to those who visited
Sebastopol ! The long lines of tents, the thatched
hovels of the native servants, the rows of horses tied
by the heels, the parks of artillery, the English soldier

---

* It appeared in the *Times*, and is quoted in the *Red
Pamphlet*. The author has taken the liberty to alter it a
little, as he has every right.

in his grey cotton coat and trousers (he has fought as well as ever without pipe-clay), the tall wiry Sikhs, with their long hair tied up behind their blue turbans ; the olive-complexioned Afghans, with their wild air, their gay head-dresses, and coloured saddle-cloths ; and the little Ghoorkas, their natural ugliness set off by black worsted hats and woollen coats, the truest, bravest soldiers in our pay, dreadful and hideous as death. There are scarcely any poorbeahs left in our ranks, but of native servants many a score. In the rear are the booths of the native bazaars ; and farther out, on the plain beyond, the thousands of bullocks, camels, and horses, that carry our baggage. The officers are talking by their tents, the men are loitering through the lines or in the bazaars. Suddenly the alarm is sounded ; every one rushes to his tent ; the infantry soldier seizes his musket, and slings on his pouch ; the artilleryman gets his guns harnessed ; the Afghan rides out to explore. In a few minutes every one is in his place. Troops are moved towards the points that are attacked ; they return towards evening faint and weary, leaving some of their number in the hospital-tents. The slain are sewed up in sacks, to be carried to the churchyard in the morning. The chaplain of the force is always ready, or the priest, if the dead be of the Romish

Church. A few words, a few shovelfuls of earth, mayhap a few tears, and all is done!

The general was continually urged by the hotter spirits in camp, since we were so much stronger, to attempt to carry the town. He yielded so far, that the engineer officers were directed to make plans ; and various ingenious devices, to blow in the gates and get over the walls, were submitted. It was assumed that, this obstacle crossed, we were in possession of Delhi. We could bring only three thousand men to the attack, the enemy certainly ten times as many. According to the maxims of regular warfare, the besiegers ought to be three times the number of the besieged. We could not hope to reach the walls without their knowledge. There was every proof that the enemy was well informed of our motions ; and, indeed, it was certain, that one night, when several infantry regiments were ordered under arms, the alarm was sounded an hour after in the city. The chance of a surprise hung upon the improbability of one of our thousand wavering sepoys, syces, grass-cutters, or camp-followers not leaving an open camp to bear news, for which he would be well rewarded. Even supposing we crossed the ditch and scaled the wall, the fight must be prolonged in hundreds of narrow streets, barricaded, swept by cannon, and held by an enemy who had already shewn that they were inferior to none in this species of warfare. When we could not drive the enemy out of the few summer-houses in the Subzi-Mundi, how could we clear all the massive buildings and narrow streets in Delhi, against the whole rebel force, and the armed rabble of the town? And who, in the meantime, was to guard the long line of our camp, full of sick and wounded men, and our batteries, and Hindoo Rao's Hill? Our position was getting better every day; the weak points of our camp had been strengthened, the enemy could no longer bring their artillery to meet us in the rear, nor attack us in front, without passing through the fire of our own ; they had not been able, after repeated attacks, to force our most advanced picquets on the right ; and the Jumna, swollen by the rains, covered our left flank. The health of our men was good; our rear was open; the Punjaub was quiet. We were reoccupying some of the revolted districts; we expected reinforcements from every side—a hope not then known to be groundless. The tide of rebellion was full, and must begin to ebb. And were we then to run straight upon the only peril we could foresee, to hazard the chance of our ladders being dashed from the walls, and our being driven back under the easy havoc of their artillery, with a thousand or fifteen

hundred men killed and wounded ;* the tidings of
our slaughter to be borne by their swiftest couriers to
every sepoy regiment, and every native prince in
India. The Punjaub would have risen ; **Scindia and**
Holkar would have been compelled to do something
or quit their thrones. The Bombay army would have
followed, with Scinde, and Madras, and the Nizam's
force, at no distant day.   Not all the strength of
Great Britain could then have gained India back.
Everything depended on our being constantly successful.   These rash counsels, therefore, appeared
every day more strikingly foolish, and at last were
echoed only by mouths from which one never expected
anything else.

About this time Colonel Laughton of the Engineers was superseded, and Colonel Baird Smith
arrived in camp to fill his place. He was a great
accession, as none of the engineer officers, though
some of them were men of great ability, had sufficient
weight and rank to recommend any decided course of
action. Brigadier Graves, and another old general, left
about the same time.   All that engineers could do at

---

* Much may be done in India by boldness, but very much
lost by ill success. Assaults do not always succeed.   In
attacks upon mud forts, the average of failure has been five in
seven.

present was to strengthen the camp, cut down the trees, and demolish the houses round the picquets ; to examine the ground, make fascines and sandbags, raise sappers and bands of workmen, and have everything ready for the time of assault. At this period we could not approach the city walls. Indeed, a good portion of the enemy was encamped outside, under cover of their guns.

CHAPTER VII.

On the 1st of July the bridge of boats was seen to be broken, owing to the Jumna being flooded, and a large force appeared on the other side. This was the army so eagerly expected from Rohilcund, the Bareilly brigade, and the mutinous regiments from Moradabad and Shahjehanpore, about three thousand men. They had plundered these three stations, with the treasuries, and murdered almost all the officers. They brought with them an enormous quantity of spoil. Their upstart leaders were riding in the carriages of their victims. They crossed the Ganges leisurely, and lay several days at Babooghar, near Meerut, destroying the stud buildings and killing the syces. General Hewitt at Meerut had a thousand men under him, but nothing could prevail upon him to send out a force to attack them.

We saw them encamp on the other bank of the Jumna, in tents taken from our stores. It was two days before they all got over to Delhi. The men were most of them ferried over at night, for fear of our artillery, though the place where they crossed was almost out of range. They were commanded by one Bukht Khan, an old subahdar of artillery. He was well known to many officers of that arm in camp. They described him as a big fat man, obsequious, fond of the society of Europeans, and very intelligent. He soon gained a great influence over the old King of Delhi, and was made commander-in-chief. He, however, was much opposed and thwarted by the fierce Mirza Mogul, who had been appointed to that dignity from the very beginning of the outbreak. The troops as a body were dissatisfied with the elevation of Bukht Khan, and addressed a petition to the king,* stating that he was only an officer of artillery, and not fit to command an army, and begging that Mirza Mogul should still keep the leadership. Bukht Khan advised that a separate brigade should be formed for the prince, out of the Delhi and Meerut regiments. The king, who was dissatisfied with the insubordinate conduct of the princes, favoured the wily old soldier. He was, besides, supported by a powerful and zealous portion of the Mahomedans, being a wahabi or reformer, a sect which had many adherents at that time in Delhi. Bukht Khan remained an important leader in the rebel army, till

* See King's Trial, p. 169.

he was killed at the battle of Nawabgunge, in the Oude campaign.

There was now a very large army in the hands of the insurgent leaders, probably not less than thirty thousand men.* But there was little union; the more regiments the more jostlings took place. On the whole they obeyed their officers, who were principally from their own ranks, with greater docility than most Asiatic races would have done under the circumstances; but nothing could be accomplished without a great deal of squabbling and coaxing. Every scheme of attack had to be submitted to so many, that it was liable to be communicated to us by

* Hodson calculated the strength of the rebel army at 36,000 men ; Norman, 30,000, about the middle of August. The editor of Hodson's Letters says, "It was ultimately ascertained that there were 70,000 or 75,000." From official returns it appears this was greater than the number of troops who mutinied. 58,230 is the number given ; 26,750 disbanded or disarmed, 5000 would likely cover all the irregular soldiers or volunteers in Delhi. It is, however, possible this last calculation is too low. A great many jahadis or devotees came to Delhi, but turned back when they saw that no provision was made for their subsistence. Very gross exaggeration is noticeable in newspaper estimates of the enemy's numbers throughout the war.

The following is the report of the strength of the Bengal army before the mutiny, 1st April 1857 :—

Cavalry—European, 1,418.　　Infantry—European, 19,686.
　　　　Native, 26,411.　　　　　　　　Native, 141,632.

our spies before it could be executed. Any plan that
required co-operation was sure to miscarry, one party
being beaten off before the other came up. Men who
threw themselves into dangerous positions could not
rely upon the help of their comrades to bring them
off. If the system of seniority had spoilt our own
high commands, it had done the same with theirs.
Old and worn out subahdars became colonels of regiments. Sometimes, however, they were degraded for
men of greater vigour and ability. They still kept
up the type and traditions of their old regiments.
Native doctors, who had studied in our Presidency
colleges, and had been trained in our hospitals, tended
the wounded ; but not many of this class had followed their regiments. They had had four commanders-in-chief, and often two or three would fight
and intrigue for the leadership. They said, however,
that we were worse off, and had put two Lath Sahibs
to death, because they could not carry the town.
Perceiving that a great deal of information was betrayed to us, they were very suspicious. Native
Christians, or people who could speak English, were
seized and blown away from the guns (a lesson we
had the honour of teaching them), on the merest
conjecture, and men were continually being seized as
spies. They hanged one of their own golundazes

because he had got a mine dug under a bastion. Spies were placed around some of their principal leaders. A great part of the Sikhs in Delhi, it was known, wished to come over to our side; but they were carefully watched, and had no chance of escaping save during action, when they feared that the Europeans would kill them. A great many desertions took place. Of course any equivocal fight was claimed as a victory, although the citizens could not fail having a poor idea of the triumphs of the sepoys, since they witnessed most of the battles from the walls. Plenty of boasting went on in the bazaars, as no one liked to contradict men who carried loaded guns with them, and considered murder a mere amusement. They brought on one occasion an elephant, and on another two guns which they pretended to have taken in our batteries. Their spies, too, often brought in most absurd stories, such as that we had nothing to eat but grain (which is ordinarily used for horses), and that their bombs went through the air, crying "coffin, coffin," and burst with murderous effect. Such imaginary successes could not destroy the natural influence of actual defeats. They became dispirited, and were continually fighting with one another. Those regiments which had got no plunder envied and railed at their richer brethren. "The king," says a native, who lived a month in Delhi during the siege, " sends sweetmeats for the forces in the field ; and the guard at door of city—plunder it like the property of an enemy."

" The bravery of the royal troops deserves every praise ; they are very clever indeed. When they wish to leave the field of battle they tie a piece of rag on their leg, and pretend to have been wounded, and come into the city halting and groaning, accompanied by their friends."*

Part of the soldiers were leading a dissolute life, breaking into the houses of citizens and debauching their wives and daughters, ordering their husbands and fathers out to fight. Only the best of the sepoys would go to battle. The king paid them at first four annas a day, and one rupee for each trooper. In the beginning of July he was compelled to reduce it one half, and often the troops were days at a time without food.

The king held durbars in the alabaster pillared hall

---

* Our information about the state of Delhi is taken from many sources, news letters and oral communications from spies, as well as from accounts of natives and native Christians after the capture. The quotations are taken from the short description of a native, in the *Lahore Chronicle*, July 25, 1857. The Trial of the King, published as a Blue Book, gives much information on all points.

of his ancestors. The vast chamber was filled with cushions, on which sat chiefs, moulvies, and courtiers, mixed up with the sepoy officers, who took rank according to the date of their commissions under a power, whose medals they wore on their breasts, and whose cannon were booming in their ears. The gaudy screens and banners half clad the naked old hall, with its wan splendour and broken mosaics. The memory of ancient days was too strong; the tinsel draperies seemed like funeral serge—the walls, worn and mouldy, like a sepulchral vault. A spectral doting black old wretch, crouched upon the lofty throne of Aurangzib, deploring the mischiefs he had brought on his own head, and phrasing Mahomedan cant about the might of destiny and the will of God. The Orientals are not legitimists. At first his authority had been much respected, but soon began to fade. The sepoy leaders did not trust him, and upbraided and browbeat him in full divan. His grandson, the heir apparent, who, with the shahzadah Mirza Mogul, was the real head of the court, was at open feud with Bukht Khan, the sepoy general. The king complained that the sepoy officers galloped their horses through the passage to the Hall of Audience, while the highest officials of the English had always dismounted and come on foot. He tried shutting the gates, leaving only a wicket to pass through ; but they made them be opened. He was also much disgusted at their attending his durbars negligently dressed and with their arms.

"The princes are made officers to the royal army —thousand pities for the poor luxurious princes. They are sometimes compelled to go out of the door of the city in the height of the sun ;—their hearts palpitate at the firing of muskets and guns. Unfortunately, they do not know how to command an army ; their forces laugh at their imperfections, and abuse them for their bad arrangements."

Sometimes the princes and courtiers would come into the batteries, when the firing was slack, with gay shields on their arms, and wrapped in jewelled Cashmere shawls ; but a round shot would send them down the slope tumbling over one another.

"The noblemen and begums, together with the princes, regret the loss of their joyful days. They consider the arrival of mutineers at Delhi as sudden misfortune for them. The princes " (accustomed to a courtly Persian dialect) "cannot understand the sepoys without an interpreter. His Majesty is very much alarmed when a shell has burst in the castle, and the princes shew his Majesty the pieces of it. Many of the royal family have left the palace through

fear." A short time after the king removed his
zenana out of the city to the kootub. He sent an
emissary into our camp, and offered to betray the
sepoys, to throw open the gates, and admit our troops
into the palace, provided his own safety and that of
his family should be guaranteed, and his former pension continued. The offer was forwarded to the Chief
Commissioner for his advice and decision. Sir John
Lawrence thought it might be accepted, if the king
and princes could clear themselves of the murder of
Europeans. But it was surely better to keep clear of
all negotiations, than to neutralize them by a condition, which we could not have rendered operative,
even had it been accepted, without exposing ourselves
to the suspicion of bad faith. Lord Canning, with
more dignity, but perhaps with a less keen sense of
our difficulties in the North-west, forbade any such
bargaining being listened to.* At the same time,
the court was straining all its resources of fanaticism
and eastern diplomacy to destroy us. The king had
still many devoted adherents—native chiefs who had
joined their fate with his, or who wished to make their
fortunes by him ; fakirs, who would run the risk of
being blown away from the guns, to preach rebellion

* This fact was noticed in Parliament, and admitted, with
the qualification, by the idolaters of Sir John.

all over India ; fanatics, who saw the green mantle
of the Iman Ali, and heard the clank of his charger
in the jungles as they sped on their way. Patriots
are not common in India ; but there might be some
who rose against the subjection of their race. Learned
moulvies from all parts flocked to Delhi to excite
the soldiers by their oratory. The mosques rang
with militant harangues. A kind of Mahomedan re-
vival took place ; high-caste Hindoo soldiers were
converted to El Islam ; even Brahmins broke their
threads. The Imaun Mendhe was coming to chase
the infidels from the earth, and begin the millennium
of the faithful. There were many able and astute
heads too in Delhi, who understood all the arts of
statesmanship. Great efforts were made to gain over
the native princes, and to induce those who wished
ill to the British to commit themselves. Envoys were
despatched to Cabul and Cashmere, and two men sent
in the disguise of religious mendicants to Persia. A
soothsayer, who had great reputation at Court, kept
up their spirits by promises of speedy relief from that
quarter. It was the subject of conversation in the
palace night and day ; and the approach of the Shah's
army by Cabul was again and again reported, till at
last the news writer quoted the proverb, " A Brahmin
only believes in the promise of a feast when he sees

H

it." Everything was done to bring all the mutinous regiments to Delhi, especially the Gwalior Contingent; and to corrupt the Bombay army, whose ranks were full of Oude sepoys. The Gwalior mutineers were detained by the art of the Maharajah till the siege was over. Though completely at their mercy, he managed to save the lives of all the Europeans who had taken refuge with him.

The authority of the king stretched over a great part of the revolted districts, and was acknowledged nominally in Rohilcund and Oude;* but the meshes of the net were loose and often torn. He might send

---

* Khan Bahadur Khan sent a petition and vakiel through the medium of Bukht Khan. He sent also an elephant, a horse with silver ornaments, and a hundred and one gold mohurs, as presents. P. 164.

Three or four of the Lucknow mutinous regiments addressed petitions to the king, in which they stated they would proceed to Delhi after they had made themselves masters of Oude, and added that they had besieged the British in Baille Guard. Kudrat-ulla Khan Risaldar, accompanied by a hundred sowars, also brought a petition from all the Oude troops, and was introduced into the king's presence by Bukht Khan. He presented the coin recently struck in the name of Bahadur Shah. The impression on the coin was as follows :—

"Siraj-ud-din Bahadur Shah Ghazi has struck in gold the coin of victory."

The petitioners stated that they had elevated a son of Wajid Ali Shah on the gaddi, on the condition that he should be the Wazir of Bahadur Shah, and acknowledge allegiance

forth governors of cities and provinces, and reverse old decisions in favour of his own adherents, but the villagers would not pay tribute till they saw who gained, and rarely obeyed any one save their own head men. He could plunder the country round about Delhi, but could not protect his adherents in Hansi and Hissar, or near Meerut and Saharunpore, from the Company's troops. There was no order even in Delhi. All was dirt and confusion. In the streets violence and murder were common and unpunished. During the four months there were as many kotwals or police magistrates. The king wished justice should be administered by muftis and sudr-ul-sudrs, who should be under his own control only. It was impossible, however, to prevent the princes or soldiers from interfering, or to make them submit to any civil authority. There was a fierce riot between the Hindoos and the Mahomedans, because the latter wished to kill a cow. The Mahomedans were very much displeased that their king would not uphold them in doing so, in spite of the idolaters. The sepoys swaggered about, plundered and sometimes murdered the

to that king. They added that they had caused the prince to write down an agreement to that effect, and had further explained to him that he had been raised to the throne subject to the sanction of the king. P. 161. See evidence of Hakim Uhsun Ulla, physician to the king. Trial.

bunneahs for demanding the price of their goods.
The king had to interpose to prevent them picqueting
their horses in the Chandney Choke. They were continually breaking into the houses of the richest, under
pretence of seeking for Europeans concealed in them.
Few shops in the bazaar were open ; the merchants
in the neighbourhood had found it advisable to leave
their premises. " The citizens are extremely sorry
for losing their safety, and curse the mutineers from
morning to evening ; poor people and workmen
starve, and widows cry in their huts." Bukht Khan
tried to check the license of the soldiery, but one
man could do little. The sepoys could lodge where
they pleased, and when not engaged in the field, it
was difficult to exert any restraint over them. The
report, however, brought by spies and fugitives of our
stern doings in the Punjaub kept their force united ;
and, after all, they held well together, considering the
many temptations to discord, and the conduct of some
of the most civilized nations under circumstances less
untoward.

On the 2d of July, three Poorbeah officers made
an attempt to bring over Coke's regiment to the
enemy. Addressing themselves to a Sikh officer, and
bewailing the inevitable downfall of the English rule,
they added, " what is the use of us staying here ? Let

us kill as many of the Feringhees as we can, and
make away to Delhi. See how few they are! They
will all be shot in the end. From the King of Delhi
our reward will be magnificent, and our name will be
great." The Sikh assented to everything, but afterwards denounced the men. One of them was a native
officer with the order of merit, a renowned soldier,
and a man of great influence. It was feared his arrest
would suffice to bring on a mutiny. He was brought
to the Head-quarter camp ; a court-martial was instantly formed : " Never mind reporting the proceedings," said Chamberlain, " I shall do so myself." The
Sikh gave his evidence, and the men were sentenced
to be hanged. They were asked if they had anything
to say, why death should not be pronounced upon
them. The native officer answered with a scornful
laugh, he did not know of what he was accused. In
truth there was some reason for doubt, yet delay
would have been madness. One native is perfectly
capable of swearing away the life of another through
pure malice, much more a Punjaubee that of a Poorbeah, especially when he gains rank by his death ;
but our position compelled us to act with decision
even in doubtful cases. The whole thing was over
in half an hour, and the Poorbeah company, to which
they belonged, was paid off. The men met their fate

with indifference, only asking to be shot instead of hanged.

Affairs far more questionable than this pained nobody's conscience. Distrust, exasperation, and continual bloodshed, had made both men and officers suspicious and cruel. A Poorbeah's life was thought less of than a dog's : one day an officer at picquet caused seven harmless villagers to be shot as spies. Two men were hanged because they said our raj was at an end. An officer sent a note, saying he was suspicious of one of his soldiers ; the man was led away forthwith to be hanged. A courier ran forward to a European sentinel, holding up a letter in his hand, which he had brought at the hazard of his life. The soldier took the letter from him, and then told him to fly ; the man turned about to run, when the ruffian shot him through the back.

Bukht Khan moved out on the 3d July, and towards the evening advanced upon Alipore, one march to our rear. He expected to find our convoy of wounded men going to Umballa, and very nearly surprised a squadron of Punjaub cavalry, who got away in time.* A force of about three hundred horse,

* Mr. Rotton says that the Sikh guard at Alipore, fifty or sixty men, were all slain. This was a false report. Mr. Greathed in his letters, makes the same mistake. On this point, see Letter in *Lahore Chronicle*, July 8th, 1857. Mr.

eight hundred foot, and twelve guns, was put under
the command of Major Coke (who had gained great
distinction in the skirmishes of the Peshawur border),
to intercept him. The enemy were now returning
from Alipore along the further side of the canal.
After lying under arms till daylight was well advanced,
we crossed the bridge that was in our possession, and
came in full sight of the sepoy force crossing a wide
plain towards Delhi, several large bodies of cavalry,
with artillery, covering their foot. Our light guns
were brought into action; but were ordered to un-
limber almost out of range. The enemy returned our
fire, and their infantry and cavalry moved off leisurely.
Our foot did not come up in time to close with them.
A few who had lagged behind, sought refuge in a village, where they were all killed. The plunder taken
from Alipore fell into our hands, with a number of
other articles, including a complete field case of
surgical instruments. The unfortunate village was
sacked, and the troops returned to camp with a spe-
cious appearance of success, driving oxen laden with
spoil, and hauling goats and calves along with them;
Coke's regiment showing remarkable knowledge of
the art of securing and carrying off their plunder.

Rotton is also in error, when he says, that we killed about a
hundred of the enemy; no more than forty or fifty could
have perished.

Some women, whom they wished to take with them, were rescued by the Europeans. Our men returned completely exhausted by the heat; indeed many of the 61st sank down beneath trees, and our elephants had to be sent from camp to carry them in.

A body of the enemy, who had been sent out to support Bukht Khan, attacked us with some cavalry as we approached the Subzi-Mundi, but were repulsed. A chief from Kohat, who had raised eighty horse to assist us, was unfortunately killed.

Everybody in camp blamed Coke for the failure of this enterprise. His infantry came up as quickly as they could through the muddy ground, but they were a quarter of an hour too late. "It is always these quarters of hours," Napoleon said, "that decide the fate of an action." At any rate the enemy had gained no glory. It was amazing, that the largest reinforcement they had received should be content to spend two days in the field in pillaging the baggage of a few horse-men, and should make off after having lost it.

On the morning of the 5th, Sir Henry Barnard, who had been indisposed through the night, and whose constitution was sinking under incessant anxiety and exposure, shewed unequivocal symptoms of cholera. The disease appears to have struck him down with more than usual force. All attempts to

support him against it were vain; and at three
o'clock the chief, who yesterday could move thousands
of armed men, was lying dead in his tent; his flag
was struck, his voice never to be heard again. His
fate was very affecting. Arriving in an upcountry
station a few weeks before the native army disappeared
in mutiny; knowing nothing of the language, character, or habits of the people, with whom he had to
deal; called, by the death of General Anson, to lead
a large force for the first time, he was obliged to de-
pend upon others both for advice and instruction.
This gave an appearance of indecision to his measures,
and caused to himself the most cruel anxiety. He
was a courteous gentleman and a gallant soldier, and
was regretted all over the camp;—for his mild and
generous disposition and heroic courage had made
him loved, even by those who criticised a procrasti-
nation which they traced to him, without being able
to shew either that the line of conduct was wrong, or
that he was the cause of its being pursued. He was
buried with as much ceremony as we could afford.
The rude wooden coffin was borne to the churchyard
on a gun-waggon, and lowered by the men of his
Lancer escort. Every one pitied his son Captain
Barnard, who had served as an aid-de-camp with the
force. He left soon after to make his way to Europe.

CHAPTER VIII.

On the death of Sir Henry Barnard, the command recurred to General Reid, who was scarcely in good enough health to hold it. Many of the more active duties were given to Chamberlain, whose influence was paramount. His first proceeding was a wise one, and ought to have been adopted long before. All the bridges crossing the canal were blown up. A large escort was sent out to destroy one over the Nuffjugher canal cut, which was accomplished before the enemy knew where we were going. The Pool Chudder aqueduct, through which the canal water flowed into the city, was also broken. The enemy were now shut out from our rear, and supplies became more plentiful in camp, as the country people could no longer take their carts over the bridges to Delhi. Van Cortlandt's force in the Hansi and Hissar district was also doing us good service.

On the morning of the 9th July, the enemy's fire suddenly became unusually hot; a number of new pieces were brought into position on the bastions; shot and shell poured on our batteries, and some bombs

were thrown into the camp.   They turned out in
great force, but we were on the alert.   Almost abreast
of the mound, on our right hand, but a little farther
to our rear, was a raised ground, covered by a Mahomedan cemetery, thickly planted with trees ; beside
it was a fakir's house.   Between it and the mound
ran a path among some gardens, to the trunk road
leading through the Subzi-Mundi.   A sowar was
stationed at the end of it as sentry ; and by the
foot of the mound there was a picquet, consisting
of two horse artillery guns, under Lieutenant Hills,
a body of the Carabiniers, commanded by Lieutenant
Stillman, and some cavalry of the 9th Irregulars,
under a native officer.   The mound battery was generally covered with spectators ; but, as it was raining
hard, every one that possibly could had taken shelter.
Some native horsemen were seen approaching, and the
officer beside the guns was asked to fire upon them.
He was unwilling to do so, as they might be friends.
One of the 9th Irregulars was sent out to see who
they were, but did not come back.   In a moment
about a hundred and fifty sowars swept round by the
fakir's enclosure upon the picquet.   The carabiniers
turned and fled without firing a shot, leaving their
officer behind.   The 9th Irregulars sat passive on
their horses ; Lieutenant Hills ordered his guns to be

unlimbered, but there was no time. The idea of
creating a diversion for a moment, by charging the
enemy, came into his mind. He spurred his horse
upon them, cut down one or two, but was presently
unhorsed. The artillerymen galloped off with the
guns towards the park, and the enemy's troopers rode
away to the rear. Hills was left lying on the ground ;
his sword had flown out of his hand, and a sowar was
stooping over him to kill him, when Major Tombs,
who had run out of his tent on the first alarm, seeing
the danger of his subaltern, fired his pistol about the
distance of thirty yards, and dropped the man. Hills
was on his legs, and had again got his sword, when
they saw another sowar going off with the young
officer's pistol. They both set upon him ; he was a
nimble fellow and good swordsman, and for a minute
kept them both at bay. He brought Hills to the
ground with a severe cut on the head, and made a
powerful stroke at the other, dividing his pugarie and
forage cap to the hair, when he received the deadly
thrust of Tombs.*

* I believe this to be the most correct account of the affair
hitherto published. A shorter one was given by the author
in the *Times*. Mr. Rotton's is very confused. Norman is in
error in believing the artillerymen did not run away. A
friend of mine saw them doing so, though it was fiercely
denied by the artillery officers at the time. Where, for-

While these two heroes were gaining the Victoria cross, the sowars rode up to the tents of Renny's black troop of artillery. "Get your guns ready," cried they, "and come away with us to Delhi." The artillerymen answered, "Who are you that give us orders? We obey only our own officers." They called on Major Olpherts' troop to fire through their bodies upon the enemy. The alarm brought some men of the hospital tents of the Jullundur artillery, and three of them were sabred. One officer was thrown over, and escaped by counterfeiting death. A fellow, seeing a horse belonging to the apothecary standing near, changed his saddle, and left his own hack instead. The alarm was sounded abrupt and loud, but there was little need for it. The camp followers, whose booths and little tents had taken the form of a tiny bazaar behind the artillery lines, were flying in all directions, to escape the 'Dihliwallahs,' who killed several of them. The Sikhs were plundering their deserted shops. The servants were running to the

sooth, were they when Tombs and Hills were struggling with the sowars? Some said the enemy were joined by the Irregulars. This was not the case; only five went away with the mutinous cavalry, and one of them was wounded. They, however, did nothing against them. I give this account on the faith of my friend and of Major Tombs, whose story I had once the honour of hearing.

officers' tents with their arms and horses. **Bullets**
were hissing about from foes and **bewildered friends.**
The enemy remained but a short time in our camp ;
a long series of alarms had taught the soldiers to turn
out at a minute's notice, and the report, that the 9th
Irregulars had played traitors and were sabring our
men, filled their breasts with fury.

The sowars began to find the place too hot. Renny
had shot several of them with his revolver ; **the guns**
on the mound were turned upon them, and a shot
came now and then from the 1st Fusiliers, who were
forming, of themselves, to oppose them. Captain
Fagan of the Foot artillery, rushing out of his tent,
caught a horse, and gathering together a few of the
carabiniers, killed about a dozen of them. Most of
them turned back the way they came. Some left
their horses and escaped across the canal ; about
thirty dashed along the road by the back of the
churchyard, and over the bridge, cutting down a
European and some natives on the way, and off
across the plain. They passed Hodson, with a body
of cavalry, on the road to Alipore, telling him they
belonged to the 9th Irregulars. About **thirty-five of**
them had fallen, including the man who led them
to this daring exploit.

The Lancers, who formed a part of our picquet to

the rear, would have pursued, but at that very time were threatened by a party of the enemy. The infantry, finding no one to fight with, turned their rage on a number of defenceless servants, who had collected for refuge near the churchyard. Several wretches were butchered, some hiding behind the tombs. One woman was shot through the breast. It is idle to say they mistook them for sepoys; so many sanguinary fights and executions had brutalised our men, who now regarded the life of a native as of less value than that of the meanest of animals; nor had their officers endeavoured, either by precept or example, to correct them. Next day twenty-three syces, companions of those who had been killed, took the road to their homes. Men of humanity were shocked, and this made the most reckless reflect. There were ten natives for every European in camp. In every troop of artillery there were four times as many natives as Europeans; in the cavalry two men for every horse; without them the work could not go on. An inquiry was made into the affair, which, however, ended in nothing. The spirit of exasperation, which existed against natives at this time, will scarcely be believed in Europe. Servants, a class of men who behaved on the whole throughout the mutiny with astonishing fidelity, were treated even by many of

the officers with outrageous harshness. **The men beat**
and ill-used them. In the batteries they would make
the bheesties, to whom they shewed more kindness
than to the rest, sit out of the works to give them
water. Many of the unfortunates were **killed.** **The**
sick syces, grass cutters, and dooly bearers, many of
whom were wounded in our service, lay for months on
the ground, exposed to the sun by day and to the cold
at night ; and it was with difficulty that one or two
medical men could get, for those under their care, a
few yards of canvas, or a reed hut, under which they
might huddle together. The tone of conversation at
mess, carried on in the hearing of numerous servants,
was too often wild and fierce. A general massacre of
the inhabitants of Delhi, a large number of whom
were known to wish us success, was openly proclaimed. Bloodthirsty boys might be heard recom-
mending that all the native orderlies, irregulars, and
other poorbeahs in our camp, should be shot. These
sentiments were not those of all, nor of the best and
wisest, but few ventured to gainsay them.* It was

* If the reader is doubtful of the correctness of this, let
him mark the spirit of Mr. Cooper's " Crisis in the Punjaub."
The following appeared in the *Lahore Chronicle* of 8th July,
at that time the only established newspaper in the **north-west,**
every issue of which was full of such, headed—" Death to the
Pandies," " Wanted, a hangman," " How to finish the muti-

even found impossible to make the most violent understand, that no one wished the guilty to escape, but that some rude precautions ought, if possible, when we conquered, to be taken, not to mingle the innocent in the same fate. The accusation of weakness was made against those who tried to stop this dangerous tide of feeling, as if cruelty could not be the fault of a weak mind, and clemency the sign of a strong one ; as if being carried by the stream was any proof of self-reliance. One must, however, remember

neers," " Sparing the rebels," &c. " Dear sir, what will your soft-hearted advocates of pardon to the rebels and mutineers say to the following passage of Holy Writ ?—' O daughter of Babylon, happy shall he be that regardeth thee as thou hast served us ; blessed shall he be, that taketh the children and throweth them against the stones.'" What would the Peace Society have done in such a state of affairs as now existed at Delhi ? It is necessary to note that there were no members of that Society in India ; and no one in England would read the *Lahore Chronicle,* and nobody wished rebels, at that time at least, to be spared, Mr. Colvin's proclamation having been hooted to death. Even the mutineers themselves never expected to obtain mercy. The assumption reminds us of the beginning of a satire in an Indian journal upon some people, who, it appears, wished mercy for the Nana (when he was at large)—"Forgive the Nana Sahib, forgetting the atrocity ; although in truth he far surpassed a tiger in ferocity." One gentleman proposed that the bodies of the mutineers should be burned after death. Mr. Rotton says, "The day concluded with the destruction of every one of the rebels composing the force." What can this mean ?

that the provocation was unparalleled.   There wa.
scarcely an officer in camp who had not lost som
near relation, many of them murdered in the mos
perfidious manner ; and perhaps the one-half of then
were fighting against their own mutinous soldiers
from whom they had escaped.   Human nature coul
not be more severely tried ; and the prudent man wil
hesitate to say, whether he would have borne it bettei
Nor can one help admiring the haughty and unbending
attitude, the entire absence of conciliation, assumec
by the English in those dreadful times, although h
may be sorry that a high ideal was disfigured by th
baser feelings with which it was blended.

In the meantime, our picquets in the Subzi-Mund
found it difficult to hold their own.   They wer
attacked by a large body of the enemy, some of whon
got up on the flat roof of a high house overlookin
the serai, which we held.   What a mistake not t
have burned it before !   The roof and courtyard o
the serai were instantly untenable.   Troops were sen
to the house ; the door of the courtyard was broker
open, and several attempts made by our Sikhs to figh
their way up the narrow staircase that wound to th
top.   A jemadar and several men were killed ;
round shot, which struck the roof from the mound
battery, seems to have made the enemy relax in thei

resistance. Twenty of them escaped by a back door, putting those who guarded it to flight, and killing two Sikhs. The rest were bayonetted by our soldiers; fourteen bodies were counted next morning on the roof, which the exaggeration of rumour had raised to fifty over night. A number of our own men, who had advanced too far, were surrounded in a serai by a large body of the enemy, and had to cut their way out. The fighting went on for several hours, but the enemy saw the difference between their holding the Subzi-Mundi against us, and our holding it against them. At some points they brought their artillery to bear upon us. It ended by our troops driving them back, when they suffered severely from the fire of our batteries in returning to the city. Our loss was two hundred and twenty-three men hors de combat, among whom was one officer killed, and eight wounded. The loss of the enemy could scarcely have been under five hundred. One hundred and thirty-eight bodies were buried by our men. Many visited the Subzi-Mundi next morning, to see the scene of fight or to strip the slain. Many dead were lying about,—corpses of strong muscular men, some of them wearing the scarlet coat, which we had so long thought the badge only of a friend, and some in native dress, their white cotton robes soaked in the blood of their death-wounds, their bodies nibbled over by the bites of jackals, and covered with swarms of flies. Nine corpses were lying in a pit to be buried, each stiffened into the attitude in which death had been met, heaped confusedly the one on the other.

Much talking took place about the behaviour of the 9th. There was no doubt that the inroad into our camp had been planned between some of the 9th Irregulars and the 8th in Delhi. Every one thought they should at least be disarmed, and the faithful Golundazes rewarded. The contrary measure found favour with Chamberlain, who had once served with the 9th. They were sent to the Punjaub, many of them deserting on the way,[*] and Renny's artillerymen ordered to be disarmed. Much representation was made to stop this latter measure. The answer was, that it was in accordance with the policy of the Punjaub (to help enemies and disarm friends). No native corps in India had better proved their attachment to us than these veterans. They had been with Nott at Candahar, and fought for us through the Punjaub campaigns. In the late mutiny at Jullundur, they had fired into the ranks of their mutinous comrades. Several occasions had occurred before

---

[*] The Punjaubee portion of them mutinied after the fall of Delhi, but was cut up by the Poorbeahs who stood staunch.

Delhi, when they might have taken their guns over to the other side. It has already been told how, when the sowars were before their tents, they had entreated Major Olpherts to fire, although they were between the enemy and his guns. All that could be said against them was, that a few recruits had deserted. The order was given, and had to be obeyed. They brought their guns into our park, the tears in their eyes. They begged to be allowed to return to their homes, they had nothing to do in the camp now; they had worn themselves out in our service, and shame was their reward. Everything was done to soften the measure. Major Turner, who, as commander of all the horse artillery before Delhi, had to see it carried out, was much affected. This excellent officer had formerly served with the troop. They were allowed to retain their swords, and ordered to serve in the batteries, which they did with the utmost bravery and fidelity to the time of assault, when they were sent in with the stormers to turn the guns captured in the bastions upon the enemy.

The rains at this time were pouring almost unceasingly upon our canvass roofs; when the sun broke out, everything was green and beautiful, but among the rank and hasty vegetation, malaria was beginning to combine its poisonous gases. Ague was more common, recurred oftener, and with a deadlier type. Cholera became more frequent, especially with two regiments. The immense swarms of flies and other

whom were too weak to drive them away. The constant exposure suffered by the men was very trying. Many patients were sent to the hospital from the picquets, where they had but poor shelter. Fighting was almost the only change we had from picquet and sentry duty.

About this time we got news from Agra, that on the 5th, the Nemuch Brigade had advanced upon that city, the only one in the Doab remaining in our possession, and the seat of the Lieutenant-Governor, whose sway was now confined to a few villages. The men of the Kotah contingent, who had up to this time stood by us, mutinied and joined the Nemuch force, which consisted of two native regiments, a troop of horse artillery, and some light cavalry. They all moved upon Agra, and encamped near a village about four miles off, some two thousand men led by Hindoo Subahader.* None but Europeans now remained by us, four hundred and fifty of the 3d Europeans, Captain D'Oyley's battery, and about fifty mounted

* This affair is described from the Mofussilite, July 15th and 22d, 1857.

volunteers. It was determined to attack them,
They were in front of the village with eleven guns.
Our force met them with a half battery on each wing,
supported by the volunteer horse. A long artillery
fight took place, and the enemy was driven back, but
not followed up. Our foot was kept alternately
advancing and lying down. We had two tumbrils
blown up, and a gun dismounted. The enemy sent
some cavalry to turn our flank, which was met by
our guns and the volunteer horse. Captain D'Oyley
'was mortally wounded, but continued giving his
orders, till at last, beginning to faint away, he said :
"They have done for me now ; put a stone over my
grave, and say that I died fighting for my guns."
The infantry was allowed to advance at last, and the
guns turned on the village. The enemy were driven
out, and a gun taken and spiked. But our own
cartridges were now all fired away, and our troops
were compelled to retire, harassed by their horsemen
and artillery, to which we could not reply, as our
ammunition waggons were empty. Some of the
enemy's horse reached the cantonment before us, and
set the bungalows on fire, causing our countrymen in
the fort to imagine that our troops had been all cut
off. Our loss was nearly one hundred and fifty men.
All the Europeans took refuge in the fort, leaving a

great deal of property, which, with a little more leisure and warning, might have been carried away. The Lieutenant-Governor with his suite was mixed up with the rest. Most of the Mahomedan servants disappeared. The ladies cooked the food, and the men carried the water. The station was given up to plunder for two days, and four thousand prisoners in the jail were let loose. Some native christians and clerks were murdered; and placards were posted upon the walls of the city, offering a hundred rupees for every European's head. The mutineers then left for Delhi, where they arrived towards the end of July. The news of their success was received with a salute of twenty-one guns from the walls, which was twice repeated to make us mark it in camp; 'and within the palace walls,' says a Persian newspaper of the city, 'the musicians played upon their English flutes, clarionets, and drums, in token of rejoicing, on the occasion;' "a memorial was also received from the officers of the Jhansi regiments, reporting the slaughter of the immoral infidels, and an answer was written."

Except the continual fire of the enemy's artillery, nothing had disturbed us till the 14th July, when they vowed to carry our batteries, and came out in great force to storm the picquets, under Hindoo Rao's and the Subzi-Mundi. They brought two guns to bear upon our right. Our men, under good cover, kept them back for several hours, making great havoc among them, and losing only twelve men, when Chamberlain appeared. He ordered the infantry and two troops of horse artillery into the Subzi-Mundi. The Goorkhas descended from the fatal hill; a cheer, running along the gardens, thickets, and rocks, told the length of our line. The enemy were supported by the fire from their walls; grape thrown from their large guns fell up to eleven hundred yards,* but our men pushed on. One native officer was seen sitting on his horse, waving his arm to cheer his men. Our troops recoiled from a wall lined with the enemy. Chamberlain, leaping his horse over it in among them, dared his men to follow. They again gathered courage, and drove the enemy through the gates with immense slaughter. Our force was within two hundred yards of the walls, when such a shower of grape and musketry was poured upon us, that we were compelled to fall back. This was done in some confusion. The enemy came again out at the gates, infantry, cavalry, and artillery. A body of their horse advanced to charge. They were again turned by some infantry of the 1st Fusiliers and Guides, brought together by Major Jacob, Hodson, and Greville. Their guns were

* Norman.

left deserted, but the gunners applied the port-fire, and discharged a shower of grape at the moment, and ere our men could be again steadied, they had limbered up and were taking them away.[*] The affair was over in a few minutes. The road was choked up with retreating guns, slain ammunition camels, horses, and men. There was some difficulty in getting off the wounded. Many soldiers were seen bearing their comrades in their arms. Lieutenant Thompson of the Horse artillery was shot through the leg while trying to prevent one of his men from falling into the hands of the enemy, who carried away four European heads as trophies to Delhi. We had seventeen men killed, and sixteen officers and one hundred and seventy-seven men wounded. The courage of the dooly bearers was deserving of high praise. A large number of this class of men, principally Kahar by caste, was attached to every hospital. Their duty was to bear the wounded on litters out of action, and from the batteries. In this work they shewed that singular mixture of courage and timidity met with among natives. Many of them were killed and wounded, and their doolies sometimes riddled with shot. Chamberlain had his arm shattered below the shoulder; he could gain no fresh reputation for courage,

* These particulars are from Hodson (letter, July 16th.)

and was blamed by many for rashness. The men were getting very discontented with this kind of work. They were ready to carry any position, however strong, from which the enemy must be driven; but to carry a strong position a dozen of times, only to see it abandoned and re-occupied, is what no soldier will do without losing heart.

CHAPTER IX.

ON the 17th July General Reid, whose health had
now fairly broken down, left for Simla. The command of the force was given to Brigadier Archdale
Wilson. This was received with much pleasure, but
some surprise. He was not the senior general in
camp; but had distinguished himself much, especially in the actions at Ghazeecoodeenuggur. He
was known as an excellent artillery officer, and a
man of sense and great determination of character.
Time had turned his hair to iron grey, but did not
yet press down his tall spare form. Perhaps his
name stood better with the army than that of any
officer of his rank, save Brigadier Showers. The
duties of Adjutant-general fell again (Chamberlain
being wounded) on the Assistant-adjutant-general
Captain Norman, a most intelligent and active officer,
whose name is now well known to every one.

About the same time, a regiment of native infantry and some cavalry, with half a field battery,
joined the mutineers. They had come in from

Jhansi. All the Europeans there had taken refuge in the fort, but were treacherously persuaded to quit it, and barbarously murdered. It was said they had a young English girl with them as a prisoner. Stories of ladies being still alive in Delhi were often repeated in camp, as if some people felt a pleasure in the romance. They were all untrue.

Our position was being strengthened every day. Breastworks were erected along the ridge, and the guns taken from the enemy placed at intervals. The houses around our picquets were, as far as possible, demolished, and the trees cut down.

We were again attacked on the 18th. The firing was very brisk; but as long as we kept under cover, we suffered little harm. Towards the afternoon some infantry and artillery, with the guides, were sent into the Subzi-Mundi. The enemy retreated with little loss towards the Eedgah, evidently wishing to draw us as far from the camp as they could, among the narrow roads surrounded by gardens with high walls. One sepoy behind a tree wounded two of our artillerymen. We drew our men off with some difficulty, followed by the enemy, and might have suffered heavily, had it not been for the address of Hodson. We had two hundred and eighty men hors de combat —three officers wounded, and one killed. The loss of the enemy was not great. A Mussulmani woman was taken, after having fought desperately. She had by her own statement renounced, for that of a jehadin or fanatic, a profession for which her advancing years had rendered her unfit. The general allowed her to go away ; but, on reflecting a little, sent after her again, and she was conveyed prisoner to Umballa. About this time Hodson was trying to effect the release of an unfortunate woman, the sole survivor of a very large family destroyed by the cruelty of the rebels. Two of her children had been killed in her sight ; she had been snatched from death by an Afghan lad to nurse her wounded infant. The poor little thing died in his zenana. The mother escaped at last in the dress of a boy, and was kindly received by the only lady in camp. What a contrast between the Teutonic and Oriental notions would have been brought out, if that bloodthirsty prostitute had actually crossed our sentries, released by the first fantastic feelings of the general, while this poor woman, innocent of any offence, could scarcely steal out of this den of murderers.

The never-ending game of leaving our own position to fight the enemy in theirs, was getting more and more intolerable to every one. The men grumbled roughly, in the hearing of their officers, at the way their lives were wasted, and sometimes could not be got to advance,   Men and officers were too often mixed up together ; discipline was getting very much relaxed.* One who saw the hardships they endured, found difficulty in treating them with severity.   This loss of authority was noticed as much in the Queen's regiments as in those of the Company, but still a great deal of mismanagement must have been necessary to produce the formidable combination, that afterwards appeared among those of the latter.

On the 20th we were informed that the enemy were intending to take away some saltpetre hid in the Subzi-Mundi.   The possessor came in and told us where it was.   A party was sent out to cart it off,

---

* A story told about this time well illustrates this, but will scarcely be relished by military readers.   A very brave and manly officer from a sepoy regiment did duty with a European one.   Accustomed to softer men, he, it appears, used a tone of command which the soldiers did not relish, coming from a stranger officer.   They managed to convey their opinion to him, which, of course, was fiercely checked. A voice came out of the ranks :—" Sind him back to his ould mutinous saypoy rigimint."   Search was made for the offender, who was not to be found.   The officer, enraged, said he would rather send them all to camp and hold the picquet himself, than command such a mutinous set of fellows.   A few minutes after there appeared on a wall, a chalk drawing of him holding the picquet against a whole army of sepoys, horse, foot, and artillery.

and twenty cart-loads were taken away. More importance was perhaps attached by us to this than by
the enemy. We would fain have believed they were
failing in powder. Saltpetre, however, as is well
known, is a plentiful ingredient in the soil of immense
tracts in India, though sulphur is not common. It had
long been rumoured that the enemy were getting out of
percussion caps, and were trying to make detonating
powder. It was now said that the native merchants
in camp were buying caps from our soldiers and
selling them for immense prices in Delhi. On
inquiry, this was found to be untrue. In fact, they
had no want either of powder or caps ; and our spies
in the city would write anything they thought
pleased us.

On the 21st a great onslaught was expected.
According to our spies, the enemy had sworn to wade
up to the knees in our blood. Preparations were
made to prevent their doing so ; but it would appear
they abandoned the project. On the second day after
an attack took place on the Metcalfe picquet, in which
we had one officer killed—Captain Law, attached to
the 1st Punjaub Infantry—and six officers wounded.
We lost for a time the services of Colonel Seaton and
Captain Money, of the horse artillery. No officer in
camp had done more work in the field, and had been

oftener under fire, than Captain Money. And no troop of horse artillery was more desperately exposed at Delhi, and, indeed, during the whole war, than the 2d troop, 3d brigade, which he commanded. It now fell to Captain Blunt.

We got news from Meerut that the country round about was now being brought back to our rule. We had been much harassed by a notorious old malcontent named Shah Mull, who raised the peasantry against us, and was a terror to our friends. He had gained the title of the King of the Goojurs. A party of troops was sent from Meerut to clear the country between that place and Saharunpore. Shah Mull collected a large body of men and attacked them, but was killed in the engagement by one of the volunteer horse. The news of his death dispersed his followers, and had a wonderful effect in pacifying the whole country. Successful expeditions were also sent against Walidad Khan, the Rajah of Malighar, who had gone out to collect tribute, and hold the country near Hauper for the Badsha against the refractory villagers about Saharunpore and Roorkhee. The number of the insurgents, who were killed in these expeditions, must be computed by thousands. Quarter was never dreamed of on either side. We succeeded in collecting the revenue, and the turbulent peasantry, if not submissive, abstained at least from active annoyance.

We had, up to this time, remained in a strange state of ignorance of everything that was going on towards the Calcutta side. We knew that all available troops had been collected, and that the China expedition must soon arrive, and believed they would be marched up as fast as possible across country to our aid. Reports now and then reached us of reinforcements concentrating at Cawnpore, or lingering at Allahabad. Sometimes it was said they were eight or ten marches off, but this always turned out false. Hodson, with his usual daring, wished to make a dash with some cavalry and artillery to Cawnpore, and bring the reinforcements up. But about this time we got a glimpse of our real situation. The mail from Europe arrived with a report of the noble speech of Lord Ellenborough on the mutiny at Meerut ; but, alas ! nobody seemed to mark the full wisdom of his words ! Troops coming by the Cape were little to us, perishing away at half the world's distance. Many were deeply disappointed that no arrangements were made to send two or three regiments by the Red Sea. We, however, felt that a beginning ought to have been made by the Indian Government. If they had sent ships to Suez it would have roused the apathy of ignorance, with which the most stirring Indian news are ever received in England. We then heard the dismal tidings of the fate of Sir Hugh Wheeler's party at Cawnpore. Surrounded, without prospect of relief, in an untenable position, they had, in the hope of saving the women and children under their protection, come out of their position on the faith of a capitulation with the Nana, Rajah of Bithour, which bore prevarication on the very face of it,* and had been all massacred with a ferocity and treachery, rare even in the black pages of oriental history. We tried to discredit the first rumours, but a courier from Lucknow brought it in the handwriting of Sir Henry Lawrence. A little after came the news of the victories of Havelock over their base and cowardly murderers, and of the dreadful butchery of the women and children that had remained in their hands at Cawnpore. Some fugitives from that place, who never stopped till they reached Delhi, brought the news of the dreadful

---

* The conditions were :—" All soldiers and others unconnected with the works of Lord Dalhousie, who will lay down their arms and give themselves up, shall be spared and sent to Allahabad." The Nana was known to many in camp. He had, the year before, taken a journey to the North-west with his vizier Azimoolah, who spoke English and French fluently, and who had visited Sebastopol during the siege, and conversed with the Russian generals during a truce.

revenge, the resistless prowess, and awful appearance of the Highlanders, whom they compared to goblins.

The fact that the victory of Futtypore was gained without the loss of a single European life from hostile weapons, impressed us with the idea that they had no real enemy to contend against. A little after we heard of the further victories of Havelock, and confidently expected that only three weeks' marching intervened, to prevent us having their aid in the assault of Delhi. But our hopes were dashed by the news of the death of Sir Henry Lawrence, and the necessity of rescuing the garrison of Lucknow. When we heard that Havelock, with all his victories and daring and suffering, could not reach his beleaguered countrymen in that capital, we again perceived that our only hope lay in ourselves. The disastrous consequences of the annexation of Oude became clearer than ever. But for this we should have had the forces of that kingdom on our side ; and but for this, many thought, we might perhaps have had no mutiny at all.

The enemy in the meantime not liking to attack us in front, prepared to throw a bridge over the canal, and thus pass to our rear. Their troops were seen from Hindoo Rao's house to defile for hours by the Eedgah. They could not have been less than fifteen

thousand men with thirteen guns. An attack was at
the same time to be made on our front, while Bukht
Khan, with this body, fell upon us behind, after cutting off our convoy.* A movable column was prepared to act against them, and sent out at night to
take in the convoy, with five hundred Goorkhas,
from Alipore. By the feeble light we saw the whole
country was under water for miles, the trunk road
rising a few inches above it. Next morning, on
returning to camp, we heard that their bridge had
been swept away by a flood, and that after having been
out two days in the rain without food, they had come
back to Delhi in very bad humour and spirits. It
was as well we did not meet them ; the force sent
out was scarcely strong enough. Their numbers were
afterwards ascertained to have been twenty thousand
men.†

On the 1st of August the King used to come out
of the city to the Eedgah, to celebrate the festival of
Bukra Eed. It was the fashion for him, on that day,
to slay a camel, to commemorate the intended sacri-
fice of Ishmael by Abraham, as the Mahomedans tell
the story. This time the festival was kept within the
palace walls. It is a great day in Islam, and the

* See King's Trial, p. 56.
† *Ibid*, p. 56 ; No. 25.

believers in the Prophet were much excited by the
wild words of fanatic moulvies and fakirs, while the
hopes of the Hindoos were played upon by pro-
phecies from holy Brahmins. A saint of the caste
announced that Mahadeo had placed the guards of
Hunyman around the English camp :—*

> No white face can move out,
> Therefore advance your guns without fear :
> The camp shall be destroyed like Lunka by fire.
>
> *   *   *
>
> Fight without ceasing day and night,—
> Protect from injury our mother the cow.
>
> *   *   *
>
> I have searched the leaves of the book
> Nisput Jee Jurria,
> And find that Saneechur (the God of Vengeance)
> Has descended on the heads of the English.

On the evening of the 2d of August, they came in
immense force against our batteries, and the attack
continued all night. The fighting was especially
fierce at the Sammy-house, a post which we had fortified strongly, about nine hundred yards from the Moree
bastion. The enemy swarmed up to our works,
cheered on by criers from the minarets in the city
mosques, whose voices were distinctly heard through
the din and distance. They had brought out about a

---

* Taken from Mr. Cooper's Crisis in the Punjaub, chapter viii.

dozen of field-pieces, which they used in the wildest manner. The firing from them and the batteries in the bastions, and our guns returning with grape and shell,—the incessant discharge of musketry, and the yells of the natives, made the most alarming roar and clamour. The heights were lighted up with flashes from our guns. The enemy came on with unusual intrepidity; every moment it seemed they would be within our works. They were driven back again and again by volleys from our men, who kept close behind the breastworks with fixed bayonets, calling on the enemy to come on. A bugleman among the sepoys shewed great courage, bringing on his companions up to the breastworks, sounding the assembly, advance, and double. It ceased at last, and he was found next morning lying dead, with his bugle in his hand. Few people slept in camp that night; there the alarm was greater than on the ridge. All our picquets were strengthened, and the men kept under arms. The enemy retired towards morning. They must have suffered very severely,—one hundred and thirty-five bodies were counted round the Sammy-house. We had only forty-six killed and wounded.

The enemy were very much depressed by this disgraceful failure. A moulvie had the courage to tell them at one of their councils, that they had risen to

gratify their own ambition, not for their religion ;
and now that they had failed, had better make the
best terms they could. They were dissatisfied with
themselves and one another, and trembled at the
fate into which they had run. The king accused the
sepoy leaders of coming into his city only to bring
about his ruin. They complained that they were not
properly supported. The Nemuch Brigade were much
shocked to see such a gloomy state of affairs on their
arrival, and their leaders were not disposed to submit
to the command of Bukht Khan. The king's treasury
was now exhausted, and his authority as little respected as that of any prince who has nothing to
give. The old man issued an order, detailing the
insults he received from the soldiers, and the excesses
they used towards his people. Two or three regiments, he said, had encamped within the walls of the
city, and thoroughly desolated several of the bazaars.
" They force locks and shop doors, and openly carry
away the property from the shops, and they forcibly
loose the horses of the cavalry and take them off.
They commit these excesses in the face of the fact,
that all cities taken without military operations have
ever been exempted from sack and slaughter. Even
Jangiz Khan and Nadir Shah, kings execrated as
tyrants, gave peace and protection to such cities as

surrendered without resistance. Moreover, the men of the army go about threatening and intimidating the royal servants and the inhabitants of the city. . . . . . Again, although repeated orders have been issued to the infantry men occupying the royal farash-khana, and the regiment of cavalry staying in the garden, to vacate these places, they have not yet done so. These are the places which not even Nadir Shah, nor Ahmad Shah, nor any of the British Governors-General of India, ever entered on horseback." "Wearied and helpless," he goes on, "we have now resolved on making a vow to pass the remainder of our days in services acceptable to God, and, relinquishing the title of sovereign, fraught with cares and troubles, and in our present griefs and sorrows assuming the garb of a religious mendicant, to proceed first and stay at the shrine of the Saint Khwaja Sahib, and, after making necessary arrangements for the journey, to go eventually to Mecca."* He wrote a letter to the Nawab of Jhujjur, as the selected from amongst all well-wishers, to help him with soldiers, carts, and camels, for his intended pilgrimage, being, like most natives in the Northwest, excessively ignorant of geography. The power was divided between the sepoy leaders and his sons,

* *See* Trial, p. 128 and 25.

who opposed and hindered one another. **Only the**
officers now received pay. The men **helped them-**
selves from the stores of the merchants. Many were
leaving for their homes; they would demand increased
rank or some new post, and desert if it were not
granted. The king ordered a council to be held on
the state of the treasury. Two expedients* were
proposed to raise money—to try a forced loan on the
merchants, and that a column should be sent out
through the revolted districts to raise the usual land
revenue. The last proposition was not carried out;
but the unfortunate merchants in the city were
ordered to lend large sums of money at twelve per cent
This was the third time that such a contribution had
been called for ; and as many of them had had their
shops and houses plundered, it may be supposed that
some were unable, as all were unwilling, to furnish the
sums demanded. Several who refused to give their
due share, were imprisoned. A petition from several
merchants under arrest is preserved. They prayed to
be delivered from the durance in which they were
placed, stating that they had suffered heavy and ruinous losses from the destruction of commerce, consequent to the disturbed state of the country and the

----

* See sixteen papers on the loan in King's Trial. We got
much information of what was doing in Delhi from our old
Kotwal, who came into our camp about this time.

plunder of their mercantile stores, with the burden of their former debts, and had been for twenty days compelled to support twelve hundred mujahids or devotees, come to fight for the faith. But the merchants were believed to favour the English; no pity was shewn to them. Some of them tried to bribe the soldiers to rescue them, and one sepoy actually came to the guard and threatened to shoot the men there, if they would not let one of them go. He promised to return in the evening with a posse of his comrades and set him free. All that the king ventured to do on hearing of this was to strengthen the guard. The collection of the loan was a privilege eagerly contested between Bukht Khan, the princes, and the court : much confusion, and no doubt some embezzlement, arose from their conflicting claims. The amount that got into the treasury was soon spent.

On the 7th of August, their powder manufactory was accidentally blown up. The Vizier Hakim Ahsanoolah had been visiting it a few minutes before. Suspecting treachery they rushed to his house, burnt and plundered it and a few more in the neighbourhood. The minister himself took refuge in the palace of the king.* They felt that though action always

* Mr Cooper tells the story thus—" A great protegé of the king, and a bitter and fanatic enemy of the British, Hakeem

brought defeat, inaction brought discord still more
ruinous.   Large bribes were offered to induce the
mutinous soldiery to make another attack.   Cupi-

Ahsanoolah Khan, had been cleverly out-diplomatized by
Rujjub Ali, Meer Moonshee." He " addressed his Mahomedan
friend in a letter couched in terms which, if the letter fell
into the sepoys' hands, must infallibly lead them to infer the
treachery of the Hakeem ; and if not discovered by them, the
Hakeem's allegiance might be diverted to the British side.
Very shortly after the receipt of the letter the Hakeem paid
a visit to the Begum Sumroo's house, wherein was deposited
the rebel powder manufactory. It exploded. This roused
the suspicions of the sepoys, who rushed to the Hakeem's
residence, searched it, and found the letter of Rujjub Ali,
whereon they plundered the premises, gutted them completely, and finished by conflagration. The Hakeem narrowly
escaped with life by darting to the palace. Great divisions
were the result of this brilliant piece of tactics. The king's
authority was spurned ; he wished to abdicate. The enemy
lost all unanimity, strength, and concert." We cannot receive
this as authentic history. It gives an unnatural order to
events, to make the world revolve round the Moonshi's letter.
The story tells perfectly well without it, and very ill with it.
How could Rujjub Ali foresee that the magazine would accidentally blow up, or that the sepoys would rush to the
Hakeem's house, and read his letters *before* plundering it ?
The letter did not really compromise the Vizier. Is a minister
compromised by a letter thrown in at his door, or is it likely
that, if it had been of such a character, the Hakeem would
have taken so little care of it ? The whole story rests upon
the authority of Rujjub Ali himself, who was at the head of
our intelligence department under Hodson, and had of course
no reason against being believed to have turned the wheel on

dity, however, can not create valour. The sepoys felt surer of being killed or put to flight, than of money coming out of the king's empty treasury. Only a few of the somewhat more noble sort volunteered to go out and fight the Feringhees for a week. General Wilson, not strong enough to storm the city, and seeing that external pressure alone kept their force together, wisely relaxed it, till he should be able to apply it again with crushing violence. The officers in command of the picquets were warned not to expose their men, nor use artillery against the opinion of the officers of that arm. Our fire in the batteries was suffered to languish. If any officer there commenced a cannonade, the general would send to ask why he was doing so. This policy was now approved of by almost every body, and the army began to respect their old general more and more every day.

Some attempts were made to destroy the enemy's bridge of boats over the Jumna by infernal machines

the spoke of which he sat. Hodson had something else to do besides examining the story ; but Mr. Cooper takes it up with enthusiasm, and gives a translation of the letter in an appendix. To those who have faith that these sepoys found a letter, or that it was this identical letter they found, it must be very interesting. Our view is confirmed by the quotation from a Persian newspaper, given in the King's Trial, p. 110, which says nothing about any letter being found in the Vizier's house.

floated down the river. They failed, as such experiments almost always do. We had prepared boats to enable us to throw a thousand men across, but the opposite bank still remained completely in the hands of the rebels, and the country was at their mercy.

From this side they began to throw rockets into our camp. They did little harm, beyond compelling Coke's men to shift their tents a little farther from the river. Captain Fagan was sent to direct the same kind of missiles at the Goluudazes, to shew we also had rockets, but ours were not nearly so good as theirs ; and, as the officer himself remarked, they were good enough to scatter among tents, but not to throw at a small party of men.

The sepoys, who had engaged to fight us for a week, gave us more embarrassment. They brought guns, which, from amongst the trees, played upon the Metcalfe picquet. We had suffered some loss and much annoyance, when, on the 12th of August General Wilson, with some reluctance, determined to send a force out to take them. Everything was wisely arranged with the greatest secrecy. A strong body of infantry, composed of Europeans, Sikhs, and Goorkhas, with a troop of horse artillery, and a squadron of the Lancers and Guides, were ordered to assemble, as if to take in some convoy. Brigadier

Showers was put in command. Our heavy guns on
the ridge were ordered to fire, whenever the musketry
began, into the only bastion on the walls that commanded the spot. At half-past three in the morning
they took the road to the Metcalfe picquet, and passed
on quietly towards the spot where the newly erected
battery was supposed to be. The artillery went along
the road, with the infantry on either side. The
enemy had not thrown out sentries farther than
fifty yards from their position. Their force consisted
of a troop of horse artillery and some foot, and occupied the building known as Ludlow Castle. It was
still dark, and our men slipped on so quietly amongst
the trees, that their advance was not noticed till they
were challenged by the sentry, who was shot dead on
the spot. The enemy were awakened by the rattle
of musketry. Surprised, and perhaps outnumbered,
they still fought stoutly and well. Many of them
were killed, issuing from the houses where they had
been sleeping. They got a shot or two fired from
their field guns, but this did little harm to the scattered line of their assailants, who advanced in
skirmishing order. The guns were taken in flank by
the 1st Fusiliers. The gunners stood stoutly to them.
Putting their backs to the waggons, they laid about
them with their swords till they were killed. Three

native officers were found dead beside them, one of whom wore a medal for distinguished services. One gun escaped, with two limbers; another was caught on the strain of starting. Three more were taken, with one limber. Our men then fell upon the enemy in the houses where they had sought refuge, forced their way into them, and killed all they met with. The sepoys fought with spirit, till our men, climbing over into the courtyards, and pushing into the rooms, came to arms-length with them, when those who had their guns loaded fired; the rest clasped their hands in supplication, which did not much avail. The Goorkhas might be seen mimicking them, and laughing, on their way back. A good deal of spoil was taken from the slain. About two hundred and fifty of the enemy were killed. Our loss was serious. Brigadier Showers was wounded, as also Major Coke, in the act of seizing one of the guns. An officer was killed, five wounded, and one hundred and nine men hors de combat. It fell most severely upon the Fusiliers and Coke's corps. Our artillery and cavalry were never brought into play. Showers was a great loss to us. Unpopular, as the brigadier of a station, owing to the sternness of his character, he had gained the admiration and good will of every one before Delhi, by his coolness and gallantry, and by the pre-

sence of mind and intelligence, which never deserted
him under the hottest fire. Of all kinds and degrees
of courage this is the rarest. In the confusion caused
by his being wounded, we had returned without
the very guns for taking which the expedition had
been planned. Our force must have passed very near
them, and, indeed, several soldiers said they had
actually seen them lying deserted among the trees.
They opened fire upon us twenty minutes after we
had fallen back, and annoyed our picquets at Metcalfe's House many a day after. Large bodies of the
insurgent troops came out of the city gates, as if
to revenge the disgraceful loss they had suffered,
and their batteries opened from the walls. "All
Delhi may fire," said old Jan Fishan Khan, "but they
still remain with their noses cut off."* His nephew,
Meer Khan, had been in the thick of the affair, and
rode back beside the guns, grasping his magnificent
beard, and telling his exploits to every one who
understood Hindustani. This gallant Afghan had
gone as a volunteer into almost every action since the
rising at Meerut. At the night attack on the batteries
numbers of the enemy had fallen by his rifle.

Our soldiers returned in triumph, riding upon the
guns, and were received with friendly congratulations

* Greathed's Letters from Delhi.

K

from every side. The camp had been awakene
the firing, and every one off duty crowded to mee
victors and see the guns.

The same day Brigadier-General Nicholson en
the camp, having ridden on before his column, v
entered on the 14th of August. It consisted of
tain Bourchier's European horse battery, Her Maj
52d Light Infantry, the remaining wing of the
(in all about one thousand Europeans), the 2d
jaub infantry, and the Moultance horse. They
with a joyful welcome. We had now eight thou
men of all arms in our camp, one-half Europ
with eighteen hundred in hospital, and we
enjoy some repose after six weeks' incessant figl
Every one wondered to find himself alive. A
leisure brought more comfort and cheerfulness. F
began to be found in camp, and games of quoits
draughts to be got up. In the evening, wou
officers appeared lying out on their couches to
the air, and listen to the bands of music which
necessities of the times had spared. Of society
was of course plenty ; the camp was a pleasant ch
from the dull stations in the North-west, and
mess-tents were merry with young officers tal
and laughing. Alas, how many of these were la
ing over their graves !

It was noticed about this time that the powder used for priming in the batteries was mixed with earth. Suspicion was directed against two khulashies, who were tried by a court-martial on the charge of having adulterated it to help the enemy. It seemed strange they should have ventured to remain in camp after having done so, or have chosen a time when firing was going on so very languidly. They were condemned to death on presumptive evidence, and hanged the same day. It would be unfair to blame the judgment without having heard the proceedings; but some officers, who were acquainted with them, openly stated their belief, at the time, that these men had fallen victims to a suspicious imagination, such as had destroyed so many in the days of the fancied Jesuit plots.*

Against all bad treatment of the natives the general declared war. He had published in the order-book the trial of a serjeant, accused of the murder of one of the camp servants. He was

* I am not sure to what extent the powder was adulter-ated. I never heard of a piece of artillery "flashing seven times," or "the vent of the guns being filled with powdered glass." Surely it would have been easier for the men to spike them at once and make off. The affair had none of the importance some writers have given to it. It may have been made with saltpetre carelessly separated from the soil, from which it is dissolved.

acquitted, but the general stated his determinatio
protect the natives in the camp from ill usage. '
became known to every Hindustani, and had a ˙
good effect both on them and on the Europe
The officers, too, became more disposed to check
roughness of their men, and to appreciate the v;
of the aid which we might derive from the pe
of the country.

CHAPTER X.

WE have already exposed the dangers which threatened those in the Punjaub, who were holding all this time the country to our rear, and must now relate how these dangers were met. The system of government there was considered to be the best existing application of European polity and justice to an Asiatic nation. At the head of affairs at Lahore was the Chief Commissioner, Sir John Lawrence, already known as a man of great ability, knowledge, courage, and determination. The different districts were under deputy commissioners, drawn from the best officers in the army and civil service, to whom were committed more power and responsibility, and fewer printed directions, than were given to the functionaries of what were called the " Regulation districts." Our communication with Calcutta was completely cut off; that with Agra also ceased, shortly after the Lieutenant-Governor had issued an amnesty to the less guilty amongst the rebellious sepoys, who should throw down their arms. This proclamation burst

like a soap bubble ere it left the building in whi(
was blown, and served but to shew that Mr. C(
had mistaken the times, and to cover with obl(
the last days of a good and estimable statesman,
died amidst the wreck of the institutions whicl
had laboured to build for the welfare of a pe(
who now threw off his authority. Sir John Lawr
thus became, for the time being, the absolute rul(
the Punjaub. He was not fearful of the responsib
thrown upon him, but accepted it at once as a m
of salvation. Our system of communication,
post and our telegraph, as a rule, remained unbr(
between Lahore and the extremities of the Punj
We thus had the advantages of centralization v
out its weaknesses. The hand that moved the v
was not too far off, for the eye to follow and
brain to comprehend the full bearing and resul
the orders it sent. Sir John had the sense to ur
stand the value of a larger measure of authoril
those under him. Almost every deputy commissi
of a district held the powers committed to a Ro
consul in times of danger and emergency, *ne*
detrimenti respublica capiat. As already said, t
were men of great ability in the Punjaub, to w
advice and assistance Sir John Lawrence owed m
Foremost amongst them must be placed the nam(

Mr. Montgomery and General Nicholson. The Chief Commissioner's confidence in his subordinates helped himself. Every one felt, what he had never felt before, that if he did his duty fearlessly and well, he would be supported and rewarded by the Government at Lahore. The sense of terrible and pressing danger prevented men from looking farther. Nobody cared to linger on the doubt, whether the Governor-General at Calcutta might suspend him for some vigorous measure, unauthorized by general order, or the Auditor-General, to the delight of his Bengal clerks, leave him to disburse the pay and equipments of some new levy out of his own salary, because he had not sent all the vouchers and certificates mentioned in the Pay Office regulations. They felt too deeply that the massacre of themselves and their families might follow an attempt to carry on the formalities that hampered decisive action.

Of course, amongst ourselves we could count upon perfect union and integrity, valuable weapons against the corruption and discord of the different classes of those who wished us ill. Besides being in possession of actual authority of the most absolute kind, the British in the Punjaub had every disposition to exercise it unsparingly. They had passed their lives ruling men, and had no speculative

scruples to hinder them from acting with decisioi
no out-of-door bias to turn them from their duty. '
fear of unpopularity, and the desire of averting
possibility of an unfavourable judgment with j
terity, must have their effect even upon the most ri
less tyrants in a European country ; but our offic
had no such feelings. Native opinion and na
prejudices are nothing to the European in India.
knows his reward will come from a country thousa
of miles off, and his acts be judged by the politic:
and historians of another race. Moreover, the ‹
tinnal massacres and cruelties that were taking p
farther down, steeled their hearts against all ɪ
They regarded, not incorrectly, all the sepoy regim‹
as so many would-be traitors and murderers, thirs
for their blood. If they felt any pity for the sc
of mutineers and deserters hanged or shot every ‹
they concealed it very successfully. From the J
cial commissioner at Lahore, who, when the ⸮
Native Infantry fled and were all destroyed, ɛ
being made prisoners, said, that he wished the o
three regiments would run their heads into the s
fate, to the young scholar who had gained his wr:
ship by competition at Leadenhall Street, every
talked in the same strain,—to ‘pott,’ ‘polish
‘saf karna ;’ i. e., make clean or exterminate, a ɭ

'bag' of Pandies, was the desire of every heart. Orders for the execution of deserters or mutineers were written in round terms, and signed with initials, where formerly a sepoy could scarcely be put under arrest without reports in quintuplicate. One hair of a European now weighed more than the head of a native.

All this severity, however, fell only upon the sepoys. With the people of the Punjaub we had no quarrel. There is every reason to believe that they appreciated the benefits of our rule, and shrunk from returning to Asiatic dominion of whatever kind. They regarded the affair as a contest between us and our native army for the possession of India. They remembered too well what a military rule was, to desire its return. National independence, it was clear, they would not gain from Poorbeah pretorians, whom they mortally hated. The native chiefs, too, in the Punjaub, knew well enough that our old army could never serve *their* purposes.

Their attitude, or rather their policy, therefore, was expectant, with a leaning to the stronger side. If we could not help ourselves, we must not expect their aid. He that would rule the Punjaub must be strong, bold, and pitiless ; as has been well said,— the clank of his war horse must be heard two miles

off. Another affair such as those at Meerut and J
lundur, would have convinced the people that th
was no strength in our hands, and they would h
risen remorselessly against us.

The first proof that we could deal sternly w
rebellion was given on the Peshawur frontier,
which all eyes were turned. Who was to have
valley—the Feringhees, the sepoys, the hill tribes,
Dost Mohammed of Cabul? The garrison of t
important place consisted of two European foot re
ments, and two troops and two batteries of artille
seven regiments of Hindustani infantry, and four
cavalry.

A week after the mutiny at Delhi, the 5ĩ
regiment at Murdan mutinied, and the 10th irregu
cavalry refused, when ordered, to charge the
Intercepted letters shewed, at the same time, that t
native troops at Peshawur were determined to ri
They were disarmed at once. Colonel Nichols
with a troop of horse artillery and some Punjaut
levies on whom we could count, went after and sc
tered the mutinous regiment. At the same time, t
10th irregulars were ordered to Peshawur. On t
road it had been arranged they should fall between
body of Her Majesty's 27th going the same way, fro
Rawul Pindi, and some Moultanee horse on t

march to Delhi. Together they fell upon the evil-disposed troopers, stripped them of their horses and weapons, and conveyed them prisoners to Attock.

The destruction of the 55th was most thorough, —a hundred and twenty killed fighting,—a hundred and forty taken, forty of whom were blown away from the guns,—a punishment which we had the doubtful honour of reviving and teaching to the rebels at Delhi. Some of them escaped to the hills, and were for a while received by a tribe in the Swat, who, however, soon tired of them, and brought the most of them in for the fifty rupees offered for their heads.

The effect of this vigour was immediately apparent. Recruits, who had before held back, now came in. The news, joined to the disarming of the native regiments at Moultan, disposed the whole Punjaub to believe in our star and to help us. It was determined to employ the military spirit of the people as far as we safely could. A native chief, Rajah Jowahir Singh, offered a body of troops, which was at once sent, under the command of General Van Cortlandt, about the beginning of June, to reoccupy the Hansi and Hissar territory to the north-west of Delhi. He was opposed by large bodies of irregular troops drawn from the lawless inhabitants of that wild district.

On the 17th of June he defeated a large **force,**
them, and afterwards took some strong **intrenc**
villages. Reinforced by the Rajah of **Bikaneer, wh**
rule extended over the wide desert **country to**
west of this slip of territory, he **gained** possessio**r**
the town of Sirsa, which was found sacked and **l**
burnt, and afterwards of Hansi and Hissar. The **(**
tricts around were reoccupied, and some drea**d**
crimes came to light that sent a chill of **ho**r
through every European breast.* The bones of **(**

* Take the following as a specimen of what **we ha(**
bear :—" Mrs. —— and her five children were murdered by
chokeedar, whom Mr. ——, only a month before, had res**c**
from starvation ; his name is Bolee Bux, and he belong**.**
the turbulent race of Ranghurs. A few minutes before
Hansi sowars came to Mr. ——'s house, Mrs. —— with
five children hid themselves in some bushes about a hund
and fifty yards north of their residence. When the sov
arrived and inquired for the family, the gardener put t**l**
on a wrong scent, by saying they had taken refuge in
fort ; the rebels therefore sacked and burned the place,
went in search of their victims and booty. Shortly a**l**
wards, the bloodthirsty hellhound of a chokeedar arri**v**
and made diligent inquiries after his mem-sahebs and b**i**
log, and, being informed where they were, he repaired
them, and without any qualms of conscience, he slew e**v**
one. I have seen the bloody spot, and the bones of the
tims collected and interred in Mr. ——'s garden, and sh**i**
of Mrs. ——'s gown, and of the clothes of her children,
blood-stained, are still hanging on the bushes."—Lette**i**
Lahore Chronicle, July 25, 1857.

countrymen, murdered in these places, had not been all carried away by the vultures and jackals. They were collected and laid in the grave. Their murderers took to flight, and our friends gained courage to stand by us. General Van Cortlandt shewed an equal ability in crushing armed opposition, and in employing the more difficult arts of diplomacy and conciliation. Many attempts were made to seduce his native troops, whom nothing but fidelity restrained from marching into Delhi. The resistance he met with in these districts was both determined and prolonged, and it was not before the fall of Delhi that he succeeded in completely pacifying them. But the advantages we derived from his holding this country to our rear will be appreciated by any one, who notes its position on the map. It gave us at the same time a most gratifying proof, that our Sikh levies could well be trusted.

It was also determined to form a movable column to disarm the native regiments in stations where there were no European troops, and to be ready to march upon and put down any outbreak in the country. It was drawn from Sealkote, and consisted originally of Her Majesty's 52d, a troop of horse artillery, a field battery, a wing of the 9th cavalry, and a native regiment of infantry. At the head of it Brigadier-General Chamberlain marched to Lahore, thence to Umritsur, striking terror everywhere by his severity. Having been appointed to the Adjutant-generalship of the army, vacant by the death of Colonel Chester, he was succeeded by Colonel Nicholson. Arrangements were made to convey as many of the infantry as possible on ponies and waggons, for taking men by forced marches in the month of June was as destructive as a series of engagements. At Phillour he disarmed the native regiments with the column. They were, it was suspected, only waiting a chance to attack it. Another from Hoshiarpore piled arms at the same time. The column then returned to Umritsur to watch the still armed regiments in the northern stations. Here they heard the news of the mutiny at Jhelum.

Of the two regiments there, one had been marched away and disarmed, but the other, the 14th Native Infantry, refused to give their arms up. A force was brought against them, two hundred and fifty men of Her Majesty's 24th, three horse artillery guns, and five hundred Moultan levies, horse and foot. Their number was swelled to twelve hundred by armed police and chaprassies. The mutineers had kept a hundred Sikhs, belonging to the regiment, the whole night in the mainguard; they however escaped before the

engagement, and fought with fury against their Poorbeah comrades. The 14th kept in their lines, and
defended themselves with desperation. No combat
during the whole war was contested more fiercely.
Fighting every foot of ground, we drove them out of
their lines. The gallant leader of the attack, Colonel
Ellice, was dangerously wounded. The enemy made
off to a village on the banks of the Jhelum. An
attempt to carry it was repulsed, and one of our guns,
which had been brought up to make a diversion in
favour of the infantry, fell into their hands. They
evacuated the village during the night. A great
many sepoys were afterwards caught, and brought in
by the villagers. A hundred and eighty are said to
have escaped into Cashmere, a hundred and twenty
of whom were given up after the death of Golab
Singh, on our engaging their lives should be spared.
Fifty of the prisoners taken at the time were shot by
the force, and twenty-five blown away from the guns.
Two hundred and fifty bodies were counted in the
lines and village. The sepoys shewed the greatest
courage ; and if every Poorbeah regiment in the
Punjaub had stood at bay like the 14th, it had been
bad for us. The prisoners executed met their fate
with the greatest composure. One said to the artillery officer at the guns, "You need not tie me on,

Sahib, I shall stand." It was impossible not t(
so much misguided heroism. If they were fai
to us, they were true to one another. Rumou
this desperate affair at Jbelum, and of the procee
of the movable column, were said to have kind
mutiny at Scalkote, a large military station o1
borders of Cashmere. Brigadier Brind there
protested against the removal of all the Euroj
but had rather chosen to risk everything than a
his suspicions so far as to disarm the native regi1
left in the station, which he appears to have t1
almost to the moment of his death, for he was
dered along with several other Europeans.
cavalry, as usual, shewed themselves the most l
thirsty, but, on the whole, the mutineers seemed
sparing of life here than they had been elsev
The station was plundered, and, heavy with
they leisurely took the road towards Delhi.
had counted on being joined by the native tro(
two neighbouring stations, but fortunately in
Their ignorance was so great, that they offere(
two colonels their usual pay and allowances, i
would keep the command of their regiments i
the King of Delhi. Sealkote lies almost strai;
the north of Umritsur ; and Nicholson, on hear
the mutiny, after disarming their companions (

9th cavalry, whom he had with his column, at one march in the sun brought his men forty-four miles, up to the banks of the Ravee. The enemy were about fifteen miles off, crossing at a ferry. They were allowed to do so unmolested. No one brought them word that the European force was approaching. When they had got over they were immediately attacked, and defeated after a vigorous resistance. If it had not been for the flight of some new levies of cavalry, destined for Hodson's Horse, they might all have been cut off that day. A large body of them took refuge on an island in the Ravee, where they were caught by the sudden swelling of the river, and watched by our force and the villagers around.

On the 4th day, Nicholson managed to get his men across on another part of the island, and had them formed before the enemy had had time to make any opposition. They were at once charged and driven into the river. Most of those who escaped to the other side were seized or put to death by the villagers. The destruction of the mutineers was most thorough. The greater part of their booty fell into our hands, and the camp-followers taken with them were punished. The faces of the disaffected were darkened, and our star shone clearer. Our Hewitts and Johnstones were forgotten for our Cahmberlains and Nicholsons. The people in the Punjaub marked these things well, and began to think our rule was not fated to pass away.

The most vigorous measures of repression were at the same time used ; passports were introduced ; the gates of cities, the bridges, and the ferries, were watched ; suspicious looking travellers were arrested. An unusual number of fakirs seemed to have come from the disturbed districts. They were turned back or thrown into prison. Most of the Poorbeahs in the Punjaub were known to be against us. The Government did not wait for overt acts of rebellion. A large proportion of them were employed in our civil courts. These were cleared of their shadows at once, a happy riddance to those who knew their arrogance and corruption. The baffled wretches were sent at once down the country. Some two thousand five hundred were expelled from Lahore during that year. The native press had begun to shew a bad spirit, but was at once put under censorship. All the editors, save one, were Poorbeahs. Letters addressed to sepoys and suspected persons were opened. "The number of seditious letters thus discovered," says the Punjaub Report,[*] "was alarmingly

* General Report on the Administration of the Punjaub Territories from 1856-7 to 1857-8 inclusive, etc. etc. Many facts in this chapter are taken from this interesting document.

great. The treason was generally couched in figurative or enigmatical language. A strange interest attached to these revelations, as shewing what the natives really said of us among themselves at that juncture. It was abundantly manifest that the sepoys and others really did believe, that we intended to destroy their caste by various devices, of which the impure cartridge was one ; that the embers of Mahomedan fanaticism had again begun to glow, and that we were observed to be but a mere handful of whites amidst a vast population of Asiatics. These things, often before imagined in regard to natives, were now veritably seen, under their own hand, in letters never intended for European eye." Wherever we suspected that weapons existed, a search was made for them, and the towns in our hands in the Cis-Sutlej states were disarmed. Sixty-nine thousand stand of arms were taken. Restrictions were put upon the sale of sulphur and saltpetre, and iron-bound clubs prohibited. "Treason and sedition were dogged into the very privacy of the harem, and up to the sacred sanctuaries of mosques and shrines. Learned moulvies were seized in the midst of a crowd of fanatic worshippers. Men of distinction and note were 'wanted' at dead of night. There were spies in the market-place, in the festival, in the places of worship, in the jails, in the hospitals, in the regimental bazaars, among the casual knot of gossipers on the bridge, among the bathers at the tanks, among the village circle round the well under the big tree, among the pettifogging hangers-on of the courts, among the stone-breakers of the highways, among the dusty travellers at the serais."[*]

The civil government of the country went on as usual. A European could travel alone in perfect safety by every road from the Indus to the Sutlej. The revenue came in as usual ; and it was even announced that we were able to raise a loan, for rupees were becoming scarce, and our officials had to be put on arrears. It could scarcely be called a voluntary one. Everything short of personal violence was put in action to wring money from the merchant class. Threats of hanging, and of breaking up their doors, were necessary to overcome their distrustful avarice. No one who knows what an excessively bad set of men these are, will have any sympathy for them. But in the villages much discontent and oppression were brought on by the thanadars, who assessed people, not according to their real wealth, but under consideration of the bribes they themselves received. Sir John wished to raise

[*] Mr. Cooper's Crisis in the Punjaub.

a contingent of Sikhs, when he saw reason to believe that they could be trusted with arms, but he could not obtain more than a limited number. The Manjha Sikhs, who had formed the pith of the army of Runjit Singh, hung back. They had not yet made up their minds what to do.

Every one was startled by the news that, on the 30th of July, one of the regiments at Lahore, the 26th Native Infantry, which was disarmed and carefully watched, had taken flight from the station. A fanatic sepoy had raised a tumult in the lines and killed the commanding officer, Major Spencer, one of the old class of sepoy officers, who had passed his life cultivating the good offices of his men. The serjeant-major was at the same time murdered. They had escaped, under cover of a dust-storm, before the Europeans had time to arrest them. After they were clear of the station pursuit was impossible, as there were still three regiments to watch, who were evidently premeditating a similar move. However, as all the rivers were swelled by the rains, it was confidently hoped, from the first, that their chance of reaching Delhi was small. The next day they appeared at a ford on the Ravee, about twenty-six miles from Umritsur, but on trying to cross it, met with a most determined resistance from the tehseldar of a neigh-

bouring village, with a body of armed police, backed
by a crowd of the stalwart peasantry of the district.

"At four o'clock, when the district officer, Mr.
Cooper, arrived with some eighty or ninety horsemen,
he found a great struggle had taken place ; the gore,
the marks of the trampling of hundreds of feet, and the
broken banks of the river, which was sweeping along,
augmented with the late rains, in vast volume, all
testified to it. Some one hundred and fifty had been
shot, mobbed backwards into the river and drowned,
inevitably too weakened and famished, as they must
have been, after their forty miles' flight, to battle with
the flood. The main body had fled upwards, and
swam over on pieces of wood, or floated on to an
island about a mile off from the shore, where they
might be discovered crouching like a brood of wild
fowl." Two boats full of armed men were pushed off
to the island. "The boats straggled a little, but
managed to reach the island in about twenty minutes,
a long inhospitable patch, with tall grass ; a most
undesirable place, with a rising tide, to bivouac on for
the night, especially if wet, dispirited, hungry, without food, fire, or dry clothing. The sun was setting
in a golden splendour, and as the doomed men crowded
down, with joined palms, to the shore, on the approach
of the boats, one side of which bristled with about

sixty muskets, maugre sundry revolvers and pistols, long shadows were flung athwart the gleaming waters. In utter despair forty or fifty dashed into the stream and disappeared, rose at a distance, and were borne away into the increasing gloom." An order not to tire upon them seemed to have disposed the sepoys to offer no more resistance. They surrendered passively, allowing themselves to be bound and borne away in gangs to the shore, and were brought in without a single escape, and lodged in the village police station. They amounted to two hundred and eighty-two, besides a number of camp followers. The magistrate, Mr. Cooper, sent away all the Poorbeah Mussulman horsemen to Umritsur, to celebrate the feast of Bukra Eed, which took place next day, as it was feared they would rise to prevent the execution of the captive sepoys, which had been resolved on. " Having taken down the names of the sepoys in succession, they were pinioned, linked together, and marched to execution. A firing party was in readiness. Every phase of deportment was manifested by the doomed men, after the sullen firing of distant musketry forced the conviction of inevitable death—astonishment, rage, frantic despair, the most stoic calmness. One detachment, as they passed, yelled to the solitary Anglo-Saxon magistrate, as he sat under the shadow of the police station performing his solemn duty with his native officials around him, that he, the Christian, would soon meet the same fate!—then, as they passed the reserve of young Sikh soldiery, who were to relieve the executioners after a certain period, they danced, though pinioned, insulted the Sikh religion, called on *Gungajee* to aid them, but only in one instance provoked a reply, which was instantly checked.

"About a hundred and fifty having been thus executed, one of the executioners swooned away ; he was the oldest of the firing party ! and a little respite was allowed. Then proceeding, the number had arrived at two hundred and thirty-seven, when the district officer was informed that the remainder refused to come out of the bastion, where they had been imprisoned temporarily a few hours before. Expecting a rush and resistance, preparations were made against escape, but little expectation was entertained of the real and awful fate which had fallen on the remainder of the mutineers, who had anticipated, by a few short hours, their fate. The doors were opened, and behold, they were nearly all dead men ! Unconsciously to all, the tragedy of Holwell's black-hole had been re-enacted. No noise had been heard during the night, otherwise relief would have been given. Forty-five bodies, dead from fright, exhaustion, and fatigue, but principally suffocation, were dragged into light, and consigned, in common with all the other bodies, into the one common pit, by the hands of the village sweepers."

Mr. Cooper's candour is wonderful ;[*] but a few more touches would have completed the parallel between the Black Hole of Calcutta and the prison of Ujnala. We have heard, on the best authority, that a cry for water came from the sufferers. Mr. Cooper had retired to rest, but, on being informed of it, ordered water to be given to them, which, however, was not done. The door, like that of the Black Hole of Calcutta, opened inwards.

The remainder of the regiment was almost entirely destroyed. Forty-one men, who were taken prisoners, were sent to Lahore, where they suffered death by being blown away from the guns.

This terrible event soon passed out of men's minds in the North-west, distracted by urgent anxiety, and rendered pitiless by continual alarm and suspicion ; but after it had gone forth to the world, it excited much feeling in England. Mr. Cooper was even attacked in the most embittered terms in Par-

* It is his own work, " Crisis in the Punjaub," we have been quoting.

liament, and defended with little heart by Lord
Stanley. A more thorough and elaborate justification
was put forth by Sir Robert Montgomery. With him,
and with Mr. Cooper, the impartial historian must
agree, though it is surely unnecessary to follow them, in
regarding the slaughter of so many men as a desirable
occurrence. If there was anything to condemn, the
blame lies with the people in England. Those who
send a few soldiers and magistrates to subdue and
keep down at all terms a population of a hundred
millions, may easily guess that this can never be done
without a telling amount of bloodshed. If it was the
duty of the Punjaub Government to quell insurrection, it was their duty to use the means they thought
necessary for doing so. What else could Mr. Cooper
have done with his prisoners? His own men were not
to be trusted, and there was a regiment of sepoys at
Umritsur, who, though disarmed, were still to be
feared, from the weakness of the European detachment there. To have conveyed them to that station,
and kept them in confinement, would have increased
the danger of our position, while the numerous disarmed regiments in the Punjaub would have gained
courage to try their own luck, when they heard that
imprisonment was the worst fate that awaited them
in case of failure, a temporary misfortune from which

the expected victory of their comrades down country would soon relieve them. It was necessary to do something as a warning to the others, but what was done was only justice. The men were mutineers and deserters caught in the very act, and as such deserved death.

When a magistrate must perform an awful duty like this, in which the natural pity of the human heart has to be overruled for the good of society, he has a just right to the sympathy, countenance, and, admiration of others. Men take it for granted that there must be a cruel struggle between pity to humanity, however erring and guilty, and the duty a judge has delegated to him. But if we know that no such struggle existed, our admiration is replaced by disgust. We can admire the stern sense of justice and patriotism, which drove Brutus to send his own sons to execution ; but what would be our feelings if we heard that he rejoiced at their death, and made himself merry upon their arrest ? In such a position Mr. Cooper has placed himself. Part of his narrative is told in so flippant and heartless a manner, that it is clear he wishes all to understand he had no feeling for the fate of the men, whom it was his dismal privilege to destroy in cold blood. He has taken great trouble to go down to posterity in this grisly character, and, it is to be feared, has succeeded. No man ever more thoroughly murdered his own reputation.

The effect of this execution on the Punjaub was very great. The disaffected scarcely dared to draw their breath, and wished they could recall the whispers they had breathed to one another. The disarmed sepoys in the northern stations lost all hope of escaping, but it failed to deter a similar attempt being made at Ferozepore.

The men of the 10th Light Cavalry there, who had been disarmed and dismounted, seized the guns of a field battery while the gunners were at dinner. They were immediately retaken, but the troopers carried away many of the horses, and dashing into almost every stable in the cantonment, about two hundred managed to mount themselves and get off to Delhi.

About the end of August we had another terrible proof of the desperate fanaticism of the disarmed regiments. One of them, the 51st Native Infantry, mutinied, while search was made in their huts for concealed weapons, apparently on the spur of the moment, and with no chance of gaining anything but destruction to themselves. Almost the whole regiment were killed or executed by court-martial. This

was the last of the terrible scenes which were
played during this year in the Punjaub. The total
number of executions was two thousand three hundred and eighty-four;* and yet all was not sufficient
to make our hold on the country secure. Symptoms
of a wide spread disaffection again met the experienced eye of the Chief Commissioner. The powers
of secret combination of the natives of India are
unfathomable. Nothing that could be laid hold of
was detected.

Sir John Lawrence, however, thought that some
day a general rising would take place, under which
his weak legions must certainly sink. The unexpected length of the siege of Delhi began to make the
Punjaubees doubtful of our final success. As long as
we could hold our own and reward them, they were
willing to assist us; but more they would not do.
Their wounded soldiers came back to the Punjaub,
boasting they had saved us again and again from
destruction. They began to ask whether this was
worth their while? Our hopes of troops from Eng-

---

* Shot by military authority   628
   ,,   ,, civil authority .   .   .   1370
Hanged by military authority   .   .   86
   ,,   ,, civil authority   .   .   300

Punjaub Report, p. 9. This, of course, does not include the
Meerut and Delhi districts.

land were never realized ; at least they never came our way. The Bombay army was in a state of great excitement. Dangerous conspiracies had been discovered at Poona, Satara, and other places. In one station it had come to actual mutiny. Military executions were becoming frequent there too. The Madras army was also turning discontented ; and the possibility of a general rebellion all over India was passing into probability. Sir John Lawrence saw the only remedy was to remove the cause of uneasiness, and sent down all the troops he could gather to Delhi. At the same time he pressed by every post the necessity of carrying the place, at whatever cost, upon the mind of General Wilson, whose view of the danger of our position there was lugubrious in the extreme.

CHAPTER XI.

THE enemy now appeared at a loss how to attack us, and we enjoyed a little more quiet. They had plenty of riflemen, who were continually starting up among the rocks and bushes beside our batteries, firing into them and making off. We thus lost men and officers whom we could ill afford. Their cannonade was particularly directed against our Mosque picquet, and they were evidently establishing themselves again in Kissengunge, but it was resolved to let them alone.

About this time a stranger, of very striking appearance, was remarked visiting all our picquets, examining everything, and making most searching inquiries about their strength and history. His attire gave no clue to his rank; it evidently never cost the owner a thought. Moreover, in those anxious times every one went as he pleased; perhaps no two officers were dressed alike. It was soon made out that this was General Nicholson, whose person was not yet known in camp; and it was whispered, at the same time, that he was possessed of the most brilliant military genius. He was a man cast in a giant mould, with massive chest and powerful limbs, and an expression ardent and commanding, with a dash of roughness; features of stern beauty, a long black beard and deep sonorous voice. There was something of immense strength, talent, and resolution in his whole gait and manner, and a power of ruling men on high occasions, that no one could escape noticing at once. His imperial air, which never left him, and which would have been thought arrogance in one of less imposing mien, sometimes gave offence to the more unbending among his countrymen, but made him almost worshipped by the pliant Asiatics.* He seemed to disdain any other

* He was actually canonized, while alive, by a brotherhood of Fakirs on the Hazara frontier. Their history is given in full in the *Friend of India, October* 18th, 1860 :—"Nicholson left the district in 1850 for England, and then the sect was founded. They looked to him as the Sikhs to Nanuck, as their Goroo, and called themselves by his name, ' Nikkul Seynees.' They wore saffron-coloured garments, and round black hats, as their distinguishing garb. Their worship consisted in singing a kind of dirge, every verse of which echoed the refrain ' Goroo Nikkul Seyn.' They were a quiet, inoffensive people, and lived in the enjoyment of their faith till 1856. Then their Goroo arrived in person, on his way to Cashmere, and great were the rejoicings of his disciples. They hastened to offer him homage, but when they persisted, he ordered some of them to be flogged. This only increased their reverence. They declared that they deserved the flogging—that they had,

than a ruling part, speaking rarely in ordinary society. Such a man would have risen rapidly from the ranks of the legions to the throne of the Cæsars ; but, in the service of the British, it was thought wonderful that he became a brigadier-general, when, by seniority, he could only have been a captain.

On the 14th of August a body of the enemy's horsemen was known to have taken the road to our rear. Hodson was sent out to watch them. He had with him his own regiment, which now, with the help of his friends in the Punjaub, amounted to two hundred and thirty-three sabres. Though many of the sowars were untrained to handle their arms on horseback, and their half-broken horses were difficult to form, they were good men, and had a very warlike appearance, dressed in their ash-coloured tunics with

by their unholy lives, naturally incurred the wrath of their saint. The result was, that they practised increased austerities, and manifested more devoted zeal. When Nicholson fell gloriously before Delhi, and the news reached his devotees, the effect was remarkable. Their leader declared he could not live in a world where there was no Nikkul Seyn, and, going to his hut, destroyed himself, cutting his throat from ear to ear. Another followed his example. A third said he would go to Nicholson's God, started off to Peshawur, waited on the missionaries ; was received as an inquirer, and in course of time was baptized. He may now be seen engaged as a teacher in the mission school."

scarlet sash. He had also a hundred of the Guides and Jheend horsemen.

The first day they managed to surprise a number of the enemy's Irregulars in a house. It was set on fire, and all shot as they were driven out by the flames. They then marched for Rohtuck, and defeated some cavalry supported by matchlock men from the town. He encamped on the outside, not being able to make an attack from want of infantry. Next morning Baber Khan, a chief of the Ranghur tribe, appeared with about three hundred Irregular horse, and nine hundred matchlock men. Hodson, when he heard of their approach, sent away his baggage, and then drew off his men into the plain as if he were taking flight. The enemy pursued in disorder. Suddenly he turned and gave the word : " Threes about and at them." * His horsemen instantly wheeled round, and scattered the enemy in a moment, who never stopped till they got to Rohtuck. Great fears were felt in camp that his boldness would carry him too far. He brought his men safe back however, with only thirteen wounded.

On the 24th, a large body of the enemy from Delhi, with eighteen guns, took the road towards Hansi, with the intention of falling upon our new

* See his own letter, 19th August.

siege train, which was coming down from Ferozepore. A column was formed by us of about two thousand infantry and cavalry, with sixteen horse artillery guns. The command was given to General Nicholson.

It set off at break of day. The march was a toilsome one; the whole country was flooded, and the rain still poured. The road was a mere bullock track through a series of swamps. The guns went up to the axle in mud; often the artillerymen had to put their shoulders to them in order to push them on. The troopers were besmirched to the crown of their helmets; the infantry soldiers could scarcely pull their feet after them; and the camels were continually slipping and falling in the mire.

They had made one such march, when it was found that the enemy were about twelve miles in front, at a place called Nujjufghar. Their sowars had pursued our scouts several miles. The spirits of our men lightened, and the road seemed to improve. The people in the villages turned out to gaze at them in silence as they passed. An hour before sunset they reached a stream, which was swollen to a river by the rains, and took the horsemen up to the knees. It was difficult for the infantry to cross. The enemy here commenced firing. They were drawn up parallel to the road which we were taking, their left wing resting on a serai with four guns, their right on a bridge across the stream. They had nine guns to the right front, which now began to play. Their leaders no doubt expected, that our troops would immediately form and advance across the fire of their artillery. Nicholson, however, having stationed his guns on the road, which was pretty well covered, marched all the infantry past. He then ordered four guns of Captain Blunt's troop to move on their nine to keep them in play, and, covering his flanks with some cavalry and artillery, led the infantry against the serai on the left, near which were four guns. His short address was preserved by one of the soldiers of the 61st.* " Now 61st, I have but a few words to say. You all know what Sir Colin Campbell said to you at Chillianwallah; and you must also have heard that he used a similar expression at the battle of the *Alma*, that is, 'hold your fire till within twenty or thirty yards of that battery, and then, my boys, we will make short work of it.'" To this they gave a general cry, that they would endeavour to act to his desire. Our troops came on accordingly, and carried the serai with a charge, then changed front and swept down the enemy's line towards the bridge. This unexpected movement had completely confounded the rebels, who took flight and

* *Lahore Chronicle*, September 9, 1857.

made for the bridge ; Captain Blunt's guns, which had met theirs with the highest daring, following them close. They had limbered up their own guns, and taken them at a wild gallop to the bridge, but the wheel of the foremost caught. It could not be pushed backwards for those behind, and the pursuers pressing close on secured the whole thirteen. A strong village in the rear was still occupied by some of the enemy. The 1st Punjaub Rifles, who attacked it, were driven · back, and their commander killed. It was evacuated during the night. It was quite dark before the battle was over, and the whole force had to lie all night on the plashing ground without any food. We blew up the bridge and returned to camp next morning, the enemy having made off to Delhi. Our loss was about one hundred men hors de combat ; three officers were dangerously wounded, two of whom died.

It turned out that it was the Nemuch Brigade we had routed. The Bareilly one was some miles behind, under General Bukht Khan, who was soundly abused for not having come to the support of those engaged. On their return, the king treated them with the greatest indignity, and refused to admit them into the city. They requested food to be sent to them, and promised to go out again if new guns were supplied. The king sent them flour (with a message that grain was good

enough for them) and seven field guns. They declared they could not go out with so few, and here
their boast ended. In the absence of our column
an attack was made on the camp by the rebels in the
city, who, however, retired on finding they had been
deceived in the report, that our position was denuded
of its defenders, to make out Nicholson's force. To
save the bad effects of this defeat in Delhi, a story
. was invented and actually believed, that the country
people had risen upon us and taken back the guns.
The truth, however, soon came out and caused great
dejection.

Their army became less manageable than ever.
Our spies again and again warned us of meditated
attacks, which they had not the heart to carry out.
The king once more sent a messenger to our camp
with proposals of a treacherous capitulation, but could
not obtain even the promise of his life.

On our part, though the troops were not so hard
worked, a new danger, which had long been foreseen
by our medical men, began to appear, and quickened
the determination of our General to hasten the
assault, which was anxiously pressed on by Sir John
Lawrence from Lahore, and by the powerful voice of
Nicholson in camp. Delhi had long been known as
one of the most unhealthy stations in India, and by

an unlucky blunder the cantonment had been placed in the very worst part. The ridge seemed to have served to dissipate the malaria, which blew from the marshy country beyond. The side on which we were encamped was known to be much more liable to fever than the city. During some years, whole regiments had been prostrated by it at once, and this season would most probably be an unusually bad one, as we had broken the banks of the canal, and half the country was undrained. It had already tried our brave fellows sorely. A man would be borne into the hospital from picquet shivering with ague, which perhaps he had stood out for a time in secret, get a doze of quinine, and, if the next paroxysm did not appear, would be sent out for duty the day after. Those who were ill never got a chance of fairly recovering. But our danger was so terrible, and our men so few, that it could not be helped. It is the well known nature of malaria, to render its victims ever more and more defenceless against its attacks. The men had continual relapses, and ever of a deadlier type. Cholera, too, became more common, and never failed killing its worn-out prey. When the rains dried up, and the sun again began to act on the heaps of carcasses and the rank vegetation, the proportion of men in hospital rapidly increased, and as the season was always becoming more sickly, it was an easy calculation to find in what time the greater part of our force must be laid up. A regiment which had come in six hundred strong, was in three weeks brought down to two hundred and forty-two out of hospital.* The unwearied exertions of the medical men in camp, and the heroic courage some of them shewed in the field and the trenches, will ever be gratefully remembered by those who fell under their care. The gaps among them from sickness and wounds could fortunately be filled up by the surgeons of abandoned civil stations, and those who had escaped from their mutinous regiments. Moreover, a large force, consisting of the mutineers from Mhow and Indore, was reported to be on full march upon Delhi; and though the Gwalior contingent was still idling away its time, it might every moment advance, either upon us or on Cawnpore, and was strong enough to turn the scales wherever it struck.

Sir John Lawrence, deeply acquainted with the tortuous policy and dispositions of the native chiefs and leaders in the Punjaub, judged that they would wait to see the result, if they felt sure a decisive blow would be struck at Delhi. All our hopes rested on the success of our assault. What would happen if

* Norman.

it failed ? What would happen if they did not wait ?
Sir John weighed the dangers, and chose the greatest
for himself, but, as he judged, the least for the
empire. No doubt, a rising in the Punjaub could
overwhelm the weak guards he had at Lahore and
Umritsur, and give himself and his staff to the fate of
the Commissioner at Delhi ; but he determined to
risk the danger, and send down the last soldier he had
to help the assault. On the 6th of September the
last reinforcements we could receive entered camp—
some detachments of artillery, and of the 8th foot
and 60th Rifles, with the 4th Punjaub Rifles, and a
wing of the Belooch Battalion. The shadow of the
arm uplifted at Delhi was the only fear that rebellion
now saw in the Punjaub. Fortunate for us in this
terrible crisis that we had a statesman at Lahore, who
had the knowledge and genius to work out such a
calculation, the daring to act upon it, and the reputation to enforce it on others. The Chief Commissioner also procured the assistance of a contingent
from the Maharajah of Cashmere, Runbeer Singh,
who had lately succeeded Golab Singh, in exchange
for a recognition of his title to the throne. They
amounted to above two thousand men, mostly Dogras
and Rajpoots. But though they looked brave enough
in their gay garments, with their fine shields and

long matchlocks, they were not the men to cope with the sepoys, whom we had ourselves trained to fight against us. They were encamped in the Subzi-Mundi. Counting them, our entire force was now nearly eleven thousand men, with about three thousand in the hospital tents. The number of the British troops was three thousand three hundred and seventeen. Many regretted the danger of bringing such large bodies of natives together, even on our side.

The enemy were by no meaus to be despised ; they were certainly three times our number, were much superior in materiel and artillerymen, of whom we had only five hundred and eighty, and they occupied a very strong position. The moment we should attack them, it might be expected, all disumion would cease, and they would fight behind that wide mass of ramparts and buildings, with the energy and courage of despair. Many in camp were sure they would run whenever our bayonets went over the wall, but this only proved that judgment and common sense are rare acquirements.*

* Hodson (letter, September 6th), though by no means without these gifts, held this opinion. The author, who published a different opinion *before* the event, has a right to note this fact.

CHAPTER XII.

GENERAL WILSON at last made up his mind; Delhi was to be attacked without delay. Our assault was of course to be made on the north side, opposite to the camp. We chose, contrary to the expectations of the enemy, the part on our left nearest the river. This was defended by the Moree, Cashmere, and Water bastions, which were connected only by a parapet wall, on which guns could not be mounted. It was clear, then, that if we could silence the bastions, we could breach the wall without any opposition. The enemy ought to have attended to this. They had plenty time and means for heaping up a rampart on the north side, which could bear any number of guns they wished to mount, and then, from their great superiority in artillery, our fire must at once have been snuffed out. As it stood, so long as we could muster more guns upon the batteries than they could upon these three bastions, we were sure of being able to keep their fire under. It was then of importance to make our breach ere

they could mend their blunder, which they would
doubtless do quickly, when they saw its necessity.
Our batteries were to be constructed of fascines up
to the embrasures, above that of sandbags. The
engineers had an immense quantity of these ready
and filled with earth.* They had also remedied our

* In describing the work in the trenches, we have acquired much information from Captain Medley's " Year's Cam-
paigning in India." That gentleman, a distinguished officer
in the Engineers, has most thoroughly made this part of the
history of the siege his own. It is to be regretted he was not
called to Delhi at an earlier period. The military reader who
wishes a detailed account of the plan of assault must go to
him, this book being intended for popular reading. We,
however, give Colonel R. Baird Smith's description of the fortifications. The land defences " consist of a succession of bas-
tioned fronts, the connection being very long, and the outworks
limited to one crown work at the Ajmere gate, and Martello
towers, mounting a single gun, at such points as require some
additional flanking fire to that given by the bastions themselves. The bastions are small, generally mounting three
guns in each face, two in each flank, and one in embrasure at
the salient. They are provided with masonry parapets about
twelve feet in thickness, and have a relief of about sixteen
feet above the plan of site. The curtain consists of a simple
masonry wall or rampart sixteen feet in height, eleven feet
thick at top, and fourteen or fifteen at bottom. This main
wall carries a parapet loopholed for musketry, eight feet in
height and eight feet in thickness. The whole of the land
front is covered by a beam of variable width, ranging from
sixteen to thirty feet, and having a scarp wall eight feet high.
Exterior to this is a dry ditch of about twenty-five feet in

scarcity of sappers, by raising and organising a corps of Muzbee Sikhs, and a large body of coolies, or day labourers, at high wages.

The ground, which was intersected by numerous and now dry water-courses, sloping towards the river, and covered with old buildings and groves of trees, might be expected to shelter us as much as it had heretofore done the skirmishers of the enemy. As we had too few artillerymen, volunteers were called upon from the Lancers and 6th Dragoon Guards to work the batteries, and all the gunners of the Horse artillery were ordered into the trenches. The Sikh artillerymen sent by Sir John were a great gain to us.

We had already dug a trench to the left of the Sammy house, with a four-gun battery, which could bear upon any troops sallying from the Lahore or Cabul gates, and thus cover the flank of our approaches. This, moreover, served to mislead the enemy, who, imagining we were going to make a second parallel under Hindoo Rao's hill, allowed us to occupy the ground on the left, before the mistake was

width, and from sixteen to twenty feet in depth. The counter-scarp is simply an earthen slope easy to descend. The glacis is a very short one, extending only fifty or sixty yards from the counter-scarp ; using general terms, it covers from the besiegers' view from one-half to one-third of the height of the walls of the place."

discovered.　On the night of the 7th September a battery was silently traced out, seven hundred yards from the Moree bastion.　Our fascines and sandbags were carried down on the backs of camels.　The engineers then commenced to build the battery, cursing every sound ; but the working of so many men and camels could not be carried on without a dull noise, which attracted the attention of the enemy.　A flash comes from the Moree, and then the powerful whirr of a volley of grape, and the drop of two or three of our workmen.　They fired twice more with the same effect, and then ceased.　They probably imagined that it was one of our working parties cutting down the thickets around, whom a shot would frighten away ; and we were left to work on, if possible, more cautiously than before.　In spite of all our engineers could do, when dawn appeared, only one gun was mounted.　The enemy, seeing what we had been doing, instantly opened a terrible fire.　Our men, however, kept well behind the parapets, and, though access and egress were extremely dangerous, managed to save themselves till the platforms were ready, and the guns mounted and unmasked.　It was beautiful to see how our guns made the old masonry fly.　The enemy soon disappeared from the bastion.　When complete, this battery consisted of five eighteen-pounders and one howitzer to the right, with four twenty-four-pounders to the left, which were to play upon the Cashmere bastion. It was commanded by Major Brind.

Next evening we seized Ludlow Castle with a strong body of troops, and traced out a battery to breach the curtain wall between the Cashmere and Water bastions. It was quite ready on the 11th of the month. On the night of the 10th, we sought a place for a second breaching battery, and lighted upon a large building, an old custom-house, about a hundred and sixty yards from the Water bastion, which the enemy in their wonderful supineness had left standing. The work was immediately commenced behind it. Pandy, perceiving his error, did all he could to drive away our party with shot and shell. Thirty-nine men were killed and wounded that night. The pioneers still toiled on with that passive courage so common among natives. " As man after man was knocked over, they would stop a moment, weep a little over their fallen friend, prop his body in a row along with the rest, and then work on as before."* When finished, this battery mounted six eighteen-pounders.

No. 4 battery for ten heavy mortars was completed on the night of the 10th, in the Koodsia Bagh, a

* Medley.

garden surrounded by a high wall, and looking out on the Jumna. It was directed by Major Tombs.

The enemy stuck to their guns most manfully, but on the 12th all our batteries were unmasked. No living thing could remain within their bastions, and the curtain wall crumbled down before our breaching batteries in clouds of dust. Fifty guns and mortars belched forth their storm upon the city. They had once said they would worry us to death, but now we had them by the throat. Not a moment passed, night or day, that was not filled up by the roar of artillery. Yet so accustomed had our men become to it, that the wearied gunners would fall asleep a few yards from the working guns, and even the wounded in hospital did not lose their rest amidst the din. It was beautiful in the dark clear night to watch them from some quiet part of the ridge. The line of flashes from our batteries, the hollow boom of the shells, their explosion within the hostile works, with the rousing din of so many pieces of ordnance, filled the breast with a strange trouble. One could not help wondering at the in-genuity of the destructive little bimana, who were putting in action engines louder than the thunder, and, in their own range, more terrible than the hur-ricane.

The enemy saw their danger; grasping one another's hands, they swore to fight faithfully as long as they drew breath. They could not work their bastion guns against us, but they used all the means in their power to check our approaches. They formed a trench along the whole front, which they filled with skirmishers, and from the trees and broken ground they kept up a ceaseless shower of musketry. The crown of our parapets was shattered with bullets, and the mantlets that closed our embrasures while we were loading, were pitted with holes. Few felt at their ease going to and from the batteries. They got some guns placed in the Talewarie suburb, from which they could enfilade our two right batteries; and they managed to reach those on the left with mortars from the other side of the river. They knocked a hole in their curtain wall to get a gun to bear on us from the front, and sent rockets into our batteries from one of their Martello towers. They made sallies, too, from the gates, which were driven back by the grape of our battery at the Sammy house, and by the guards in the trenches. They also gave us much annoyance by bringing out field-pieces at night to enfilade our position at different points. These changed place too often for our guns to retaliate on them. We did our best to keep their skirmishers back, ploughed up the ground with **grape, and sent** bombs into their rifle pits ; twenty of them were killed by the explosion of one shell.

Our men, accustomed for three **months to work** in the batteries, were skilful in using the cover they had.   Experience, caution, and presence **of mind** save many lives in the trenches.   The nature of the ground helped us much.   The ravines and water courses, that ran parallel to our works, formed so many ready-made trenches and passages, by which our supports could move up, and our wounded be carried away.

The rains were fairly over, and the moist **heat** tried the strength most severely.   The exertion was terrible, and many sunk under it.   Very much re-gretted was the loss of Major Turner of the Horse artillery, whose strength, worn out by a long struggle with sickness, gave way at last.   Those who kept up bore everything cheerfully.   The prospect of the long and toilsome siege being soon over, the steady suc-cess of their operations, and the satisfaction of escap-ing with life and limb, made them cheerful and sanguine.   After a weary day's work, they would eat their dinner with a good appetite, and have a plea-sant chat behind some half ruined wall, or under an old gateway.   It was pleasant to note the courage of the depreciated natives who brought them their food, and the nervous demureness of the servants, who, in irreproachable costume, came with the officers' meals. All the artillery of course remained in the batteries day and night. Delhi, on the other hand, was full of fright and confusion. The streets were choked with carts and camels trying to leave the city. But the gates were shut by the King's order, and no one allowed to go out. An attempt was made by their cavalry to drive off our camels from the rear of the camp. Carriage was beginning to be of great value. The native chiefs and sepoy leaders met in council, but could not conceal their terror from one another. The King, in presence of all, tore his thin grey beard, and called down curses on those, who had brought him to this by their cowardice and discord.*

Our loss during the six days the trenches were open was three hundred and twenty-seven. Especially regretted was Captain Fagan of the Foot artillery, the best shot in the trenches, bravest of soldiers and finest of fellows, who was hit through the forehead while looking over his gun at the Customhouse Battery. The daring of Major Brind was as remarkable as his escape was wonderful. He would

* See Crisis in the Punjaub.

get up on the parapet, point out where the enemy were thickest, and watch the effect of his men's fire, while the bullets seemed to sweep every place but the space he occupied. He seemed to believe himself invulnerable, to live on the excitement, and to rest on his work, scarcely ever quitting his battery. No efficer at the same time was more attentive to the safety of his men, or shewed them more kindness.

The plan of attack was sketched by Colonel Baird Smith, but he being wounded at its commencement, the whole direction of the work fell upon Captain A. Taylor, who admirably executed his dangerous task.

The breaches had now got pretty wide, and on the night of the 13th two engineer officers were sent to examine each of them. They stole through the enemy's skirmishers, descended into the ditch, and managed to make out that the breaches were practicable, although they might both be much improved by a longer cannonade. Our artillerymen, however, were so much exhausted, and the enemy's flanking fire began to be so annoying, that it was determined to make the assault at once. Besides, they were known to be working at a new battery behind the curtain wall, which would have been ready in two days, and driven us out of our trenches.* The inhabitants of the city had been ordered by beat of drum to assemble in the direction of the Cashmere Gate, bringing iron picks and shovels with them ; and, as afterwards turned out, they were preparing a new enfilading battery to the right for seventeen guns. The assault would then have been impossible. The chief engineer advised that it should not be put off, and our infantry was divided into five columns of about one thousand men each, to carry the city in different places.

The First was composed of detachments of the 75th, 1st Fusiliers, and 2d Punjaub Infantry, to storm the breach near the Cashmere bastion.

The Second was made up from her Majesty's 8th, the 2d Fusiliers, and 4th Sikh Infantry, to carry the breach in the Water bastion. It was commanded by Brigadier Jones.

The Third column, from her Majesty's 52d, the Kumaon battalion, and the 1st Punjaub Infantry, was to blow open and enter by the Cashmere Gate.

The Fourth, under Major Reid, was to assault. Kissengunge, and enter by the Lahore Gate. He had with him the Goorkhas and Guides, some companies of European troops, and the Cashmere contingent.

* See Captain Medley, op. cit.

The Fifth column, consisting principally of native troops, was destined for a reserve.

At four o'clock in the morning the different columns took their appointed places. The direction of the storming had been left to Nicholson. The First column was marched silently down to the Koodsia Bagh ; the Second a little to the right ; and the Third waited on the high-road, which leads to the Cashmere gate. Our batteries redoubled their angry roar, throwing shells to drive the enemy away as far as possible from the breaches. The morning was just breaking ; the thunder of our artillery was at the loudest, when all at once it hushed. Every one could hear his heart beat. The artillery had finished their task. Guided by the engineer officers, the stormers marched on with a deep and steady tramp. The Rifles ran forward in skirmishing order, and the heads of the first two columns issued from the Koodsia Bagh at a quick walk. No sooner were their front ranks seen, than a storm of bullets fell upon them from every side. At the breach by the Cashmere gate, for some minutes, it was impossible to get ladders down into the ditch. The enemy dared them to come on. The ladders are thrown down, and the men jump after, and raise them against the escarp. Many are struck down ; the feeble moans of the dying, the groans of the wounded, the shouts and struggles of the living, mingle together. Lieutenant Fitzgerald of the 75th, is the first to mount the breach. He instantly fell dead on the spot. But there are plenty stout hearts behind. They are in at last, and the glorious old colours go over the broken wall. The Second column had also burst through. That line of ramparts, which had so often turned back our pursuing bayonets, was now our own.

The Third column had, in the meantime, advanced toward the Cashmere gate, and waited the signal of the explosion. The party, to whom the blowing in of the gate had been committed, consisted of two officers of Engineers, three sergeants, and eight native sappers, with a bugler to sound the advance, if successful. This work was to have been done before dawn, but, through some mistake, it was broad daylight before they reached the spot. Lieutenant Home walked through the outer barrier gate, which he found open, and crossed the broken drawbridge with four men, each carrying a bag of powder. The enemy, in alarm, shut the wicket, and Home had time to arrange his bags and jump into the ditch. The firing party followed with four more bags of powder, and a lighted port-fire. The enemy now understood what we were about. The wicket was opened ; through it,

from above, and from every side, came the bullets of
the sepoys.   Lieutenant Salkeld was wounded in two
places, but passed the light to Sergeant Carmichael,
who fell dead while attempting to fire the train.
Havildar Madhoo was also wounded. It was done
by Sergeant Burgess, who immediately sunk with a
mortal wound. Sergeant Smith ran forward to see if
it was right, and had just time to throw himself in
the ditch, while bugler Hawthorne bore away Salkeld
upon his back, bound up his wounds, and carried
him to a place of safety. The explosion took instant
effect, and our column burst through the shattered
gates. The four heroes who survived were recom-
mended for the Victoria Cross, which only two of
them lived to receive—Salkeld dying of his wounds,
and Home, who had escaped such terrible dangers
unhurt, perishing by accident about a fortnight after.
These men were no desperadoes tired of their lives,
who volunteered for the service in place of committing
suicide. They got their orders as the most available
men, and executed them with a simple heroism never
surpassed in the history of the most illustrious
nations of the earth.

The European quarter of the city was now in our
hands. Unfortunately, the warehouses of the merchants who sold European goods were full of wines

and brandy. Our men had been allowed a double dram of rum before the assault, and flew thirstily upon the liquor in the stores. Many of them were quite intoxicated ; others, instead of following their officers, went here and there seeking for plunder. Men of different columns and regiments got mixed up with one another.

The First and Second columns swept along the circuit of the walls, taking the Moree bastion and the Cabul gate. They were guided by men, who had been driven away from their homes here by the mutiny, and who now returned for revenge. When they approached the Lahore gate, they found they had to push through a lane which would admit only four abreast. It was barricaded and swept by some pieces of artillery, and the enemy were firing from the houses. Our men recoiled. Nicholson came up, and ordered a new attack. Major Jacob, of the 1st Fusiliers, assured him it was impossible to carry the passage without artillery ; but Nicholson's lion heart was beating too high with the pulse of victory ; he would not listen to anything like delay. He ordered an advance, and the officers to the front. This had not the desired effect. The companies behind, no longer under the eye of their officers, staggered by the loss they had suffered, and demoralized by plunder, would not come on. Every one who shewed himself was struck down ; Lieutenant Speke was killed, **Major Jacob** mortally wounded, Captain Greville severely, **and** the hero Nicholson shot through the chest. He ordered himself to be laid in the shade, and said he would wait there till Delhi was taken. But it soon **became** clear that this would not take place so quickly. Two guns were indeed taken and spiked, but we were obliged to abandon the attempt to force the passage, and fall back upon the Cabul gate.

The Third column had been guided by Sir T. Metcalfe, in the most gallant and skilful manner, by a circuitons road through some gardens, to the Chandney Choke, the principal street of Delhi. A very destructive fire was poured upon them from the houses, but they made their way to the Jumma Musjid. It was full of men, its gates blocked up, and, towering above their heads on its massive terrace, could be reduced only by the heaviest artillery. They were obliged to fall back with great loss. Cannons were pointed down the streets, that led from the part of the city still in the enemy's hands. The guns in the captured bastions were turned upon them, and everything done to secure our new position.

The Fourth column met with a worse mishap. They were to attack Kissengunge and join Nichol-

son's column at the Cabul gate. Major Reid was
waiting for three guns which had been promised him,
when the enemy attacked the Cashmere contingent.
He hastened to their support. The suburb was
full of houses, and had been very strongly fortified.
The Cashmere contingent was completely routed,
and took to flight with the loss of their four guns.
The whole fire of the enemy was turned on Major
Reid's force; he himself fell wounded in the head,
and his Goorkhas would advance no farther. We
were compelled to retreat. A body of the Guides
was surrounded in a house, and would have been
destroyed, had they not been gallantly brought off
by the Belooches. The enemy poured out after us.
There was great danger of their breaking into our
empty camp, or turning the flank of our storming
parties. But the guns that were still mounted on
Hindoo Rao's poured shrapnel amongst them, and
Chamberlain, now a little recovered from his wound,
reassured the scared infantry, like Tancred saving the
Crusaders' camp from the fury of Solyman; and
Brigadier Hope Grant brought up his old Lancers with
three regiments of Punjaub cavalry, and Hodson's
Sikh and Patan sabres, from the rear of the batteries, leaping their horses over the sandbags to save
our assailing force from being taken in rear. The

enemy turned out in large numbers of all arms, and avoiding the open ground, poured a staggering fire upon our cavalry and artillery, helped by the Burn bastion and Talewarie guns. Our troopers could neither charge from the difficulty of the ground, nor retire, to leave the position in the hands of the enemy. They were obliged to sit in their saddles, and wait till some infantry could be spared to come to their relief. The horse artillery did what they could to keep the enemy back, but they became every moment bolder, and spread out, mending their sight and taking better aim. The steadiness, with which the cavalry confronted this most anxious position for two hours, is as deserving of praise as the courage of the infantry, who carried the breaches. The Brigadier and four officers composing his staff had their horses killed under them ; two of them were wounded. Tombs lost the half of his now scanty and war-worn guns' crews.° At last some foot was sent up, by whose help the enemy were driven back.

A melancholy procession of doolies had been trailing all day to our hospitals, which were crowded to the doors with wounded. A field hospital was established in the church, where the doctors had their operating tables, amputating limbs, tying arteries, and

* See Hodson's Letter, September 15, etc.

resecting joints. Victory and misery, how are they mingled together! Honour truly hath no skill in surgery. The mutilated heroes were borne away to camp, to sink and die, or mayhap to recover, to learn to walk on crutches, or keep up a weakly existence a few years longer on the wretched pittance allowed by Government to its disabled soldiers. As the day closed we could count more exactly our gains and our losses—eleven hundred and four men and sixty-six officers hors de combat, beside those who fell in the Cashmere contingent, of whom we had no returns. The 1st Fusiliers had lost nine officers; of seventeen serving with the Engineers only seven remained for duty; and our greatest General was lying waiting for death. We were in possession of little more than a quarter of the city. The enemy were firing on us from the palace and Selim Ghar; and, from the failure of the attack on Kissengunge, our camp was in great danger of being assailed. Our men, too, had lost their discipline; many were dead drunk, and guards allowed themselves to be surprised and murdered. Before a determined enemy our position was worse than ever. General Wilson was completely unnerved by exhaustion and anxiety, and, it is said, wished to withdraw the troops to their old position and wait for more reinforcements; but, fortunately for his own reputation, and for the existence of our empire, he yielded to the pressing advices of some members of his military council.

The task of carrying the rest of the town was an easier one than had been surmised, and was worked out with great skill and caution. The palace and Selim Ghar were bombarded; such places as we wanted to seize were cleared of the enemy by a cannonade, before they were occupied. We got along several streets by sapping the inside walls, which were generally made of clay. On the 16th the magazine fell into our hands. Its immense stores seemed quite unaffected by the drain kept on it during the siege. It still contained two hundred pieces of ordnance. Large quantities of percussion caps were found, shewing the falsehood of the numerous stories we had heard of their scarcity. The same day the enemy left Kissengunge. It was clear their numbers were oozing away. Only the more determined now remained. On the 17th no more than three or four thousand of their troops were in the city, but our progress was still slow. Our men were disorderly and unmanageable; and even the sense of the danger of our position could not keep them to their ranks. Delhi was a very wealthy city. Though the plunder of kingdoms had long ceased to enter by its gates, its situation made it the great emporium of the commerce of the North-west. It was full of the costliest merchandize, and contained the palaces of many rich Mahomedan sirdars. The poor Sikh soldiers, from their reed hamlets in the jungle, had dreamed of carrying away jewels and treasures, that would make their families rich for ever. The less imaginative cupidity of the Europeans was equally strong, and there was great danger that the men, who were needed to drive the enemy from his last barricades, might be cut off in detail, dispersed among the mansions and ware-houses of the wide and wealthy city. The intoxicating liquors in the European merchants' stores were de-stroyed at once, lest they should fall into the hands of the men. It was deplorable to see hundreds of bottles of wine and brandy, which were sadly needed for our sick, shivered, and their contents sinking into the ground. Wine, which had fallen to threepence the bottle, soon rose again to six shillings.

General Wilson had done his best to obviate the danger. He had promised that the plunder of the city should, when realized, be distributed to the army. Prize-agents had been appointed. This had a great effect in restraining the more honourable of the sol-diers, and in giving every one a motive to keep the rest from plundering. Guards were placed at all the gates we held, who seized everything that was attempted to be passed through, principally the more bulky and less valuable articles. The Sikhs were not so easily foiled. They got bullock waggons to be driven at night to the walls, and dropped their booty down to their friends below. Many women, too, were seized and carried away by them. It was not till the spoils of Delhi were seen passing up to the Punjaub, that the news of its capture was fully believed in the great Mussulman cities to the north-west.

Most of the inhabitants had fled, and some painful scenes were thus avoided. Large numbers of deserted women, with their children, clinging to one another for protection, many of them evidently unaccustomed to walk, passed out by the Cashmere Gate, and through our camp. Our men treated these with kindness and sympathy, but many of the citizens were shot, clasping their hands for mercy. It was known, too, that a large proportion of them had all along wished us well. Helplessness ought to be respected in either sex, especially in those who have never done us wrong. It is as unmanly for an officer to drive his sword through a trembling old man, or a soldier to blow out the brains of a wounded boy, as to strike a woman. But though people talked wildly and fiercely, and though among so many soldiers there were some who shewed the spirit of the gladiator, the fears of those who anticipated the most violent excesses were fortunately not realized. One cannot help thinking, that no nation in the world would have shewed more moderation under the provocation endured. On the morning of the 19th, Lieutenant Hodson rode round by the Eedgah, and entered their camp on the other side of the city, near the Delhi gate. It was silent and deserted. Ammunition, clothes, and plunder strewed around shewed that it had been abandoned in haste. Several wounded sepoys were found and put to death. On the same day the gates of the palace were blown open ; only a few fanatics were found inside, determined to live no longer, and a large number of wounded, who were bayonetted—the closing scene in the royal halls of the emperors of Delhi.

On the morning of the 20th the Lahore gate, which had been deserted by its defenders, was occupied by our troops, and before night the whole of Delhi was in our hands. The city people had fled or been turned out, and our shrunken force was left alone guarding that wide circuit of walls, which now contained no enemy save some lurking fanatics or wounded sepoys, who were from time to time dragged forth and slain.

The Head-quarters had been, several days before,

shifted to the city, and were now settled in the palace. The tents of many of the regiments, too, had been brought down to or within the walls, and soon the last of them were struck, and the old parade ground left bare. It was not four months since the first tent had been pitched there, but a life's load of struggling and patience, and victory and mourning, seemed to lie between. And where were our brothers, who had come in the flush of hope and pride and bounding vigour? Now sleeping in that crowded little graveyard.

Old soldiers, who had fought at Cabul and in the Punjaub, said that a month at Delhi was more than a year's hard fighting any other where. We had put to flight a disciplined army four times greater than our own. The same men had gone out more than thirty times, to fight an ever fresh and swarming enemy. We had taken a strong city defended by a more powerful artillery, in a sickly season and under a tropical sun. We had saved a falling empire. This, then, was glory, which future ages would look upon and wonder at, and the present acknowledge with gratitude. The last of these hopes we soon found deceitful, at least as far as actions shewed. The war was barely over, when ten thousand of the soldiers who had saved India left the army, whose name they had rendered glorious, on a doubtful quarrel with the Government, which transferred them, without their consent, from the ranks of the Company to those of the Crown, withholding the bounty it granted freely to the rawest recruit; and Lord Canning announced in General Orders, that their period of service would not be recognised if they again entered our ranks—services painfully given, lightly forgotten. A few months after, many of the conquerors of Delhi and Lucknow were starving in the streets of our great cities, without even a medal to prove they had fought, while the Government held their prize-money in its coffers, and was showering rewards on native nawabs and ranas, the Lord Lovats and Secretary Murrays of the rebellion. About three years later, by a vote of Parliament, in disregard of the promises of the Ministry, and against the advice of all the greatest Indian statesmen then living, the Indian army was stripped of its privileges and separate existence. Future ages will no doubt have their own heroes to praise, mayhap to reward; but, whenever the wise and noble-hearted turn over the page of history for a bright and glorious example, they will rest awhile on those that record the achievements of the "Delhi Field Force."

CHAPTER XIII.

THE insurgents had no longer the walls of Delhi to take refuge behind, but there was still a large army which would never submit, save on terms which we were unwilling to offer. The king, too, had escaped, and it was to be guessed that the Mahomedans of the North-west would do their best to prevent the old prince, whom they considered the lamp of Hindostan, from falling into the hands of his deadly enemies. Natives of India, however, have a great clinging to their homes, and the old man felt his unfitness to be borne about, a houseless fugitive, the mark of continual pursuit, without any fixed place of refuge. It was ascertained that he had retired to the neighbourhood of the Kootub.° Negociations for his surrender were begun. They were principally carried on by Rujjub Ali, who had done most of the work in the intelligence department during the siege, and was a

* The Kootub is a beautiful and lofty fluted column, about five miles from Delhi, one of the most graceful as well as the oldest monuments of Mussulman splendour in India.

man of very great sagacity and astuteness. In affairs of this kind, nothing can be done save through a native medium. A European would be sure to be deceived, lose the thread of the intrigue, or break it off in impatience. Another agent in this work, who no doubt played an important part, from the very large reward he afterwards received, was Mirza Elihee Bucksh, the father-in-law of the late heir-apparent, who had died some months before the mutiny. Through them an offer came from Zeenat Mahal, the favourite wife of the king, that she would persuade him to surrender, on condition that he and the princes should be restored to the position and amenities they held at the commencement of the mutiny. This was what, in a native bargain, is called the spoken price. It soon subsided into a paction, that the king should give himself up, if his own life and that of her son should be guaranteed, and that they should not be exposed to any personal indignity.

It was not without much difficulty that, through the persuasion of Chamberlain, General Wilson could be prevailed on to allow Hodson to make the attempt to bring in the king. He set out with fifty sowars to the Kootub. The road led through the ruins of Old Delhi, amongst which most of the population of the city had taken refuge. When he arrived near the

spot, he placed his men within an old gateway, and
sent Rujjub Ali and another native envoy to the king,
who was surrounded by his attendants and faithful
followers, within the precincts of the tomb of Humayon, one of the most unfortunate of his ancestors.
Like most Mahomedan buildings, it was perfectly
defensible, and the king had so large an escort, that,
if the negociation failed, nothing could be done by
force. Indeed Hodson's small party would have been
in great danger. After two hours' arguing, reassur-
ing, and stipulating, Rujjub Ali announced the success
of his mission. A covered palanquin issued from the
deep shade of the old gateway, containing the Begum.
It was of course not searched. Behind, in another,
came the king. Hodson dismounted and demanded
him to deliver up his arms. The old man asked
if he was Hodson Behadur, and would repeat the
promise from the general that his life would be
spared. Hodson did so, and added that he would
kill him like a dog, if any attempt were made at rescue. The trembling old creature put the sword he
had with him into the powerful hand of Hodson.
The boy Jumma Bucksh, the son of the Begum, did
the same. The sowars then gathered round the
palanquins, and the bearers were ordered to move on.
Close behind came a large crowd of Mussulmans,

their dark faces deepened by the spectacle of their king being carried off by a single white man with a handful of Punjaubees. Very little would have turned them upon the party. Hodson afterwards said that he had never felt a ride longer in his life. The slow shuffling pace of the bearers, their continual changing of their shoulders, and the pressing on of the crowd behind was most aggravating to his patience. The sowars kept close round the palanquins, and Hodson's calm and quiet demeanour daunted the ever-rising indignation of the throng. No attempt at rescue was made. The crowd fell behind one by one as they neared the city ; and when they came to the Lahore gate, Hodson and his fifty sowars rode alone beside the palanquins. The king was borne through the gate and down the Chandney Choke to his own palace, where a few days before his short and guilty reign had terminated. Here Hodson delivered his prisoners to the civil authorities. His reception by General Wilson, on reporting his success, was not so warm as the nature of it seems to have merited.* "Well, I am glad you have got him," said the old

* The friends of Hodson were much dissatisfied at the manner in which General Wilson, in his despatches, arrogated the whole credit of the affair to himself. They themselves do not hesitate to pass over, in exactly the same way, the leading part which the Moonshi Rujjub Ali took in the matter.

General, "but I never expected to see either you or him again." He was allowed, at the intercession of the officers present, to keep the two swords taken with the king, one of which bore upon it the name of Jehangir, the other marked with the seal of Nadir Shah.

Next day Hodson had the same difficulty in obtaining the consent of General Wilson to lead out a party to take three of the princes, the leaders of the rebellion. General Wilson, at this time, seems to have commenced to reject all advice, having accepted so much during the assault. " Even poor Nicholson," Hodson writes, "roused himself to urge that the pursuit should be attempted. The General at length yielded a reluctant consent, adding, ' But don't let me be bothered with them.' I assured him, it was nothing but his own order which bothered him with the King, as I would much rather have brought him into Delhi dead than living."

Hodson set out for Humayon's tomb, where he understood they were, with a hundred sowars, accompanied by the astute moulvie Rujjub Ali, and one of the King's family, who was willing for pardon to give his services as an informer. He also took with

With this exception, our account is mainly taken from that in Hodson's Memoirs.

him Lieutenant Macdowell. We shall give the rest
of the narrative in the words of that lamented young
officer:—

"We started at about eight o'clock, and pro-
ceeded slowly towards the tomb. It is called Humayoon's tomb, and is an immense building. In it were
the princes and about three thousand Mussulman
followers. In the suburb close by about three thousand more, all armed ; so it was rather a ticklish bit
of work. We halted half a mile from the place, and
sent in to say the princes must give themselves up
unconditionally, or take the consequences. A long
half hour elapsed, when a messenger came out to say
the princes wished to know, if their lives would be
promised them if they came out. 'Unconditional
surrender' was the answer. Again we waited. It
was a most anxious time. We dared not take them
by force, or all would have been lost, and we doubted
their coming. We heard the shouts of the fanatics
(as we found out afterwards), begging the princes to
lead them on against us, — and we had only one
hundred men, and were six miles from Delhi. At
length, I suppose, imagining that sooner or later they
must be taken, they resolved to give themselves up
unconditionally, fancying, I suppose, that as we had
spared the king, we would spare them. So the mes-

N

senger was sent to say they were coming. We sent
ten men to meet them, and, by Hodson's orders, I
drew the troop up across the road, ready to receive
them, and shoot them at once if there was any attempt
at a rescue. Soon they appeared, in a small 'Ruth'
or Hindostanee cart, drawn by bullocks, five troopers
on each side. Behind them thronged about two
or three thousand (I am not exaggerating) Mussul-
maus. We met them, and at once Hodson and
I rode up, leaving the men a little in the rear.
They bowed as we came up, and Hodson, bowing,
ordered the driver to move on. This was the minute.
The crowd behind made a movement. Hodson waved
them back ; I beckoned to the troop, which came up,
and in an instant formed them up between the crowd
and the cart. By Hodson's order, I advanced at a
walk on the people, who fell back sullenly and slowly
at our approach. It was touch and go. Meanwhile
Hodson galloped back, and told the sowars to hurry
the princes on along the road, while we shewed
a front and kept back the mob. They retired on
Humayoon's tomb, and step by step we followed
them. Inside they went up the steps, and formed up
in the immense garden inside. The entrance to this
was through an arch, up steps. Leaving the men
outside, Hodson and myself (I stuck to him through-

out), with four men, rode up the steps into the arch, when he called out to them to lay down their arms. There was a murmur. He reiterated the command and (God knows why, I never can understand it) they commenced doing so. Now you see we didn't want their arms, and under ordinary circumstances would not have risked our lives in so rash a way ; but what we wanted was to gain time to get the princes away, for we could have done nothing had they attacked us, but cut our way back, and very little chance of doing even this successfully. Well, there we stayed for two hours, collecting their arms, and I assure you I thought every moment they would rush upon us. I said nothing, but smoked all the time, to shew I was unconcerned ; but at last, when it was all done, and all the arms collected, put in a cart and started, Hodson turned to me and said, ' We'll go now.' Very slowly we mounted, formed up the troop, and cautiously departed, followed by the crowd. We rode along quietly. You will say, Why, did we not charge them ? I merely say, we were one hundred men, and they were fully six thousand. I am not exaggerating ; the official reports will shew you it is all true. As we got about a mile off, Hodson turned to me and said, ' Well, Mac, we've got them at last ;' and we both gave a sigh of relief. Never in my life,

under the heaviest fire, have I been in such imminent
danger.   Everybody says it is the most dashing and
daring thing that has been done for years (not on my
part, for I merely obeyed orders, but on Hodson's,
who planned and carried it out).   Well, I must finish
my story.   We came up to the princes, now about
five miles from where we had taken them, and close
to Delhi.   The increasing crowd pressed close on the
horses of the sowars, and assumed every moment a
more hostile appearance.   'What shall we do with
them?' said Hodson to me.   'I think we had better
shoot them here ; we shall never get them in.'   We
had identified them by means of a nephew of the
king's, whom we had with us, and who turned king's
evidence.   Besides, they acknowledged themselves to
be the men.   Their names were Mirza Mogul, the
king's nephew, and head of the whole business ;
Mirza Kishere Sultamet, who was also one of the
principal rebels, and had made himself notorious by
murdering women and children ;   and Abu Bukt
(Abu Bukr), the commander-in-chief nominally, and
heir-apparent to the throne.   This was the young
fiend who had stripped our women in the open street,
and cutting off little children's arms and legs, poured
the blood into their mothers' mouths ; this is literally
the case.   There was no time to be lost ; we halted

the troop, put five troopers across the road behind
and in front. Hodson ordered the princes to strip,
and get again into the cart ; he then shot them with
his own hand. So ended the career of the chiefs of
the revolt, and of the greatest villains that ever shamed
humanity. Before they were shot, Hodson addressed
our men, explaining who they were, and why they
were to suffer death ; the effect was marvellous—the
Mussulmans seemed struck with a wholesome idea of
retribution, and the Sikhs shouted with delight, while
the mass moved off slowly and silently."

The bodies of the princes were carried away, and
placed in front of the Kotwalie, where, four months
ago, had lain those of their unfortunate victims. The
Sikhs said that on this very spot had been exposed
the remains of Tegh Bahadur, nearly two hundred
years before, to the insults of the Mahomedan crowd,
and wondered at the fulfilment of their ancient
prophecy.

These two exploits raised the fame of Hodson to
an extraordinary height, both in Europe and in India.
Volunteers came down to him in hundreds. Many
Sikhs of rank and family did not think it beneath
them to become simple sowars in his regiment. He
was blamed by some people because he promised the
king his life ; by others because he killed the princes.

There is no use lingering over these accusations. The king would not have surrendered at discretion; and, had he been allowed to remain at large, the subjugation of the Doab would have been inevitably prolonged to an extent, which would have told most seriously on the fortune of the war.

On the 24th the hero, John Nicholson, passed away from the scene, in which he had played such a short but brilliant part. His loss was mourned by the whole army, who felt they lost in him at once their most skilful general and their best and bravest soldier. The British nation, startled by the brilliant military genius which he had so recently shewn, felt a deep regret at the loss of a man, who might have been one of its greatest captains. He died after living long enough to hear the full news of our victory, as he so ardently prayed to do. From his dying bed he had aided the last military operations with his counsels, when he could no longer lead our columns to the attack. He sleeps by the Cashmere gate, near the breach he had led his stormers through, borne to the tomb by his friend General Chamberlain, by whose orders a suitable monument was erected over his place of rest.

Our army was so much exhausted by its exertions during the assault, that no attempt was made to pursue the enemy till the morning of the 24th September, when a movable column was sent out to pacify the districts on the other side of Delhi, relieve Agra, and open communication with General Havelock at Cawnpore. It consisted of two troops and a battery of artillery, the 9th Lancers, some Punjaub cavalry, and the skeletons of H. M's 8th and 75th, (about four hundred and fifty men), with the 2d Punjaub infantry, twelve hundred strong. They found many of the towns and villages on the road plundered, and, though there were frequent claims for redress, very little joy was shewn by any one at their appearance, save by the merchant class, who hailed our arrival everywhere as a renewal of the easy old money-making times. In almost every large town they came to they had to overcome opposition. After destroying the Fort of Malagurh, the residence of the refractory Walidad Khan, who had given us and our friends so much trouble, they arrived on the 5th of October at Allygur, which was taken after some resistance. A small garrison was left there, and on the 10th of October they reached Agra.

Repeated messages from that city had reached our column, that they were there in great danger of being attacked by a powerful army of the enemy, and that we must come quickly to their rescue. A

detachment of cavalry and horse artillery had been
sent on before. The whole population of Agra turned
out to see the conquerors of Delhi come in. The
authorities there informed Colonel Greathed that
the force of the enemy could not be nearer than ten
miles, and trusting to this he relaxed his vigilance,
and allowed many officers to visit the fort. A few of
our tents were pitched, and the men lying down in
disorder, waiting for the rest, when suddenly round
shots from a dozen of guns struck through the
encamping grounds, and squadrons of sowars rode in
amongst us, followed quickly by strong bodies of
infantry. The camp followers and sight-seers who
had come from Agra flee away tumultuously to
the fort, but our soldiers had got too severe a training
in danger to be easily startled. The troopers are in
their saddles in a minute ; the guns are harnessed,
unlimbered and open fire ; the infantry are soon in
their ranks ; and all, without waiting for the word of
superior command, beat back the enemy wherever
they find them. Never was a force more completely
surprised, recovered from it more rapidly, inflicted a
more thorough defeat upon the enemy, or pursued
them with more keenness and determination. All the
enemy's guns, twelve in number, with their baggage
and camp, fell into our hands. They must have lost

at least five hundred men. The rebel army was made up of the Mhow and Indore mutineers, part of the Nemuch brigade and other sepoys, and some volunteers from Delhi, probably numbering about six thousand men. They were commanded by our old enemy Bukht Khan. It was very singular how they had managed to cross the Karee Nuddee, a river deep and difficult to ford, pitch a camp about five miles from Agra, in a country full of villages, and that the functionaries there should believe that they were ten miles off, when they were almost within sight. It was said at the time that the enemy's information was equally bad, and that they mistook the hundreds of horses and crowds of camp followers in camping ground, for a part of the small detachment of troops in Agra, and attacked us without knowing who we were, a notion most excessively improbable, which perhaps arose from the belief, that the enemy were too much dispirited by the capture of Delhi, to dare to make such a vigorous attack upon us.

It is not our intention to follow them on their march down country till they joined the Commander-in-chief. The reader who takes up the history on that side, written by so many able pens, will trace them aiding in the second relief of Lucknow, and helping to avenge the defeat of General Wyndham upon the Gwalior contingent. We must return to Delhi as we left it, abandoned by its inhabitants.

To a stranger the desolation of the great city would have been eloquent of the miseries of war. Save in the immediate vicinity of the houses in which soldiers were quartered, all was silent and deserted. There were no merchants sitting in the bazaars; no strings of camels or bullock-waggons toiling through the gates; no passers by in the thoroughfares ; no men talking by the doors of the houses ; no children playing in the dust ; no women's voices from behind the screens. Household furniture of all kinds was lying in the streets. The spectacle was made only more melancholy by traces of recent inhabitants. The ashes were still black in the hearths, and domestic animals were roaming up and down in all directions in search of their late possessors. The houses here and there burnt or shattered by cannon shot, and the fragments of shells scattered about, with rotten corpses now and then to be seen, half eaten by crows and jackals, gave a clue to the desolation around. The merchants had stuck to their shops to the last, and had been driven out only by the bombardment and the report of the fierce doings of the soldiers.

The shops and warehouses in the Chandney Choke were full of costly goods. Those containing jewellery were entered and cleaned out in a few minutes. A great deal of valuable spoil fell into private hands. From the very beginning all the property in Delhi had been declared to belong to the army, and prize agents had been appointed to watch over and realize the booty, but their means of doing so were small, and many difficulties were thrown in their way. To collect and guard such an immense amount of miscellaneous property, scattered over such a wide city, was very difficult. A great number of articles of value, such as necklaces, earrings, bracelets, anklets, and all the multifarious ornaments of native women, with piles of rupees, were found concealed under the floors, or in holes of the walls in the houses. The native servants roamed about over the city looting everywhere. The European soldiers went about selling things. They had plenty of money in their pockets, which they spent with the recklessness common to their profession. Some private soldiers kept their carriages for a week or two. The temptation now and then proved too strong even for officers. Some of them carried away, and even presented to their friends, valuable jewels and costly shawls. An immense deal of property, useless to every one but residents on the spot, was broken and wasted. For every rupee gained in the way of plunder, there were twenty lost to the citizens. The native merchants, who had followed our camp, made their fortunes by buying the goods put up for auction by the prize agents.

No one ever doubted that General Wilson's promise, giving the prize money at Delhi to the army, would be confirmed by the Governor-General. It will be remembered that it was this confident expectation that they should be no losers, and that the prize money should be equally shared amongst all, that kept the men from dispersing among the streets of the great city, and restrained the reckless cupidity of soldiers in the neighbourhood of plunder. Without such a promise we could scarcely have carried the town. Every one was astonished at a Government notification which appeared about three months after. It stated at some length that no one had a right to treat state property, recovered from rebels, as subject to the laws of prize. It must revert to the government. No mention was made of what was to be done with the property of rebels, or what could not be traced. As a reward for the exertions of the Delhi field force, they were to receive six months' batta. Every one at once concluded that the government would thus manage to appropriate all the prize money, a striking proof of the little credit its servants gave it. This caused the utmost discontent. The officers of the native troops, who had come down from the Punjaub under the belief that they would share in the spoils of Delhi (a hope which had kept them faithful during the siege), were afraid to tell their men of the Governor-General's order; and the Europeans showed their contempt and anger in the most open manner. They wrote upon the walls of their barracks, "Delhi captured and India saved for 36 rupees 10 annas;" and at one station actually went out to plunder the government bullock-waggon trains. Whatever may be said against Lord Canning, it will be acknowledged that he has a high sense of honour. A scheme so questionable could have had no chance of his concurrence, unless indeed the matter had been totally misrepresented to him. It was not until several months were over, and the dangerous excitement had somewhat subsided, that a second proclamation appeared, stating that the intentions of government had been misunderstood, and granting to the army not only the whole of the prize money, but six months more batta. That the Governor-General should have endangered the fidelity of the army, and disappointed its hopes so cruelly, merely to lay down so self-evident a truism, that state property, when captured by rebels and recovered by its own troops, belongs to the government,

seemed very strange. It seemed stranger still that
no one who read the first proclamation ever doubted
—although that question was left at least doubtful
—that the government would wish to take the whole
thirty-five lacs of prize money, instead of content-
ing itself with its recovered property, that is, the
stores in the magazine, to which the prize agents never
laid any claim. They now admitted that the government was a noble and generous one, and none doubted
that the prize money would be speedily distributed to
the army. Here again they had mistaken the intentions of the government. Three years have now
passed away, and half the men that fought at Delhi
are in their graves, but no one has yet (1861) received
a pice of the prize money,* nor any so much as a

---

* The royal warrant for the Delhi prize money appeared
in the *Gazette* of 9th February 1861, and is dated 15th
December 1860. It granted the whole of the prize money
actually realized, amounting to 34 lakhs, 61,213 rupees, to the
officers and soldiers engaged in the operations which began at
Ghazeeoodeenuggur on the 30th of May 1857, and ended
with the capture of the fort of Jhujjur, 19th October 1857.
One-twentieth of the whole was granted to the legal represen-
tatives of the late Sir Henry Barnard, to General Reid, and Sir
Archdale Wilson, and to the heirs of the late General Penney,
according to the time that they held their several commands.
    The shares are calculated on the scale of the daily pay of
each man, one share for each shilling. Native soldiers thus
get half a share, European privates one share each, up to a

medal to point them out among the soldiers of nations, who two years later gained decorations on the plains of Lombardy, as men who had conquered at Delhi and Lucknow.

The loss of their property was not the only punishment the city people had to endure. They were driven, as already said, out of their homes, and had to put up as they best could among the ruins of Old Delhi and in the neighbouring villages. Hundreds of the more feeble perished through want and misery. It was not till the end of November, that the Hindoo portion of the population was allowed to return.

major-general, who gets seventy-six shares. Even the water-carriers, bullock-drivers, and doolie-bearers are not forgotten. Formerly it was customary to allow the commander of a force as much as one-eighth of the whole prize money. This new scale, however, is, as will be observed, much more favourable to the lower ranks. The warrant is most considerate and judicious. The prize money will probably not be paid for at least two years (March 1861).

The valuable property taken in the fort of Jhujjur had been claimed by Brigadier Showers for those who entered that place, which was done without any resistance, and was indeed the natural consequence of the fall of Delhi. This was over-ruled, but all those, who had walked in there, were allowed to participate in the common prize money.

This accounts for the name of General Penney receiving so large a share. He commanded the troops in Delhi after the retirement of General Wilson, though he was never present at the actual siege.

No Mahomedans could get in at the gates without a special order, and a mark was set upon their houses, and they were required to prove their loyalty before getting back again. At the same time, no one was disposed that the more guilty should escape. Those who had distinguished themselves most during the mutiny had every opportunity to make off. It is surprising, however, how many were caught hovering about the neighbourhood ; twenty-nine of the royal house were taken and put to death. Almost the only one of note who escaped was the Prince Feroze Shah, who, as a leader in the rebel army, rivalled Tantia Topee in the rapidity of his movements. He is supposed to be still hiding in the jungles of Central India, and his name is still breathed by the Mussulmans as the last of the house of Timour. Amongst those executed at Delhi was the man, who had commanded the rebel army at the battles on the Hindun and Badle Serai.

Offenders who were seized were handed over to a military commission to be tried. The work went on with celerity. Death was almost the only punishment, and condemnation almost the only issue of a trial. The gentlemen who had to judge offenders were in no mood for leniency. The murder of their relatives in the mutinies, the death of their friends

and comrades in battle, the sight of the ruins of the
European bungalows, and the recollections called forth
by the very stones of Delhi, were enough to embitter
the heart of any one. It was sufficient to prove that
any man had helped the rebel cause with provisions
or stores, for him to be put to death. Between two
and three hundred people were hanged. All this,
however, did not satisfy the vindictive fury of some,
the 'mountain party' of the Indian mutiny. There
was a cry, that those in authority at Delhi wished to
screen the guilty, and the fact of the king's life having
been promised to him, was a valuable one for this
strong-minded faction. Having, besides, an active
imagination, they invented a few more, such as that
the king still retained his insignia of royalty, and the
prince Jumma Bucksh had two English officers to
attend him when he took a ride. With these hallu-
cinations, joined to the facts that a very deserving
Mahomedan had been appointed extra-assistant commissioner down the country, and that the city of
Delhi had not been demolished, they were able to
make a surprising amount of clamour. It was principally of an oral character, though the more highly
educated in their ranks wrote, some of them in pretty
good English, long and fiery letters, lavish of interjec-
tions and doggerel rhymes, in those Anglo-Indian

newspapers which were disposed to increase their credit by circulating them. They considered that Delhi ought to be rased to the ground (which would have been by far the most laborious work the English had as yet executed in India) ; that the ploughshare should be passed over the site of the Jumma Musjid, and a cross erected upon the spot ; that no Mahomedan should be employed by our government, though some of our bravest regiments were nearly made up of them ; that Islam ought to be confined and exasperated by insulting enactments, and Hinduism alarmed by interference with the system of caste and by chronic affronts, as if the prejudices and customs of a nation can be destroyed by law. An immense number of natives, they thought, ought to be killed. Some of them held the country ought to be christianized, and the inhabitants taught English en masse. Some could not perceive why Hindostan could not be colonized as well as New Zealand. Others would send a large European population to cultivate the peaks of the Himalayas. This party never gained the ascendency ; its advocates did not seem to rise rapidly to the posts of distinction for which they believed themselves fitted ; and its influence was always less than the noise it made. But the powers of life and death were occasionally intrusted,

during those critical times, to persons altogether
unfit to execute them. Their zeal hindered their
own purpose. The government, alarmed at an indiscriminate craving for blood and licence, which might
have changed the insurrection into a war of races and
creeds, hastened to bridle them by amnesties, which
were not all of them well timed. The Mahomedan
fanaticism was excited and kept up, the suspicions of
the Hindoos about their caste were confirmed and
aggravated, the war was prolonged and made more
bloody, and our reputation for justice and mercy was
shaken among the nations of the continent.

That such people accused the authorities at Delhi
of over leniency, will be a valuable testimony to them
in future times. The Commissioner, Mr. Saunders,
fell in for a large share of their censure. To wind
up a topic so essentially unpleasant, it is but justice
to note, that the punishment which fell upon the
guilty city, though very severe, contrasts favourably,
as a distinguished French writer* has remarked, with

---

* M. le Comte Montalembert,—we give his words (from an
English translation, the original not being at hand), " I admit
that the severe punishment inflicted on soldiers, captured
with arms in their hands, all of them voluntarily enlisted,
and bound under an oath, taken of their own free will, to
respect the commanders whom they have massacred, cannot
be compared with the chastisements inflicted on innocent and

the conduct of the most civilized nations under circumstances much less exasperating, much less blood
having been shed at Delhi (save in the field) than in
many districts, where reprisals were much less called
for. No great time, moreover, has elapsed since the
vengeance was inflicted, and yet it is already in our
power to present the British conducting themselves,
in this very spot, in singular and pleasing contrast.
In the year 1860, owing to the failure of the rains,
the corn withered on the stalk, the grass was dried up,
and a dreadful famine fell upon those districts which
had been desolated by the war. About Meerut,
Delhi, Agra, Mutia, and Rohilcund, the summer and
spring crops were entirely lost. Suppliants were
seen to drop down dead in the streets, begging for
alms ; parents sold their children for a few annas ;
people died by hundreds, whole villages at once ;

hospitable populations by the conquerors of the New World,
nor even with the rigorous punishments, decreed by our
generals of the French Empire against the populations of Spain
and of the Tyrol, engaged in the most legitimate of insurrections ;
still less to the horrors committed in Vendee by the butchers
of the convention. But, for all that, I am not less convinced
that the just limits of repression have been overpassed, and
that the executions en masse of the defeated sepoys, systemati-
cally continued after the first outburst of grief caused by
unheard of atrocities, will fix an indelible stain on the history
of British rule in India. This is no longer justice but
vengeance."

millions of human beings were said to be without bread. The rich natives hung back ; the princes and nawabs were niggardly or indifferent ; the bunneahs hoarded up their grain, and lent money on enormous usury ; but the Europeans in India shewed they were worthy to rule over it. Their charity was freely and ungrudgingly given ; their subscriptions were doubled by the local government. Their mercy was most conspicuous where their justice had been most signal. Nineteen hundred starving wretches were fed at once by the European magistrate beside the Delhi gate ; and the world saw the noble spectacle of a community feeding those, who hated and had deeply injured it.

From Delhi parties of men were now sent out to punish the refractory villagers, and columns of troops to bring the country to order, and reduce the strongholds of the different native chiefs, who had assembled troops and made every preparation to set up for themselves, in case we had been driven out of the country. The military movements were tame, as there was scarcely any opposition. Those who had been most avowedly hostile to us took to flight. Walidad Khan, whom the King of Delhi had made governor of Boolundshahr, disappeared into Rohilcund, and the Nawab of Dadree into the desert of Bikaneer. Tooli

Ram, formerly a revenue contractor, who had raised a considerable army, cast guns, and built a fort, fled away after some finessing with General Showers. Some who had tried to keep friendly with both parties, and thought they had a chance of being pardoned, gave themselves up, among them was the Nawab of Jhujjur, the Rajah of Bullnagurh, and the Nawab of Furucknuggur.

At their trials they all adopted the same line of defence. They said they always wished well to the British government, but that the hostility of their followers was so strong, that they were unable to do anything to assist us. Any acts of opposition they traced to the same cause, and said they were done without their orders. They had all, it was clear, tried to avoid breaking with both parties, but had committed themselves more or less to either cause. One of them had saved the lives of several Europeans, and had offered to come to our camp during the siege, as he was powerless to give us any other assistance. The trial of the Nawab of Jhujjur* excited much attention,

* The Nawab of Jhujjur held a large territory near Delhi, and kept up a considerable force of horsemen. At the outbreak of the Delhi mutiny, Sir T. Metcalfe had escaped and taken refuge with the Nawab, with whom he had had much friendly intercourse. He was, however, treated with great discourtesy, and dismissed to make his way alone through the excited

as he was well known to Europeans.   They were all condemned to death, which sentence was carried out at once.   The whole of the districts round about Delhi were brought again under our rule.   Though considerable reluctance was shewn, little opposition was made.

But our victory had a wider result than this.   The taking of Delhi was the turning point of the struggle. It deprived the insurrection of its head-quarters and country on a sorry pony, his horse being taken from him. The magistrate of Rhotuck had applied for assistance to the Nawab, but could obtain only a few sowars, who could not be induced to do us any service.   It was proved that he had received a visit from Nadur Bux, one of the princes of Delhi ; at the same time he must have been a most unwelcome guest. For such a public avowal of his sympathy could never be forgotten or concealed.   He seems at first to have met with a cool reception, but this soon passed away, and he received the usual honours given to a chief of high rank, and remained several days the guest of the Nawab.   It was proved that, by threats and violence, he had extorted a large sum of money from the merchants of Jhujjur, and had sent treasure to assist the royal cause, that two envoys of his had audience in the palace, and that he had sent a body of sowars under the command of his father-in-law to fight against us at Delhi.   Several friendly letters from the King to the Nawab were also produced.   His defence was, that he was but a tool in the hands of his soldiers, and that he was compelled by his officers to receive the prince.   The fact of the treasure being sent was met with a denial.   The extenuating point was, that he had sheltered and escorted to our camp a party of European fugitives.

war material, dispersed the sepoy army, and destroyed
the prestige accruing from the possession of the
capital of the ancient seat of government, and of an
acknowledged head to the political movements of the
insurgents.   It brought back the Doab to us, relieved
us from an imminent rising in the Punjaub, and
allayed the ferment in Bombay and Madras, though
the news came too late to check the mutiny of the
Joudpore legion.   The head of the rebellion was
crushed, but the body still moved.   After the news of
the fall of Delhi had been spread through the Punjaub,
an émeute took place among the wild herdsmen and
vagabonds, who assemble after the rains in the well-
nigh uninhabited country round about Googaira,
affording at that season excellent pasturage, but at
other times of the year a sandy desert.   Googaira lies
between Moultan and Lahore, and this disturbance
shut up for a time the only road by which we could
communicate with Europe.   Without aim, without
leaders, and without weapons, it was suppressed about
the middle of November after a good deal of exposure
and marching, and only served to show how strong
the bent towards rebellion had become.   This was the
only civil outbreak in the Punjaub, save an abortive
attempt of the hillmen at Murree to plunder the
bungalows there.

It has been said that while the capture of Delhi set free three thousand men to aid the Commander-in-chief to relieve Lucknow, it let loose thirty thousand trained sepoys to swell and give a shape to the irregular bands of Oude. But if the great majority of the rebel army escaped, they escaped in a different condition from that in which they had entered. They came in organised brigades and regiments, full of hope, rich with plunder, and elate with unresisted massacre and mutiny. They fled away in disorderly parties, their faces darkened, disgusted with one another, their money spent, their bravest comrades killed in battle, with but a scanty supply of ammunition, and leaving all their heavy guns behind them. Three months before, the sepoys who opposed Havelock were turning their percussion guns into matchlocks. They had no more caps. As a general rule, they all had to fight out the war with such wretched firearms, against the fresh troops that were arriving from Europe, expert at the Enfield rifle. Never again did they turn their faces to us in the field for more than a few minutes.*

Their next great stand was at Lucknow, but no

---

* The Gwalior contingent has a right to be excluded from this remark, but they never were at Delhi, and came up to Cawnpore fresh troops.

one who served at Delhi ever thought of comparing the one with the other. Hodson, in the last letter but one he ever wrote, said, " Pandy has quite given up fighting, except pot shots under cover, and runs at the very sight of troops advancing. I stood on the top of the Dilkoosha palace yesterday, and watched the capture of as strong a position as men could wish for, (which at Delhi would have cost us hundreds), without the enemy making a single struggle or firing a shot." The paucity of means, both in men and ordnance, is what gives the chiefest glory to our triumph at Delhi. At Lucknow, the Commander-in-chief had one of the most numerous and well appointed armies, and certainly the most powerful and crushing train of artillery, that ever opened fire in India, against the scanty and wretched fabrications of the native arsenals, and the ill-flanked and hastily constructed fortifications of Lucknow. No one will venture to disparage the gallant army and skilful leader, that so gloriously put an end to the war. They had difficulties enough to conquer, and gained renown enough for themselves. Nothing could exceed the steadfast bravery, which enabled them, against overpowering numbers, to accomplish the second relief of Lucknow. The wonderful celerity and success with which the defection of Scindia's army was quelled, and the heights of Gwalior carried, joined to the dreadful fatigues and dangerous exposure to the sun endured by the force, gave a character quite unique to Sir Hugh Rose's Central India campaign. But it must be cheering to all to reflect, that the two greatest struggles in the war, the siege of Delhi, and the relief of Lucknow, were fought out without the aid of a single soldier from Europe.

Our victory itself brought us reinforcements. The military population of the Punjaub no longer hung back; claimants for enlistment appeared in double the number we desired, many of them old soldiers ready for instant service. Regiment after regiment was raised, and the officers who had escaped from the mutineers put at their head, and we soon had a native army, larger than the one that had risen against us. After the war was over, people might grumble at the deficit their pay made in the revenue, but it would have been very difficult for us to march and hunt down the broken bodies of the rebels without our Punjaubee legions, who served us with unhoped for fidelity and a bravery, which placed them on a level with European troops. The help they afforded us was perfectly appreciated both by themselves and by the Poorbeahs, although evident political reasons kept our government from acknowledging it to the full.

And since, by ways so wonderful and by means so unexpected, God, who rules over all things, has given us the victory, let us hope that he will also teach us so to govern the people whom we have conquered, that our rule may be a blessing to them and not a scourge ; and that he will grant they may learn from us the virtues which they so sorely need, and, adding them to the good qualities they undoubtedly possess, may become a light and an example to the fallen races of the East.

APPENDIX.

Return of Sick and Wounded of all ranks of the Delhi
Field Force.

	11th September 1857.
Artillery Europeans	131
„ Natives	126
Engineer Brigade	214
6th Dragoon Guards	45
Her Majesty's 9th Lancers	51
Detachment 1st Punjaub Cavalry	4
2d do.	4
5th do.	10
„ 4th Irregular Cavalry	16
Hodson's Horse	32
H. M.'s 8th Regiment (part of)	124
H. M.'s 5th Light Infantry	332
H. M.'s 60th Rifles (part of)	121
H. M.'s 61st Regiment	256

H. M.'s 75th Regiment .	.	**160**
1st European Fusiliers .	.	**183**
2d European Fusiliers .	.	**362**
Sirmoor Battalion	.	**232**
Kumaon Battalion	.	**165**
Guide Corps .	.	**209**
4th Sikh Infantry	.	**121**
1st Punjaub Infantry .	.	**136**
2d Punjaub Infantry .		**76**
4th Punjaub Infantry .		**50**
Wing Belooch Battalion .		**14**

Total . **3074**

List of OFFICERS KILLED, died of WOUNDS, or WOUNDED at and near DELHI from the 30th May 1857 **to the** final capture of the place on the 20th September, **1857.**

Palace of Delhi, 23d September 1857.

Killed or died of Wounds.

Brigadier General J. Nicholson, Commanding **4th Infantry** Brigade.

Colonel C. Chester, Adjutant General of the **Army.**

Captain C. W. Russell, 54th Native **Infantry, Orderly** Officer.

Captain J. W. Delamain, 56th Native **Infantry, ditto.**

Captain R. C. H. B. Fagan, Artillery, previously **slightly** wounded.

Lieutenant E. H. Hildebrand, ditto.

Lieutenant H. G. Perkins, ditto.

Lieutenant T. E. Dickens, ditto.

2d Lieutenant F. S. Tandy, Engineers.

2d Lieutenant E. Jones, ditto.

Captain T. M. Greensill, 24th Foot, Assistant Field Engineer.

Assistant Surgeon S. Moore, 6th Dragoon Guards.

Brevet Lieutenant-Colonel R. A. Yule, 9th Royal Lancers.

Lieutenant W. W. Pogson, Her Majesty's 8th (the King's) Regiment, previously slightly wounded.

Lieutenant W. R. Webb, ditto.

Lieutenant W. H. Mountsteven, ditto.

Lieutenant J. H. Bradshaw, Her Majesty's 52d Light Infantry.

Captain F. Andrews, Her Majesty's 60th Royal Rifles.

Ensign W. H. Napier, ditto.

Lieutenant M. A. Humphrys, 20th Regiment Native Infantry, attached to Her Majesty's 50th Rifles.

Ensign E. A. L. Phillipps, 11th Regiment Native Infantry, attached to ditto, previously twice slightly wounded.

Lieutenant T. Gabbett, Her Majesty's 61st Regiment.

Ensign S. B. Elkington, ditto.

Captain E. W. J. Knox, Her Majesty's 75th Regiment.

Lieutenant J. R. S. FitzGerald, ditto.

Lieutenant A. Harrison, ditto.

Lieutenant E. V. Briscoe, ditto.

Lieutenant W. Crozier, ditto.

Major G. O. Jacob, 1st European Fusiliers, previously slightly wounded.

Captain G. G. McBarnett, 55th Native Infantry, attached to 1st Fusiliers.

Lieutenant E. Speke, 65th Native Infantry, attached to do.

Lieutenant S. H. Jackson, 2d Fusiliers.

2d Lieutenant D. F. Sheriff, ditto.

2d Lieutenant C. F. Gambier, 38th Light Infantry, attached to 2d Fusiliers.

Ensign O. C. Walter, 45th Native Infantry, attached to ditto.

Ensign E. C. Wheatley, 54th Native Infantry, attached to Sirmoor Battalion.

Lieutenant J. H. Brown, 33d Native Infantry, attached to Kumaon Battalion.

Lieutenant J. Yorke, 3d Regiment Native Infantry, attached to 4th Sikh Infantry.

Brevet Captain W. G. Law, 10th Native Infantry, attached to 1st Punjaub Infantry.

Lieutenant E. J. Travers, 2d in command, ditto.

Lieutenant W. H. Lumsden, Adjutant, ditto.

Ensign J. S. Davidson, 26th Native Light Infantry, attached to 2d Punjaub Infantry.

Lieutenant R. P. Homfray, 4th Punjaub Infantry.

Lieutenant Q. Battye, Commandant of Cavalry Guide Corps.

Lieutenant A. W. Murray, 42d Native Light Infantry, attached to Guide Corps, previously severely wounded.

Lieutenant C. B. Bannerman, Belooch Battalion.

Wounded.

Brigadier General N. B. Chamberlain, Adjutant General of the Army, severely.

Colonel A. M. Becher, Quarter Master General of the Army, severely.

Lieutenant F. S. Roberts, Officiating Deputy Assistant Quarter Master General, slightly.

Brigadier H. Garbett, C.B., Artillery, slightly.

Brigadier St. G. D. Showers, 1st Infantry Brigade, severely.

Captain H. E. H. Burnside, Brigade Major, 3d Infantry Brigade, twice slightly.

Lieutenant F. C. Innes, 60th Native Infantry, Orderly Officer, slightly.

Lieutenant Colonel T. Seaton, C.B., 35th Native Light Infantry, attached to 1st Infantry Brigade, severely.

Lieutenant Colonel R. Drought, 60th Infantry, attached to 2d Infantry Brigade, severely.

Major J. H. Campbell, Artillery, severely.

Brevet Lieutenant Colonel M. Mackenzie, Artillery, severely.

Captain E. K. Money, ditto, severely.

Captain J. Young, ditto, slightly.

Brevet Major H. Tombs, ditto, slightly twice.

Captain T. E. Kennion, ditto, severely.

Captain A. Light, ditto, slightly.

1st Lieutenant A. Bunny, ditto, slightly.

1st Lieutenant H. P. Bishop, ditto, do.

1st Lieutenant G. Baillie, Artillery, slightly.

1st Lieutenant A. Gillespie, ditto, do.

1st Lieutenant E. L Earle, ditto, do.

1st Lieutenant A. H. Lindsay, ditto, do.

1st Lieutenant C. Hunter, ditto, do.

2d Lieutenant J. Hills, do, severely.

2d Lieutenant M. Elliott, ditto, do.

2d Lieutenant P. Thompson, ditto, do.

2d Lieutenant A. H. Davidson, ditto, do.

2d Lieutenant E. Fraser, ditto, slightly.

2d Lieutenant R. T. Hare, ditto, do.

2d Lieutenant H. Chichester, ditto, do.

Lieutenant and Riding Master S. Budd, ditto, do.

Assistant Surgeon W. W. Ireland, ditto, dangerously.

Lieutenant Colonel R. Baird Smith, Engineers (Chief Engineer), slightly.

Lieutenant W. W. H. Greathed, Engineers, very severely.

Lieutenant J. T. Walker, Bombay Engineers, severely.

Lieutenant F. R. Maunsell, Engineers, very severely.

Lieutenant J. G. Medley, ditto, severely.

Lieutenant P. Salkeld, ditto, dangerously.

Lieutenant E. Walker, ditto, slightly.

Lieutenant G. T. Chesney, ditto (Brigade Engineers), severely.

Lieutenant W. E. Warraud, Engineers, dangerously.

Lieutenant H. A. Brownlow, ditto, do.

Lieutenant M. G. Geneste, ditto, slightly.

Lieutenant J. St. J. Hovenden, ditto, severely.

Lieutenant Œ. Perkins, ditto, slightly.

2d Lieutenant J. N. Champain, Engineers, slightly.

2d Lieutenant R. B. C. Pemberton, ditto, do.

2d Lieutenant P. Murray, ditto, do.

2d Lieutenant H. A. L. Carnegie, ditto, do.

Ensign (Local) L. Gustavinski, Punjaub Sappers, severely.

Ensign (Local) C. Anderson, do. slightly.

Captain C. P. Rosser, Her Majesty's 6th Dragoon Guards, dangerously.

Lieutenant A. A. de Bourhel, ditto, severely.

Captain the Hon. A. H. A. Anson, Her Majesty's 84th Regiment, attached to Her Majesty's 9th Lancers, slightly.

Lieutenant B. Cuppage, 6th Light Cavalry, attached to Her Majesty's 9th Lancers, do.

Lieutenant Watson, 1st Punjaub Cavalry, do.

Lieutenant H. H. Gough, 3d Light Cavalry, attached to Hodson's Horse, do.

Brevet Lieutenant Colonel J. C. Brooke, Her Majesty's 8th Regiment, severely.

Captain E. G. Daniell, ditto, do.

Brevet Major R. Baynes, ditto, dangerously.

Brevet Captain D. Beere, do., severely.

Brevet Captain E. N. Sandilands, ditto, twice slightly.

Lieutenant G. F. Walker, ditto, severely.

Lieutenant W. J. Metge, ditto, slightly.

Colonel G. Campbell, Her Majesty's 52d Light Infantry ditto.

Captain J. A. Bayley, ditto, severely.

Lieutenant W. Atkinson, do., slightly.

Ensign T. Simpson, Her Majesty's 52d Light Infantry, slightly.

Captain H. F. Williams, Her Majesty's 60th Rifles, severely.

Captain C. Jones, ditto, do.

Captain G. C. H. Waters, ditto, once severely, once slightly.

Lieutenant H. P. Eaton, ditto, dangerously.

Lieutenant J. D. Dundas, ditto, slightly.

Lieutenant H. G. Deeds, ditto, do.

Lieutenant P. G. Curtis, ditto, once severely, once slightly.

Ensign W. G. Turle, ditto, severely.

Ensign A. C. Heathcote, ditto, slightly.

Surgeon J. H. K. Innes, ditto, do.

Captain W. E. D. Deacon, Her Majesty's 61st Regiment, severely.

Lieutenant T. M. Moore, do., slightly.

Lieutenant W. H. W. Pattoun, do., severely.

Lieutenant A. C. Young, ditto, do.

Lieutenant C. J. Griffiths, ditto, do.

Lieutenant T. B. Hutton, ditto, slightly.

Ensign E. B. Andros, ditto, do.

Lieutenant Colonel C. Herbert, Her Majesty's 75th Regiment, twice slightly.

Captain T. C. Dunbar, ditto, do.

Captain A. Chancellor, ditto, do.

Captain R. Dawson, ditto, dangerously.

Captain R. Freer, Her Majesty's 27th Regiment, attached to Her Majesty's 75th, slightly.

Lieutenant and Adjutant R. Barter, Her Majesty's 75th Regiment, severely.

Lieutenant C. R. Rivers, do., slightly.

Lieutenant E. Armstrong, ditto, do.

Lieutenant G. C. N. Faithful, ditto, do.

Lieutenant C. M. Pym, ditto, do.

Ensign R. Wadeson, ditto, severely.

Ensign Dayrell, 58th Native Infantry, attached to Her Majesty's 75th Regiment, do.

Paymaster D. F. Chambers, Her Majesty's 75th Regiment, slightly.

Assistant Surgeon S. A. Lithgow, ditto, do.

Colonel J. Welchman, 1st Fusiliers, dangerously.

Captain S. Greville, ditto, once severely, twice slightly.

Captain E. Brown, ditto, dangerously.

Lieutenant H. M. Wemyss, ditto, once severely, once slightly.

Lieutenant J. W. Daniell, ditto, severely.

Lieutenant E. A. C. Lambert, do., slightly.

Lieutenant A. G. Owen, ditto, once severely, once slightly.

2d Lieutenant N. Ellis, do., slightly.

Captain J. P. Caulfield, 3d Regiment Native Infantry, attached to 1st Fusiliers, do.

Captain W. Graydon, 16th Grenadiers, ditto, severely.

Lieutenant E. H. Woodcock, 55th Native Infantry, ditto, do.

Lieutenant A. Elderton, 2d Fusiliers, do.

Lieutenant C. R. Blair, ditto, dangerously.

Lieutenant J. T. Harris, ditto, severely.

Captain J. C. Hay, attached to 2d Fusiliers, dangerously.

Captain D. Kemp, 5th Regiment Native Infantry, ditto, severely.

Lieutenant T. N. Walker, 60th Native Infantry, do., twice slightly.

Major C. Reid, Commandant Sirmoor Battalion, severely.

Lieutenant D. B. Lockhart, 7th Native Infantry, attached to Sirmoor Battalion, do.

Lieutenant S. Ross, 9th Native Infantry, ditto, slightly.

Lieutenant A. Tulloch, 20th Native Infantry, ditto, once severely, once slightly.

Lieutenant H. D. E. W. Chester, 36th Native Infantry, ditto, slightly.

Lieutenant A. H. Eckford, 69th Native Infantry, ditto, do.

Captain H. F. M. Boisragon, 2d in command Kumaon Battalion, severely.

Lieutenant A. B. Temple, 49th Native Infantry, attached to Kumaon Battalion, slightly.

Lieutenant C. F. Packe, 4th Regiment Native Infantry, attached to 4th Sikh Infantry, severely.

Lieutenant F. H. Jenkins, 57th Native Infantry, ditto, do.

Lieutenant A. Pallan, 36th Native Infantry, ditto, do.

Major J. Coke, commanding 1st Punjaub Infantry, do.

Lieutenant C. J. Nicholson, 31st Native Infantry, Acting Commandant 1st Punjaub Infantry, do.

Lieutenant H. T. Pollock, 35th Light Infantry, attached to ditto, very severely.

Lieutenant T. M. Shelley, 11th Native Infantry, attached to ditto, slightly.

Ensign (Local) C. Prior, attached to 1st Punjaub Infantry, slightly.

Captain G. W. G. Green, Commandant 2d Punjaub Infantry, ditto.

Lieutenant Frankland, 2d in Command, ditto, severely.

Captain H. D. Daly, Commandant Guide Corps, do.

Lieutenant T. G. Kennedy, Officiating Commandant Cavalry, ditto, do.

Lieutenant R. H. Shebbeare, 60th Native Infantry, attached to Guide Corps, twice slightly.

Lieutenant C. W. Hawes, Adjutant, ditto, slightly.

Lieutenant E. E. B. Bond, 57th Native Infantry, attached to ditto, severely.

Ensign O. J. Chalmers, 3d Native Infantry, ditto, slightly.

RETURN of KILLED, WOUNDED, and MISSING of the DELHI
neighbourhood of Delhi, on 30th May 1857, up

CORPS.	Effective Strength of all ranks on 11th Sept. 1857.	KILLED.									
		Officers.		Non-Comd. Officers.		Drummers, etc.		Rank and file.		Total.	Horses.
		European.	Native.	European.	Native.	European.	Native.	European.	Native.		
Staff	0	4	0	0	0	0	0	0	0	4	8
Artillery, including drivers, gun lascars and newly raised Sikh Artillery	1350	4	1	4	1	0	0	39	25	74	55
Engineers and Sappers and Miners (including 5 Companies newly raised Punjaub Sappers) .	722	3	2	3	3	0	0	1	31	43	0
Her Majesty's 6th Dragoon Guards (4 Troops) . . .	123	1	0	5	0	0	0	13	0	19	16
Her Majesty's 9th Lancers .	391	1	0	1	0	0	0	25	0	27	59
Detachment 4th Irregular Cavalry (disarmed and dismounted) .	78	0	0	0	0	0	0	0	0	0	0
Detachment 1st Punjaub Cavalry	147	0	0	0	0	0	0	0	1	1	1
„ 2d Punjaub Cavalry	114	0	0	0	0	0	0	0	0	0	1
„ 5th Punjaub Cavalry	107	0	0	0	0	0	0	0	0	0	1
Hodson's Irregular Horse . .	462	0	0	0	0	0	0	0	0	0	2
Her Majesty's 8th Regiment .	322	3	0	5	0	0	0	19	0	27	0
„ 52d Light Infantry	302	1	0	1	0	0	0	17	0	19	0
„ 60th Rifles . .	390	4	0	2	0	1	0	106	0	113	0
„ 61st Regiment .	402	2	0	2	0	0	0	28	0	32	0
„ 75th Regiment .	459	5	0	4	0	1	0	74	0	84	0
1st European Fusiliers . .	427	3	0	10	0	2	0	83	0	98	0
2d European Fusiliers . .	370	4	0	7	0	1	0	71	0	83	0
Sirmoor Battalion . . .	212	1	0	0	3	0	0	0	82	86	0
Kumaon Battalion . . .	312	1	0	0	2	0	0	0	18	21	0
Guide Corps (Cav. and Inf.: 302 Inf., 283 Cav.) . . .	585	2	5	0	13	0	2	0	50	72	16
4th Sikh Infantry (including Recruits)	414	1	2	0	3	0	0	0	40	46	0
1st Punjaub Infantry (including Recruits)	664	3	3	0	5	0	0	0	66	77	0
2d Punjaub Infantry (including Recruits)	650	1	1	0	3	0	0	0	38	43	0
4th Punjaub Infantry (including Recruits)	541	1	0	0	1	0	0	0	8	10	0
Wing Belooch Battalion . .	322	1	0	0	0	0	0	0	7	8	0
Pioneers (unarmed and undisciplined)	No return	0	0	1	1	0	0	0	23	25	0
Grand Total . .	9866	46	14	45	35	5	2	476	389	1012	139

FIELD FORCE, from the commencement of the operations in the to capture of the City on the 20th September.

PALACE OF DELHI, 23d *September* 1857.

WOUNDED.										MISSING.										TOTAL OF KILLED, WOUNDED, & MISSING.	
Officers		Non-Comd. Officers		Drummers, etc.		Rank and file.				Officers		Non-Comd. Officers		Drummers, etc.		Rank and file.					
European.	Native.	European.	Native.	European.	Native.	European.	Native.	Total.	Horses.	European.	Native.	European.	Native.	European.	Native.	European.	Native.	Total.	Horses.	Officers and men.	Horses.
9	0	0	0	0	0	0	0	9	2	0	0	0	0	0	0	0	0	0	0	13	10
22	1	13	2	4	0	190	47	289	62	0	0	0	0	0	0	0	2	2	4	365	121
19	1	6	10	0	0	0	50	86	0	0	0	0	0	0	0	0	9	9	0	138	0
2	0	2	0	0	0	6	0	11	11	0	0	0	0	0	0	0	0	0	0	30	27
2	0	2	0	0	0	61	0	66	46	0	0	0	0	0	0	0	0	0	36	93	121
0	0	0	1	0	0	0	2	3	3	0	0	0	0	0	0	0	0	0	0	3	3
1	0	0	0	0	0	0	5	6	12	0	0	0	0	0	0	0	0	0	3	7	16
0	0	0	0	0	0	0	3	3	2	0	0	0	0	0	0	0	0	0	0	3	3
0	1	0	0	0	0	0	3	4	4	0	0	0	0	0	0	0	0	0	0	4	5
1	5	0	0	0	0	0	5	11	11	0	0	0	0	0	0	0	0	0	1	11	14
7	0	9	0	0	0	120	0	136	0	0	0	0	0	0	0	0	0	0	0	163	0
4	0	8	0	0	0	65	0	77	0	0	0	0	0	0	0	5	0	5	0	101	0
10	0	17	0	0	0	249	0	276	0	0	0	0	0	0	0	0	0	0	0	389	0
7	0	7	0	0	0	105	0	119	0	0	0	0	1	0	0	4	0	5	0	156	0
14	0	7	0	0	0	177	0	198	0	0	0	0	0	0	0	3	0	3	0	285	3
11	0	23	0	1	0	186	0	221	0	0	0	0	0	0	0	0	0	0	0	319	0
6	0	11	0	0	0	145	0	162	0	0	0	0	0	0	0	0	0	0	0	245	0
6	0	0	3	0	1	0	210	233	0	0	0	0	0	0	0	0	0	0	0	319	0
2	3	0	3	0	0	0	30	38	0	0	0	0	0	0	0	0	5	5	0	64	0
6	10	0	43	0	4	0	168	231	33	0	0	0	0	0	0	0	0	0	0	303	58
3	7	0	8	0	0	0	98	116	0	0	0	0	0	0	0	0	0	0	0	162	0
5	5	0	7	0	0	0	134	151	0	0	0	0	0	0	0	0	0	0	0	228	0
2	4	0	7	0	0	0	96	109	0	0	0	0	0	0	0	0	0	0	0	152	0
0	2	0	5	0	0	0	54	61	0	0	0	0	0	0	0	0	0	0	0	71	0
0	1	0	5	0	0	0	43	49	0	0	0	0	0	0	0	0	1	1	0	58	0
0	1	1	0	0	0	0	128	130	0	0	0	0	0	0	0	0	0	0	0	155	0
140	49	103	99	5	5	1313	1076	2795	186	0	0	0	1	0	0	12	17	30	53	3837	378

H. W. NORMAN, *Lieutenant*,
Assistant Adjutant-General of the Army.

ABSTRACT.

	Officers.	Native Officers.	Non-Comd. Officers.	Drummers.	Rank and file.	Total.	Horses.	Europeans.	Natives.	Total.
Killed ..	46	14	80	7	865	1012	139	572	440	1012
Wounded	140	49	207	10	2389	2795	186	1566	1229	2795
Missing .	0	0	1	0	29	30	53	13	17	30
Total...	186	63	288	17	3283	3837	378	2151	1686	3837

Memorandum.—Those Officers who died of wounds during the siege are included as killed, but those returned as killed of other ranks were all killed at the time, there being no documents available to shew what number of wounded Soldiers died in consequence of their injuries.

Officers and men killed, wounded, and missing, prior to 8th September,
on which date the batteries for the reduction of the place were opened   2163

Officers and men killed, wounded, and missing, from above date until
morning of assault   327

Officers and men killed, wounded, and missing, in the assault of 14th
September   1170

Officers and men killed, wounded, and missing, from 15th September
until final capture of the City on the 20th Idem   .   .   177

         Total   3837

N. B.—Since this return was compiled, it has been ascertained that a mistake took place in the returns furnished by the 8th Foot of casualties at the assault, 17 more men having been killed than were actually entered. Owing to the numerous casualties in Corps during the siege, it is probable that some were omitted to be returned, and that the loss in several Regiments exceeds that above shewn.

                 H. W. NORMAN, *Lieutenant,*
                       Assistant Adjutant-General of the Army.

TRIAL OF THE KING OF DELHI.

T**HE** King of Delhi had surrendered himself under the promise that his life should be spared, and that he should not be treated with personal indignity. Some were very much dissatisfied that these promises were kept,—but the latter of them was scarcely so. A letter from Delhi,* dated the 14th January 1858, says,—" It is not true that the King is living in state, but, on the contrary, he is confined to a little room containing only one charpoy (or cot), and allowed but two annas (3d.) a day for his food. He is treated with great disrespect by the officers and soldiers, though Mr. Saunders is civil to him. The officers boast that they make the King stand up and salaam to them, and one of them pulled his beard." The begum and princesses of his house had come to share his prison with him. These unfortunate ladies, to whom no guilt could be attached, were exposed to the gaze of officers and soldiers, who could go into the room where they were at pleasure. To a native woman of the very lowest class this is an unutterable shame. My informant, a private soldier, who went to see the King, noticed their gilt slippers at the

* Mofussilite.

door, which surely ought to have been sufficient to prevent any one, who wished to refrain from insulting helpless women, from entering. On his suddenly going in, they all turned their faces to the wall.

It was determined that the King should be tried, though the punishment of death could not be passed upon him. It was delayed for some time on account of the feeble health of the prisoner. On the 27th day of January 1858, Mohammed Bahadur Shah, ex-King of Delhi, was brought before a military commission consisting of five European officers, assembled in the Hall of Audience, and the proceedings continued for twenty-one days, being closed on the 29th March. He was arraigned on four charges. The first three state that he, being a subject and pensioner of the British Government in India, did aid and abet Mohammed Bukht Khan, subahdar of artillery, and his son the prince Mirza Mogul, and divers others unknown, to mutiny, rebel, and wage war against the British Government — that he had proclaimed himself the Sovereign of India, seized possession of Delhi, and waged war against the state. The fourth charge accused him of being accessory to the murder of forty-nine persons on the 16th of May 1857, within his palace walls, and of encouraging in different ways the murder of Europeans. The prisoner pleaded Not Guilty.

There was some doubt whether he could be called a British subject. According to the commissioner, Mr. Saunders, he was under the control of the Supreme Government, though above that of the local authorities.

The proceedings took a very wide scope, being in fact an examination into the causes and history of the mutiny, as well as the guilt of the prisoner. Very little, however, was learned. It appeared that, by the instigation of a soothsayer called Hasan Askari, he had sent an Abyssinian to Persia with papers, which were given him in the night time and attested by the King's seal. This was about two years before. According to one hearsay statement, the same envoy was also sent to Constantinople and Russia. The soothsayer, it appears, was in the habit of promising aid from Persia, the coming of which he learned through supernatural means. One of his dreams was, that he had seen a hurricane approaching from the west, which was followed by a great flood of water, devastating the country that it passed over, and that he noticed that the King suffered no inconvenience from it, but was borne up over the flood seated on his couch. The way in which Hasan Askari interpreted this dream was, that the King of Persia with his army would annihilate the British power in the East, would restore the King to his ancient throne, and reinstate him in his kingdom ; and at the same time the infidels, meaning the British, would be all slaughtered. He also persuaded the King that he had given him twenty years more of life, which were to be subtracted from his own.

It appears that the letter to the Shah of Persia contained a complaint of the treatment he received from the English, and a request that the Shah would give him assistance. The King promised to become a Shia, remembering, no doubt, how his ancestor, the Emperor

Humay, had recovered Delhi with the assistance of an army of Persians, by a similar profession. It does not appear that the messenger ever returned, or that any answer was received.

Some examination took place into the affair of the chapatties; an officer said his sepoys imagined these were circulated by orders of our own government, for the purpose of intimating to the people of Hindostan, that they would be all compelled to eat one food,—in their eyes equivalent to embracing one faith; as they themselves termed it—" one food and one faith." This remark shews a much greater intimacy with the native mind than the explanation of Sir Theophilus Metcalfe, who regarded it as a signal " to all those who partook of one kind of food, connecting a body of men together in contradistinction to those, who lived differently and had different customs" (we suppose the Europeans, who eat fermented bread), " giving warning to the people to stand by one another." Chapatties passed from hand to hand by men of different castes—polluted food, in short, would never have been taken as a sign of brotherhood, but the reverse. It is indeed the very foundation of disunion in India, that different castes will not eat from the hand of one another.

Very little was brought out as to any correspondence between the King and the army, before the sepoys came to Delhi. Jawan Bakht, younger son of the King, who was very much disgusted with the English Government, because they refused to allow him to be made heir-apparent, in the hearing of some Europeans prophesied the massacre of the English in Delhi a few days before it took place. This, however, he said would happen when the Persians came; he never spoke about the sepoys.

According to Mukund Lal, his secretary, the King shewed, three years before, a desire to gain over the army, by giving some of the soldiers a document detailing the names of his ancestors, with a napkin dyed pink as an emblem of his blessing. This was put a stop to by the Commissioner. The witness, however, adds,—" It may be said that, from that day, a sort of understanding was established between the army and the King." It appears from Uhsan Ulla, that this practice was begun under the father of Bahadur Shah, but he denied that it had any influence on the revolt, or that any of the disciples came to produce the red handkerchief. He also said the King never had any idea that the native army would join itself to him, but the princes of the royal family used to remark, that they would go over either to Nepaul or Persia. Mukund Lal said, he did not know whether any direct proposals came from the prisoner to the army before the 11th of May; " but the King's personal attendants, sitting about the entrance to his private apartments, used to converse among themselves, and say that very soon, almost immediately, the army would revolt and come to the palace, when the government of the King could be re-established, and all the old servants would be greatly promoted, and advanced in position and emoluments."

There were no further proofs that there had been any

intercourse between the King and the army, but the presumption that such had existed was very strong. The methodical manner in which the magazine had been attacked, under the orders of the King's officers, was in itself sufficient to shew that everything did not take place by hap-hazard.

The deputy Advocate-General, Major Harriott, would entirely discard the cartridge question as a cause of the mutiny, which he appears to trace entirely to a Mahomedan conspiracy. Without repeating what we have already said on the subject, it is enough to remark, that we cannot join that gentleman in believing, that the fact of the cartridge grievance not being touched upon, in petitions to the King written after, proves that the Hindoo soldiers did not feel it before the outbreak. It is perfectly true that Mahomedan table servants will in India cook and handle pork ; but Major Harriott ought to have known that even they, regarded as the worst class of Mussulmans, would not drink water brought from the well of Zem-zem by a Christian hand. We have known a case where one of these servants had to pay for loss of caste to his brethren, because he had been seen coming out of the mess-house with a table napkin between his lips. The Indian Mussulman really believes himself to have a caste, although the more educated know it to be a Hindoo institution. We are not sure whether an order to bite cartridges greased with pig's fat would not be enough to raise a serious mutiny in the Sultan's army. That the sepoys had agreed amongst themselves to rise, all over the country, was most certainly made out, but that any particular day had been fixed seems very doubtful. Hakim Ahsanoolah remarks, that if such had been the case, they would have addressed one another in the urgent letters they wrote from Delhi :—" You promised to rise on such a day, but you have not arrived yet, so you have not kept your promise," which they never did. The King's complicity in the massacre of the Europeans was very clearly made out. When the sepoys had murdered the Commissioner, Captain Douglas, and others, they went to the King, told him what they had done at Meerut, saluted him as king, and claimed his protection. He said, " I did not call for you, you have acted very wickedly." The sepoys replied, " Unless you join us we are all dead men ; and we must, in that case, just do what we can for ourselves." The King then seated himself in a chair, and the men came forward one by one, and he put his hand upon their heads in token of protection, they saying just what came into their heads. At three o'clock that day Bahadur Shah was proclaimed Emperor of India by beat of drum and a salute of twenty-one guns.

The gentlemen above mentioned had been murdered by the immediate servants of the King, but no attempt was made to punish them, or even to shew disapproval of their conduct. The mutineers brought in all those prisoners whom they did not kill to the palace. The King assigned a certain room for their confinement, remarking at the time that it was a large capacious building. This was scarcely the case. " The building," says the Advocate-General, "is forty feet long, twelve broad, and about ten high. It is old, dirty, and dilapidated, and without the vestige of plaster ; but it is worse than that, for it is dark, has no made flooring, no windows, and is entirely without the means of ventilation or of light." The treatment they endured there is described by one of them, Mrs. Aldwell, who had escaped death by pretending to be a Mussulmani. " We were all confined in one room, very dark, with only one door, and no window or other opening. It was not fit for the residence of any human being, much less for the number of us that were there. We were very much crowded together, and in consequence of the sepoys and every one who took a fancy to do so coming and frighten- ing the children, we were obliged frequently to close the one door that we had, which then left us without light or air. The sepoys used to come with their muskets loaded and bayonets fixed, and asked us whether we would consent to become Mahomedans and also slaves, if the King granted us our lives; but the King's special armed retainers, from which the guard over us was always furnished, incited the sepoys to be content with nothing short of our lives, saying we should be cut up in small pieces and given as food to the kites and crows. On Thursday some of the sepoys came, and told the ladies that they intended to kill us all by mining and blowing up the palace. We were very indifferently fed, but on two occasions the King sent us better food."

These prisoners were fifty-four in number, and all women and children save four or five. Two days before

the event, it was known that their death had been determined on, and crowds of people flocked to the palace to
see the spectacle. The Hakim Ahsanoolah said that he
had pointed out to the King the cruelty and impolicy of
murdering these poor people. The King might easily
have taken the women and children into his zenana, where
every one agreed they would have been safe, and where
indeed there were crypts in which they might have
remained concealed, even had the sepoys dared to search
every woman's apartment in the palace. On the 16th of
May the prince Mirza Mogul came with a body of the
soldiery to the entrance of the King's private apartments,
to demand that the prisoners should be given up. He
went inside with Basant Ali Khan, while the soldiers remained without. They returned in about twenty minutes,
when Basant Ali Khan, publicly and in a loud voice,
proclaimed that the King had given his permission for
the slaughter of the prisoners, and that they could take
them away. To go on in the words of Mrs. Aldwell,
" Some of the King's special servants, attended by a small
number of infantry sepoys, came and called out to our
party that the Christians were to come out of the building,
and that the five Mahomedans were to remain. The
women and children began crying, saying they knew
they were going to be murdered; but the Mahomedans
swore on the Koran, and the Hindoos on the Jumna, that
such was not the case, that they wanted to give them a
better residence, and that the one they were in would be
converted into a magazine. On this they went out, were

counted, but I do not know the number, a rope was thrown round to encircle the whole group, the same as prisoners are usually kept together when on the move, and in this manner they were taken out of my sight, and, as I heard, brought under the pipal trees by the small reservoir in the courtyard, and there murdered with swords by the King's private servants. None of the sepoys took part in killing them. The privilege, for it was so considered, of murdering them was particularly reserved for the King's own servants, as it was believed by them the killing an infidel would ensure them a place in paradise."

It is said the Prince Mirza Majhli attempted to remonstrate, urging that the slaughter of women was not legal by Mahomedan law; but the troopers ran at him to kill him, and he had to fly for his life. The Prince Abul Bakr took an active part in the massacre; which Mirza Mogul witnessed from the roof of his house. The Mahomedan crowd, who looked on, covered the unfortunate victims with the coarsest abuse; but the Hindoos in the city said that men, who committed such atrocious cruelties, would never be victorious against the English. As if irrefragably to seal the proof against the prisoner, the massacre was thus recorded in the court diary:—"The King held his court in the hall of special audience; forty-nine English were prisoners, and the army demanded that they should be given over to them for slaughter. The King delivered them up, saying, 'The army may do as they please,' and the prisoners were consequently put to the sword." It is unnecessary to cite the proof in the other charges, the principal part of which indeed is a matter of history. The King's defence was, that he was but a helpless and unwilling tool in the hands of the soldiers and his sons.* This is brought forward entirely upon his own affirmation, and is rebutted by a number of witnesses, and a close-spun web of evidence. There is plenty of proof that his authority was treated, at least at first, with very great deference ; and when the mutineers came to Delhi he had 1200 soldiers in his own service within a fortified palace. That his own retinue was ready for rebellion could scarcely be urged as an excuse for him, for he had accustomed his servants to his long-continued discontent against the British power. It was advanced by some at this time, that his faculties were too far gone by weakness and age, to render him responsible for what had been done by the ambition of his family ; and that the spectacle of such a feeble old man suffering on the scaffold for the crimes of his children, could not be pleasing to justice. It is difficult to decide such a question without any personal knowledge. That he was very weakly during the trial was clear to every one, and it is likely that the destruction of his family, and the privations he experienced in prison, had given him a most severe blow. But there is, we think, proof enough that,

---

* His sons Mirza Mogul and Abul Bukr. This is refuted by a petition of Mirza Mogul, dated 11th July 1857, " Your slave affirms, with the solemnity of an oath, that no orders are ever issued, but such as your majesty has been previously made acquainted with."

at the time of the outbreak, he perfectly appreciated both the dangers he was exposing himself to, and the guilt that would be imputed to him in heading the rebellion. That a tremulous old man stretched out his hand to grasp a crown he could not hope long to wear, with some misgivings, is very likely. It would have been better for him and his house, if he had shewn more of the caution, with some of the obstinacy of old age.

Though we hold that, under the circumstances, it was the best policy to guarantee his life, we certainly think that, if such a promise had not been made, he ought to have suffered the punishment inflicted on many a less guilty head. "It will be for you to pronounce," said the Advocate-General, "whether this last King of the imperial house of Timour shall this day depart from his ancestral palace, bent down by age and misfortune, but elevated, perhaps, by the dignity of his sufferings and the long-borne calamities of his race, or whether this magnificent hall of audience, this shrine of the higher majesty of justice, shall this day achieve its crowning triumph in a verdict which shall record to this and all ages, that kings by crime are degraded to felons, and that the long glories of a dynasty may be for ever effaced in a day." Truly the close of that great line of kings was in darkness and in shame, without a single trait of courage or ability, as a relief to treachery, cowardice, and ferocity. When Timour Khan portrayed, with searching contempt, the character of the natives of India, when he spoke of their effeminacy, their hypocrisy, their excessive bad faith, and venality, he was tracing the features of the last of his race that ever bore a kingly name.

The court found the prisoner guilty of all the charges, and he was sentenced to imprisonment for life. It was thought at the time that this would soon be at a close, but, with that remarkable tenacity of existence which so many of his ancestors had shewn, he recovered from the illness under which he was labouring. When the road became sufficiently clear, he was escorted down to Calcutta, and then sent away to Burmah, which was selected as the place of his banishment.

VOCABULARY OF HINDUSTANI WORDS USED IN THE TEXT.

Badsha—Title of the emperors of Delhi.

Bhoorkha—The veil worn by women in the east when they go out.

Budmash—A blackguard.

Bungalow—A cottage or thatched house.

Bunneah—One of the merchant caste.

Chaprassic—Lit., a man with a badge, a policeman, etc.

Chapatty—Flour cake. Scottice, scone.

Chokidār—A policeman, a watchman.

Compound—An enclosed space, containing the house or bungalow, with servants' houses, stables, etc.

Durbār—A levee, audience.

Fakir—A beggar, a religious ascetic.

Golundaze—A native artilleryman.

Goroo—An apostle, spiritual guide.

Goroo-ka-Durbar—The great Sikh temple at Umritsur.

Havildār—A native non-commissioned officer.

Hindoo—One of the Brahminical creed.

Hindustani—A man of India, whether Hindoo or Mussulman.

Jemadār—A native commissioned officer.

Khulashie—A labourer used for pitching tents, or any such duty connected with warfare.

Kookry—A short heavy sickle-shaped hanger used by the Goorkhas, carried in a leather scabbard, with two little knives, like a Highland dirk.

Kotwalie—The police station.

Lath Sahib—The Commander-in-chief.

Lotah—A brass cooking and drinking vessel.

Mahadeo—Great God.

Maharajah—Great rajah or king.

Moonshie—Answers to the old word clerk.

Moulvie—A Mussulman preacher.

Poorbeah—Lit., an eastern; used by the Punjaubees for the inhabitants of Hindostan east of Kurnaul.

Pugarie—The roll of cloth that forms the Hindustani head-dress.

Punkah—A large fan hung from the roof, and swung by a cord.

Rajpūt—Name of the second-highest caste.

Serai—A square building, generally with four towers, enclosing a court-yard, with a well in the middle. It has numerous little chambers for the use of travellers, with loopholes opening to the outside. The

roof is flat, and it has only one outer door. It is
thus highly defensible.

Sowār—A rider; always used in the text for a native
horseman.

Suār—A pig, term of reproach.

Subahdār—The highest rank of native commissioned
officer.

Sudder—The chief, the highest; S. Bazaar, the principal
Bazaar.

Syce—A groom.

Tehseldār ⎫
                  ⎬ Native village magistrates.
Thanadār ⎭

Tope—A grove or clump of trees.

Villait—A generic name for all countries out of India.

Zamindārin—Wife of a zamindar or landholder.

Zenāna—Women's apartment, the women; answers to
Frauenzimmer in German.

INDEX.

Q

ERRATUM.

———◆———

Page 187, line 23, *for* " The minister himself took refuge in the palace of the king," *read* " was seized by the sepoys, and with difficulty delivered by the king."

CATALOGUE OF BOOKS.

PUBLISHED BY ADAM & CHARLES BLACK, EDINBURGH.

ADAMSON (ROBERT). The Cottage Garden. Second edition, fcap. 8vo, cloth, limp, 1s.

ANDERSON (Professor). Elements of Agricultural Chemistry. Crown 8vo, price 6s. 6d.

ANDERSON (Rev. WM., LL.D., Glasgow). Discourses. Second series, second edition, crown 8vo, price 6s.

—— Regeneration. Second edition, crown 8vo, price 6s.

ANDERSON (Rev. JAMES). Light in Darkness, or Comfort to the Sick and Afflicted, being a series of Meditations and Prayers, and portions of Scripture for those visited with bereavement and distress. Second edition, fcap., cloth, antique, red edges, price 5s.

APPERLEY (CHARLES). The Horse and the Hound; their various Uses and Treatment, including Practical Instructions in Horsemanship and Hunting, &c., &c. Third edition, with numerous Illustrations on Wood and Steel, after drawings by Herring, Alken, and Harrison Weir. Post 8vo, price 10s. 6d.

BALFOUR (Professor). A Class-Book of Botany: being an Introduction to the Study of the Vegetable Kingdom. In one large vol. demy 8vo, with 1800 Illustrations, 31s. 6d.

Sold also in Two Parts:—

Part I. Structural and Morphological Botany, 10s. 6d.

Part II. Vegetable Physiology, Classification, Glossary, &c., 21s.

BALFOUR (Professor). A Manual of Botany: being an Introduction to the Study of the Structure, Physiology, and Classification of Plants. Crown 8vo, pp. 700, with 820 Illustrations, price 12s. 6d.

The Botanist's Companion: or, Directions for the Use of the Microscope, and for the Collection and Preservation of Plants, with a Glossary of Botanical Terms. Crown 8vo, price 2s. 6d.

Botany and Religion; or, Illustrations of the Works of God in the Structure, Functions, Arrangement, and General Distribution of Plants. Third edition, 260 Wood Engravings, 12mo, cloth, price, 6s. 6d.; or cloth, gilt edges, price 7s.

BAYNE (PETER, A.M.) The Christian Life in the Present Time. New edition, carefully revised, and with additional Essay on the Relation of Mr. Carlyle to Christianity. Crown 8vo, price 7s. 6d.

Essays; Critical, Biographical, and Miscellaneous. Crown 8vo, price 7s. 6d.

BEESLY (E. W., M.A.) A System of History for the Use of Students. In preparation.

BENNETT (Professor). Clinical Lectures on the Principles and Practice of Medicine. New edition (the third), pp. 1005, with five hundred Illustrations, price 30s.

An Introduction to Clinical Medicine. Six Lectures on the Method of Examining Patients, &c. Third edition, 107 Illustrations, fcap. 8vo, price 5s.

Outlines of Physiology. Numerous Illustrations, fcap. 8vo, cloth, price 6s.

— The Pathology and Treatment of Pulmonary Consumption. Second edition, with 26 large Illustrations, demy 8vo, price 7s. 6d.

BLACK'S General Atlas of the World. New edition (1860), 56 maps, and Index of 60,000 names, &c., folio, half-bound morocco, gilt edges, price 60s.

School Atlas. 40 maps, and Index, 4to or 8vo, price 10s. 6d.

School Atlas for Beginners. 27 maps, oblong 12mo, price 2s. 6d.

Atlas of Australia, with all the Gold Regions. 6 maps, royal 4to, price 6s.

BLACK'S Atlas of North America. 20 Maps of the various Provinces, States, and Countries. By JOHN BARTHOLOMEW, F.R.G.S. With descriptive letterpress, and an Index of 21,000 names. Folio, price 16s.

—— Guide Books for Tourists in Great Britain and Ireland, &c.

	s.	d.
England and Wales	10	6
Scotland	8	6
Ireland (Dublin, Killarney, Belfast, separately 1s. 6d. each)	5	0
Wales	5	0
North Wales, separately	3	6
South Wales, separately	3	6
English Lakes	5	0
South of England. In the press.		
Yorkshire (paper cover 2s. 6d.) cloth	3	0
Kent and Sussex (or separately, Kent 2s., Sussex 1s. 6d.)	3	0
Derbyshire, Hampshire, Warwickshire, and Gloucester, each	2	0
Surrey. In the press.		
Highlands (Anderson's Guide)	10	6
The Trosachs, and Argylleshire, each	1	6
Argyleshire, Aberdeen, Perthshire, Moffat, Staffa and Iona, Skye, and Sutherland, fcap., sewed	1	0
Edinburgh, Illustrated	3	6
———————— cheap edition	1	6
———— Plan of the Town and Environs	1	6
Glasgow and West Coast	2	6
Tourist's and Sportsman's Companion to the Counties of Scotland, post 8vo, bound in leather	10	6
Tourist's Memorial of Scotland, Views of Scottish Scenery, royal 8vo	6	0
Where Shall We Go? or Guide to the Watering Places of Great Britain and Ireland	1	0
Home Tours through Great Britain and Ireland. In the press.		

Travelling Maps, lined with cloth, and bound in portable cases—

	s.	d.
England, 32 by 22 inches	4	6
Scotland	4	6
Scotland. Counties, each	1	0
England, Scotland, and Ireland (20 by 14½ inches), each	2	6
English Lake District, 19 by 14 inches	2	6
North and South Wales, each	1	6
Continent of Europe, railway map	4	6
India, 23 by 17½ inches	3	0

BOWDLER (JOHN). The Religion of the Heart, as Exemplified in the Life and Writings of John Bowdler, late of Lincoln's Inn, Barrister-at-law. Edited by CHARLES BOWDLER. 12mo. cloth, price 5s.

"A number of first-rate essays on most important themes, such as—'*The Atonement*,' '*Eternity of Future Punishments*,' '*Religion and Melancholy*,' '*Practical View of the Character of Christ*,' '*Spiritual Mindedness*,'" etc.

BROMBY (Rev. C. H.) Liturgy and Church History, &c. &c. Fcap., 8vo. In the Press.

BROUGHAM (Lord). Installation Address of the Right Hon. Henry Lord Brougham, Chancellor of the University of Edinburgh, with Notes. Fcap., 8vo, price 1s.

BRUCE (JAMES). Travels and Adventures in Abyssinia. New edition. Edited by J. M. CLINGAN, M.A. Five page illustrations and portrait on tinted paper, by C. A. Doyle. Square 12mo, cloth, gilt edges, price 5s.

BRYCE (JAMES, M.A., LL.D., Glasgow). A Treatise on Book-keeping by Double Entry, with an Appendix on Single Entry. Fcap. 8vo, cloth, price 5s.

—— The Arithmetic of Decimals, adapted to a Decimal Coinage. Second edition, price 1s. 6d.

—— A Treatise on Algebra. Third edition. In the press.

A   (A. W., F.E.I.S.) The Advanced Prose and Poetical Reader; being a collection of select specimens in English, with Explanatory Notes and Questions on each lesson; to which are appended Lists of Prefixes and Affixes, with an Etymological Vocabulary. 12mo, cloth, price 3s.

THE POETICAL READER, separately, price 1s. 3d.

(Rev. HENRY, LL.D., etc.) The Amateur Gardener's Year Book, a Guide for those who Cultivate their own Gardens on the Principles and Practice of Horticulture. Fcap. 8vo, cloth, price 3s. 6d.

D   (Rev. Dr.) Life in a Risen Saviour. Being Discourses on the Resurrection. Second edition, Crown 8vo, price 7s. 6d.

CARSON (A. R., LL.D.) Exercises in Attic Greek for the use of Schools and Colleges. 12mo, price 4s.

CARSON (A.R., LL.D.) Phaedrus' Fables of Æsop in Latin. New edition, with Vocabulary, edited by Rev. Wm. Veitch, 18mo bound, price 2s.

CHRISTISON (Professor). A Dispensatory. New edition in preparation.

COCKBURN (Lord). Memorials of His Time. With portrait after Raeburn. Demy 8vo, price 7s. 6d.

COOK'S (Captain) Voyages and Discoveries. Edited by John Barrow Esq., F.R.S. Seven page Illustrations, square 12mo, gilt edges, price 7s. 6d.

CREUZE (A. B.) A Treatise on the Theory and Practice of Naval Architecture. 4to, price 12s.

CUNNINGHAM (Rev. JOHN, D.D.) The Church History of Scotland, from the Commencement of the Christian Era to the Present Century, 2 vols, demy 8vo, price 21s.

DAVIDSON (Rev. Dr.) A Treatise on Biblical Criticism. 8vo, price 18s.

DEMAUS (Rev. ROBERT, M.A.) Class Book of English Prose, Comprehending Specimens of the most Distinguished Prose Writers from CHAUCER to the Present Time, with Biographical Notices, Explanatory Notes, and Introductory Sketches of the History of English Literature. 12mo, cloth, price 4s. 6d.
Or in Two Parts, price 2s. 6d. each.

—— Introduction to the History of English Literature. 12mo, price 2s.

—— The Young Scholar's Guide, a Book for the Training of Youth. Illustrated, 18mo, cloth, price 2s. 6d.

DENISON (E. B., M.A., Q.C.) Clocks and Locks. Fcap, 8vo, price 3s. 6d.

DONALDSON (JAMES, M.A.) Latin Reader of Jacobs and Classen. With Notes, etc., 12mo, price 3s. 6d.
Or COURSE I., price 1s. 9d.
COURSE II., price 2s.

—— Modern Greek Grammar, 12mo, price 2s.

DRESSER (Professor). Popular Manual of Botany without technical terms. Fcap. 8vo, twelve page Wood Illustrations, price 3s. 6d.
With the Illustrations coloured, price 4s. 6d.

ENCYCLOPÆDIA BRITANNICA. 21 vols., 4to (each vol. 24s.) Complete £25 : 4s. ; with Index £25 : 12s.

—— 21 vols, 4to, half bound, Russia extra, marbled edges, 30s. per vol., Complete £31 10s.

—— Index to Ditto, 4to, price 8s.   In the Press.

FARRAR (REV. F. W.) Julian Home : A Tale of College Life.   Foolscap 8vo, second edition, price 5s.

—— Eric; or Little by Little; a Tale of Roslyn School. Fourth edition, crown 8vo, price 6s. 6d.

FORBES (Professor J. D.) Occasional Papers on the Theory of Glaciers, with ten Plates and twenty-nine Wood Engravings. Demy 8vo, price 10s. 6d.

—— Reply to Professor Tyndall's remarks in his work "On the Glaciers of the Alps."   Price 1s.

—— Norway and its Glaciers.   Followed by Journals of Excursions in the High Alps of Dauphiné, Berne, and Savoy.   With two Maps, ten Coloured Lithographic Views, and twenty-two Wood Engravings.   Royal 8vo, price 21s.

—— Tour of Mont Blanc and of Monte Rosa.   Illustrated with Map of the Pennine Chain of Alps, fcap. 8vo, price 3s. 6d.

GRAHAM (G. F.) Musical Composition : its Theory and Practice.   With numerous Engravings, and copious Musical Illustrations.   4to, price 9s.

GULLIVER'S Travels to Liliput.   Illustrated.   Fcap. 8vo, gilt edges, price 1s. 6d.

GUNN (WM. M., LL.D.) Rudiments of the Latin Language. 12mo, price 2s.

GUTHRIE (Rev. Dr.) Pleas for Ragged Schools.   Crown 8vo.   Illustrated cover.   Price 2s. 6d.

—— The Gospel in Ezekiel.   Twenty-fifth thousand.   Crown 8vo, price 7s. 6d.

—— Christ and the Inheritance of the Saints.   Sixteenth thousand.   Crown 8vo, price 7s. 6d.

—— The Christian World Unmasked, by BERRIDGE, Edited by DR. GUTHRIE.   Fcap. 8vo, cloth antique, red edges, price 2s. 6d.

GUTHRIE (Rev. Dr.) The Street Preacher, being the Auto-
biography of Robert Flockhart. Edited by DR. GUTHRIE. Small
crown 8vo, cloth limp, price 2s.

—— (Rev. Dr.) Voices from Calvary; or the Seven
Last Sayings of Our Dying Lord. Second edition, fcap. 8vo, cloth
antique, price 4s.

JUKES (J. B.) The Student's Manual of Geology. Fcap.
8vo, with Woodcut Illustrations, price 8s. 6d.

—— School Manual of Geology. In preparation.

KELLAND (Professor). Elements of Algebra, for the use of
Schools and Junior Classes in Colleges. Crown 8vo, price 5s.

KEMP (W. S., M.A.) Exercises in Latin Syntax, adapted to
Ruddiman's Rules, with Copious Vocabularies. Part I., Agreement
and Government. Crown 8vo, price 2s.

KITTO (Dr.) Cyclopædia of Biblical Literature. Second
edition. 2 vols. medium 8vo, 554 Wood Engravings. Several Maps
and Engravings on Steel, price £3.

—— Popular Cyclopædia of Biblical Literature. In one volume,
8vo, illustrated by 336 Engravings, price 10s. 6d.

—— History of Palestine; from the Patriarchal Age to the
present time. Numerous Wood Engravings, crown 8vo, price 5s.

—— School Edition. 12mo, price 4s.; without Map, 3s. 6d.

—— An Account of Palestine. Crown 8vo, cloth plain, price
2s. 6d., cloth gilt, price 3s.

LAMARTINE (ALPHONSE DE). Mary Stuart. With Portrait,
crown 8vo, price 5s.

LAYCOCK (Professor). Principles and Methods of Medical
Observation and Research. Crown 8vo, price 6s.

M'CULLOCH (J. R.) Principles of Political Economy. 8vo,
price 15s.

—— A Treatise on Metallic and Paper Money and Banks,
written for the Encyclopædia Britannica. 4to, 5s.

—— Economical Policy. Second edition, enlarged and improved, 8vo, price 10s. 6d.

—— On Taxation. 4to, price 3s. 6d.

MACAULAY (Lord). Biographies of Atterbury, Bunyan, Goldsmith, Johnson, and Pitt, contributed to the Encyclopædia Britannica. Fcap. 8vo, price 6s.; demy 8vo, with Portrait by Maull and Polyblank, price 10s. 6d.

MACAULAY (Dr. ALEXR.) Medical Dictionary, designed for popular use; containing an account of Diseases and their Treatment, including those most frequent in warm climates. New edition, greatly enlarged and improved. By ROBERT WELBANK MACAULAY, M.D., H.E.I.C.S. Demy 8vo., price 10s. 6d.

MANSEL (H. L., D.C.L.) Metaphysics, or the Philosophy of Consciousness. Crown 8vo, pr.ce 7s. 6d.

MASSON (GUSTAVE). Introduction to the History of French Literature. 12mo, cloth, 2s. 6d.

MILLER'S (HUGH) Works, crown 8vo, each 7s. 6d.

> MY SCHOOLS AND SCHOOLMASTERS.*
> SCENES AND LEGENDS IN THE NORTH OF SCOTLAND.
> FIRST IMPRESSIONS OF ENGLAND AND ITS PEOPLE.
> THE OLD RED SANDSTONE.
> TESTIMONY OF THE ROCKS.
> THE CRUISE OF THE BETSY.
> SKETCH BOOK OF POPULAR GEOLOGY.

——* Cheap edition of the above, crown 8vo, cloth, limp, price 2s. 6d.

MILLER (Professor). Principles and Practice of Surgery. Numerous Illustrations. 2 vols., 8vo, each 16s.

MUNCHAUSEN (Baron). Numerous Illustrations. 18mo, gilt edges, price 1s. 6d.

NEILL (PATRICK, LL.D.) The Fruit, Flower, and Kitchen Garden. Profusely Illustrated. Fcap 8vo, price 3s. 6d.

NICOL (Professor). Elements of Mineralogy; containing a General Introduction to the Science, with descriptions of the Species. Fcap. 8vo, price 5s.

OSWALD (Rev. JOHN). Etymological Dictionary of the English Language. Seventh edition, 18mo, bound, 5s.

OWEN (RICHARD, F.R.S.) Palæontology, or a Systematic Summary of Extinct Animals, and their Geological Relations. 141 Illustrations, demy 8vo, price 16s.

PARK (MUNGO). Travels in Africa. Nine page Illustrations, square 12mo, gilt edges, price 5s.

PATERSON (JAMES, M.A., Barrister at Law). Compendium of English and Scotch Law. Royal 8vo, price 28s.

FILLANS (Professor). Eclogæ Ciceronianæ. 18mo, price 3s. 6d.

—— First Steps in Physical and Classical Geography. Fcap. 8vo, price 1s. 6d.

PORTEOUS (Bishop). Evidences of the Truth, and Divine Origin of the Christian Revelation, with Definitions and Analysis by JAMES BOYD, LL.D. 18mo, price 1s.

POETRY and Poets of Britain. From Chaucer to Tennyson, with Biographical Sketches, and a rapid View of the Characteristic Attributes of each. By DANIEL SCRYMGEOUR. Post 8vo, gilt edges, price 7s. 6d.

PROSE and Prose Writers of Britain. By Rev. ROBERT DEMAUS, M.A. Crown 8vo, gilt edges, price 7s. 6d.

RAMSAY (Allan). The Gentle Shepherd. Illustrated, 16mo, price 2s. 6d.; gilt edges 3s.

RICHARDSON (SIR JOHN, LL.D., etc.) The Polar regions. Demy 8vo. With Map, price 14s.

ROBINSON CRUSOE. Illustrated by C. A. Doyle. Square 12mo, gilt edges, price 5s.

RUSSELL (SCOTT). The Steam Engine. Illustrated, post 8vo, price 5s.

—— Steam and Steam Navigation. A Treatise on the Nature, Properties, and Applications of Steam, and on Steam Navigation. Illustrated, post 8vo, 9s.

RUSSELL (ROBERT). North America; its Agriculture and Climate: containing Observations on the Agriculture and Climate of Canada, the United States, and the Island of Cuba. With Coloured Map and Plans. Demy 8vo, price 6s.

SCHMITZ (Dr.) Elementary Greek Grammar. 12mo, price 3s. 6d.

SCRYMGEOUR (DANIEL). Class-Book of English Poetry. 12mo, price 4s. 6d. Or in 2 parts, price 2s. 6d. each.

SCOTT (Sir WALTER). Complete Works and Life. 98 vols., fcap. 8vo, £14 : 14.

—— Waverley Novels. The latest editions with the Author's Notes —

NEW ILLUSTRATED EDITION of 1860, 48 vols., fcap. 8vo, cloth, 96 Plates, and 1700 Illustrations . . . £10 16 0

LIBRARY EDITION, 25 vols. demy 8vo, with 204 Engravings after Wilkie, Landseer 13 2 6

AUTHOR'S FAVOURITE EDITION of 1847, in 48 vols., fcap. 8vo, with Frontispiece and Vignette to each vol. . 7 2 0

CABINET EDITION, 25 vols., fcap 8vo, each vol. containing Steel Frontispiece and Woodcut Vignette . . . 8 10 0

PEOPLE'S EDITION, 5 vols. royal 8vo, with Illustrations . 2 2 0

RAILWAY EDITION, 25 vols., fcap. 8vo, Illustrated Covers 1 17 6
Separately, 1s. 6d. each, or in cloth, 2s.

Vol. 1. Waverley, or "'Tis Sixty Years Since."	Vol. 13. Pirate.
2. Guy Mannering, or The Astrologer.	14. Fortunes of Nigel.
	15. Peveril of the Peak.
3. Antiquary.	16 Quentin Durward.
4. Rob Roy.	17. St. Ronan's Well.
5. Old Mortality.	18. Redgauntlet.
6. Black Dwarf, and Legend of Montrose.	19. The Betrothed.
	20. The Talisman.
7. Heart of Mid-Lothian.	21. Woodstock.
8. Bride of Lammermoor.	22. Fair Maid of Perth.
9. Ivanhoe.	23. Anne of Geierstein, or the Maiden of the Mist.
10. Monastery.	24. Count Robert of Paris.
11. Abbot.	25. Surgeon's Daughter— Castle Dangerous.
12. Kenilworth.	

—— Poetical Works. Various editions from 5s. to 36s.

—— Miscellaneous Prose Works. Various editions, from 26s. to 84s.

—— Life of Napoleon Bonaparte. 5 vols., fcap. 8vo, price 20s. People's edition, 1 vol., royal 8vo, price 10s.

—— Tales of a Grandfather. Various editions, 6s. to 15s.

SCOTT (Sir WALTER) Beauties of. Crown 8vo, gilt edges, price 5s.

—— Readings for the Young from Scott's Works. Fcap. 8vo, gilt edges, price 7s. 6d.

—— Life of, by J. G. Lockhart. Various editions, 7s. 6d. to 30s.

SIMPSON (Professor). Obstetric Memoirs and Contributions, including those on Anaesthesia. Edited by C. W. Priestly, M.D , and H. R. Storer, M.D. 2 vols., 8vo, profusely Illustrated, 36s.

SMITH (ADAM, LL.D.) The Wealth of Nations : an Inquiry into the Nature and Causes of the Wealth of Nations. Edited, and with Life of the Author, by J. R. M'CULLOCH, Esq. Fourth edition, corrected throughout, and greatly enlarged. 8vo, 16s.

SPALDING (WM., M.A.) An Introduction to Logical Science. Fcap. 8vo, 4s. 6d.

STEVENSON (DAVID). Canal and River Engineering. Small 8vo, 4s. 6d.

STEWART (W. C.) The Practical Angler, or the Art of Trout Fishing, more particularly applied to Clear Water. Fourth edition, 12mo, in the press.

THOMAS (Dr. ROBERT). The Modern Practice of Physic. Eleventh edition, edited by Dr. Frampton. 2 vols., 8vo, price 28s.

THOMSON (Professor). Brewing and Distillation. Post 8vo. price 6s.

TRAILL (Professor). Medical Jurisprudence. Post 8vo, price 5s.

TYTLER (P. F.) History of Scotland. Enlarged and con- tinued to the Present Time, by the Rev. JAMES TAYLOR, D.D., and adapted to the purposes of Tuition by ALEX. REID, LL.D. Sixth edition, 12mo, 3s. 6d.

—— Outlines of Modern History. Fifth edition, 12mo, 3s.

—— Outlines of Ancient History. Fourth edition, 12mo, 3s.

TYTLER (MISS M. FRASER). Tales of Good and Great Kings. Fcap., cloth, price 3s 6d.

VEITCH (Rev. Wм.)   Greek Verbs, Irregular ,and Defective.
Post 8vo, price 6s.

WALPOLE (Horace).   The Castle of Otranto.   Fcap. 8vo,
Illustrated, gilt edges, price 2s. 6d.

WARDLAW (Dr.)   Systematic Theology.   A Complete System
of Polemic Divinity,   In three vols., demy 8vo, price 21s.

WHITE (Robert).   Madeira; its Climate and Scenery.   Second
edition by J. Y. Johnson.   With numerous Illustrations, and a Map
of the Island, crown 8vo, price 7s. 6d.

YOUNG (Andrew).   The Angler and Tourist's Guide to the
Northern Counties of Scotland, with Instructions to Young Anglers.
18mo, price 2s.

RETURN TO ➤   CIRCULATION DEPARTMENT
198 Main Stacks

LOAN PERIOD 1 HOME USE	2	3
4	5	6

ALL BOOKS MAY BE RECALLED AFTER 7 DAYS.

Renewls and Recharges may be made 4 days prior to the due d

Books may be Renewed by calling 642-3405.

FOR

Lightning Source UK Ltd.
Milton Keynes UK
UKOW06f0345091217
314149UK00016B/916/P